TRADEMARK PROBLEMS and How to Avoid Them

TRADEMARK PROBLEMS and How to Avoid Them

Revised Edition

Sidney A. Diamond

CRAIN
BOOKS
CHICAGO

Published by Crain Books
A Division of Crain Communications, Inc.
740 Rush Street
Chicago, IL 60611

81 82 83   10 9 8 7 6 5 4 3 2 1

ISBN 0–87251–059–X
Library of Congress Catalog Card Number   80–70205

Printed in the United States of America

Contents

Preface

This book consists essentially of a series of case histories dealing with trademark and brand name problems taken from the feature columns I have been contributing to *Advertising Age* and its predecessor, *Advertising Agency Magazine,* for a number of years. Although these are problems of a legal nature, they have been written up in nontechnical fashion for the basic purpose of informing marketing and advertising executives about developments in a field of obvious concern to them.

This material has been arranged into chapters so that it presents a coherent treatment of many different kinds of problems that arise in the selection and protection of trademarks. Where necessary, the text has been up-dated. (For example, a number of the court decisions discussed were affirmed when appeals were taken after the columns originally appeared, and this fact has been noted.) Some editorial changes also have been made in order to unify the material.

The entire book is intended fundamentally to explain how potential trademark problems can be recognized in advance and then avoided by proper understanding and the application of proper techniques. It can be read straight through as a general treatment of the subject of trademarks in colloquial terms, or it can be used as a reference book to check specific topics of immediate interest.

In an effort to make the book more useful, an index of trademarks mentioned in the text has been included. In addition, the detailed legal references for all of the court cases referred to in each chapter have been listed in a separate section of notes so that the book also can be used by lawyers, who may wish to check the citations. The table of contents provides a detailed topical breakdown of the subjects covered in the text.

S. A. D.

Preface to the Revised Edition

After eight years it seemed time to revise the original edition of this book and bring it up to date. There have been no changes in the fundamentals of trademark law, but some points have been clarified by recent decisions, and a number of the case histories in the earlier edition had become quite old.

Approximately half of the revised edition is new. The same basic subjects are covered as in the original edition, although some of the chapters have been rearranged. Also, I have inserted new material on comparative advertising and added three new chapters covering nicknames, imitation of packaging and design features, and international problems.

Another reason for publishing a revised edition at this time is that, because of an unexpected development in my personal career, I had to discontinue the feature column in *Advertising Age*, which has been the source for the contents of the book. In the spring of 1979 I was appointed Assistant Commissioner for Trademarks in the United States Patent and Trademark Office, and it seemed wise to avoid possible embarrassments that might have occurred if something I wrote in a column were taken as an official statement. Later in the year, when I became Commissioner of Patents and Trademarks, the need to avoid any appearance of conflict was accentuated. I did contribute one "guest column" in 1980, however, and that has become the chapter called "Trademarks and the Public Interest," replacing the old "Trademarks and Consumerism." Now that I have left the government and returned to private practice, my column has been resumed.

I have been gratified by the response to the first edition, and I hope that this revision will be useful to the public.

S. A. D.

CHAPTER 1 History and Basic Characteristics of Trademarks

The History of Trademarks

The basic idea of a trademark was brought to North America by the colonists as part of their British tradition. Following the Revolutionary War, the first official interest of the new government in trademarks was expressed in 1791 when Thomas Jefferson proposed a federal trademark registration law after he had received a petition from a group of Boston sail makers asking for the exclusive right to use particular marks on their products.

The first federal law on the subject was not passed until 1870. Unlike patents and copyrights, trademarks are not mentioned in the Constitution, and the 1870 trademark law was ruled unconstitutional by the U.S. Supreme Court.

Congress tried again in 1881, basing the law this time on its power to regulate commerce across state lines. A revised statute was enacted in 1905. We are operating currently under a more modern trademark law, the Lanham Act, which was passed by Congress in 1946.

Trademark No. One was registered for a design used by the Averill Chemical Paint Company of New York on liquid paint. That registration has expired, and the oldest one in force today (it was renewed in 1974) displays the name Samson Cordage in association with a drawing of Samson wrestling with the lion. It is owned by the Samson Cordage Works of Boston.

1

Although copyrights are administered by a separate agency that is part of the Library of Congress, trademarks were placed under the jurisdiction of the Commissioner of Patents and from the beginning have been registered in the Patent Office. Among other things this rather accidental association of what really are somewhat strange bedfellows has caused considerable confusion between trademarks and patents. A law signed by President Ford in 1975 changed the name of the operation to the Patent and Trademark Office, and the title of its head became Commissioner of Patents and Trademarks.

By calling attention to the fact that patents and trademarks are two different things, the new title should help to keep them straight. The changed names also upgrade the status of trademarks by giving them separate recognition, to the gratification of trademark owners, lawyers, and others who deal with these important commercial symbols.

On December 17, 1974, the United States Patent Office issued its one millionth trademark registration certificate. By a happy coincidence, the company whose trademark application matured into Registration No. 1,000,000 is a shining example of the traditional American success story.

The Patent and Trademark Office registers trademarks in batches once a week. Of the 631 certificates issued on December 17, 1974, the one bearing the number 1,000,000 went to Cumberland Packing Corporation of Brooklyn, N.Y., for the G clef and musical staff design used in association with its Sweet 'N Low brand name for a low-calorie sugar substitute.

Cumberland is a family enterprise that started marketing individual-serving sugar packets at the end of World War II. The owner, Benjamin Eisenstadt, developed a cheaper and more efficient process for producing single-portion packages of sugar and condiments for institutional food service. In 1958, by which time one of his sons had joined the business, he made plans to add a powdered, low-calorie sugar substitute to his line of goods. Searching for a brand name for this new product, Mr. Eisenstadt remembered the well-known song, "Sweet and Low," set to a poem by Tennyson. He changed the title slightly, to "Sweet 'N Low," and decided to superimpose the words on a musical staff design.

The combined association of the familiar song title and a phrase that reminded customers of the essential qualities of the product—a sweetener low in calories—proved to be a winner. The product was introduced as a restaurant item, but individual customers were so pleased with it that they inquired about buying the sweetener for home use. Cumberland then switched its marketing focus to the retail level.

Sales of the product have increased more than 500 times since 1958. Today the words "Sweet 'N Low," accompanied by the G clef and a musical staff design, appear on half of all the low-calorie sweetening sold in this country.

Cumberland had registered the combination trademark consisting of the words and design years ago but decided (as many companies do) that the design portion of its mark was sufficiently important to justify a separate registration. The Patent and Trademark Office raised a question of whether the design actually functioned as a trademark apart from the words, but this objection was overcome by submitting copies of advertisements that emphasized the design as something to look for when purchasing the product.

And then, as thousands of pending trademark applications ground their way through the mill of Patent and Trademark Office procedure, came the happy accident that attached No. 1,000,000 to the registration for the G clef and musical staff design.

This milestone was the occasion for appropriate ceremonies at the U.S. Patent Office (which was still its name at this time). The certificate was signed personally by C. Marshall Dann, the Commissioner of Patents, the only occasion in modern times that a trademark registration was issued with a handwritten, as distinguished from a printed, signature.

Commissioner Dann paid tribute to the vital role that trademarks play in our economy. He said, "Many businesses would fail, or could survive only through a long and expensive process of creating a new identifier for their product, if they were prevented from using the marks they have used for many years."

The Commissioner added: "The producer or manufacturer is not the only beneficiary. Trademarks also protect the consumer by serving as an identification of the source of goods, pinpointing the responsibility for quality, and by guaranteeing the consistency of the quality or nature of a product."

Benjamin Eisenstadt, president of the Cumberland Packing Corporation, spoke modestly of the fortuitous circumstance that made his company the recipient of the lucky honor. He used the occasion of the presentation of Registration No. 1,000,000 to express his own views on the importance of trademarks and other kinds of intellectual property. "We must value with equal passion property rights as well as human rights," said Mr. Eisenstadt.

Mr. Eisenstadt has an interesting explanation of the function of a trademark. As he put it in his informal remarks during the ceremonial presentation of the certificate: "Each person is unique unto himself. He has fingerprints unlike those of any other human being. Trademarks are the fingerprints of American industry. They make it possible for any business enterprise to be unique and bring its uniqueness to the attention of the world. Of course, just as with any individual, the value of this uniqueness depends not on his name or fingerprints, but what talents he brings to bear in their use. So it is with a trademark. Its value can be measured only by those who are benefitted or abused by its use."

The Patent and Trademark Office estimates that the average American's daily life involves confrontation with some 1,500 trademarks. Not many consumers could define them in legal terms or in the way Mr. Eisenstadt explains them. But all of us unconsciously recognize the importance of symbols. The bald eagle immediately suggests the United States. The blind goddess balancing the scales represents justice. The dove signifies peace.

Similarly, trademarks are symbols that stand for particular products or services. Consumers come to recognize these commercial symbols by repeated exposure on labels and packages and in advertising; and they rate them in terms of the satisfaction or dissatisfaction they have experienced in the past.

Purposes and Functions of a Trademark

There is a considerable amount of unnecessary confusion about trademarks among marketing and advertising executives. The legal requirements for selecting and protecting trademarks admittedly are technical, but they are certainly not incomprehensible. The answers to six basic questions will help to introduce the subject.

What Is a Trademark?

A trademark is a word or design used on an article of merchandise to identify it as the product of a particular manufacturer. Legally speaking, a "brand name" is just one variety of trademark. A trademark may be used on all of a company's products or only on one, and it may be used in combination with other marks or by itself.

A trademark may be a coined word with no meaning at all (Kodak, Dacron, Exxon), an ordinary word that has no meaning in connection with the product on which it is used (Camel, Arrow, Dial), a word whose meaning suggests some quality or function of the product (Raid, Sure, Head and Shoulders), or a coined word suggesting what the product is or does (Kleenex, Jell-O, Panasonic). It may be a foreign word, whose English meaning may or may not have some significance for the product (Lux, Oreo, Bon Ami). It may be the name of the owner or founder of the company (Ford, Singer, Gillette), the name of some famous person selected arbitrarily (Lincoln, Cadillac, Yale), or a name from mythology or literature (Hercules, Ajax, Peter Pan). It may be just initials (RCA, IBM, BVD), or just numerals (4711, 66), or a combination of both (V-8, A-1). It may be a pictorial mark, with or without explanatory words (Four Roses, the White Rock girl, Elsie the cow). And of course these do not exhaust the possibilities.

A trademark is not a legal monopoly in anything like the sense that a copyright or patent is. Basically, a trademark's function is to distinguish between products that are available from more than one source. A trademark helps the consumer to identify the source. It is not significant if the consumer forgets the name of the particular manufacturer; it is the trademark's job merely to differentiate one competitive product from another. Thus Crest and Close-Up both are good trademarks for toothpaste; Ivory, Lux, and Dial for soap; Dash, Cheer, and Bold for detergents. Nabisco is an example of a trademark that identifies a whole line of products, many of which have their own brand names besides (Oreo, Lorna Doone, Ritz). The "house mark" Nabisco and the individual brand names legally are each separate trademarks, and so is the striking white-on-red insignia that also identifies the line of products made by Nabisco, Inc.

Trademarks are not limited to goods; they may be used for services, like transportation, insurance, entertainment, and advertising. Strictly speaking they then are called "service marks." Well-known examples are Pullman, Greyhound, and Prudential's sketch of the rock of Gibraltar. Distinctive titles of radio and television programs also are service marks and so are the identifying slogans, designs, and sounds of radio and television broadcasters (the NBC peacock, the CBS eye).

The striking feature of a trademark, then, is that it is used to distinguish between goods or services that normally are supplied by several business competitors. It is the trademark that makes it possible for the housewife, instead of just buying "scouring powder," for example, to choose among Ajax, Comet, and Bon Ami. Even if the product is a new one and available from just a single company, the trademark is a symbolic identification of the manufacturing source.

How Do You Get a Trademark?

Rights in a trademark are obtained by putting it into use. Registration comes later.

After—not before—actual use in commerce has begun, an application may be made to register the trademark in the

United States Patent and Trademark Office. Actual use in this connection means that the article has been shipped and sold across at least one state line with the trademark on it—attached by means of a printed tag or woven label, for instance. Valuable brand names sometimes fail to qualify for registration because they are used like catalogue numbers and never appear on the goods themselves; that kind of brand name technically is not a trademark at all.

There is no prescribed minimum or maximum period of time to wait between starting to use a trademark and filing an application to register it. In case of any conflict, however, the first one to use the mark is the owner, even if he was not the first to apply for a registration.

All applications for trademark registration are examined in the Patent and Trademark Office to determine whether they meet the statutory requirements. These are rather formidable, although thousands of new trademarks succeed in satisfying them each year.

In the first place, the trademark must not be confusingly similar to any other trademark previously registered or used by someone else; that is, it must not be likely to make purchasers think that there is some connection between the two products or their manufacturers.

Then there is a list of specific prohibitions against registering obscene or scandalous marks, designs that simulate the flag of any country or the emblems of certain organizations, and so on.

If a trademark is the actual name of a particular living individual, it cannot be registered without written consent (Max Factor, Pierre Cardin, Estee Lauder). Note that this does not apply to fictitious persons created for promotional purposes (Ann Page, Etienne Aigner, Betty Crocker).

A family name standing alone is not registrable at all unless it has been used to such an extent that the public understands the name represents one particular source for the product. For example, Ford clearly means automobiles produced by just one manufacturer; after so many years of use and advertising, no member of the public is likely to think when the new models come out that somebody else named Ford has gone into the automobile business. Five years' substantially exclusive and continuous use is generally accepted as sufficient proof of distinctiveness; when the period is shorter and sometimes even when it is longer, the Patent and Trademark Office may call for sworn statements showing the extent of use and public acceptance of the family name as a trademark. This is to prevent any one individual from keeping all other people with the same last name from using their family names in a competing business. But if nobody else does so, and the family name comes to mean a particular brand to the consuming public rather than just a product made by someone with that surname, then the Patent and Trademark Office will agree that the name has been turned into a distinctive trademark and allow registration.

For similar reasons a geographic name cannot be registered unless it can be proved to have become distinctive by the same standards that are used for family names. Waltham and Elgin watches passed the test long ago, but any manufacturer who started currently with, let's say, a Chicago brand of watch could expect trouble and delay in getting a trademark registration. It would not matter for this purpose whether or not the watches actually were made in Chicago.

Many trademark applications fail on the issue of descriptiveness. If the mark merely describes—or misdescribes—the goods, it is not registrable unless it has acquired distinctiveness through long-continued exclusive use like the family names and geographical terms discussed above. But brand names that tell something about the product are proposed for adoption so frequently that drawing the line between a suggestive mark (which is acceptable legally) and a descriptive mark (which is not) has become just about the most difficult problem in the whole field of trademarks. For instance, Sparkle probably would be accepted as a valid trademark for soap powder because it just suggests that the housewife will get excellent results from using it, but Kleen Kwik probably would be rejected because it simply describes the fact (if it is a fact) that the soap powder will do a fast job. Note that the deliberate misspelling does not make the trademark distinctive; the Patent and Trademark Office checks the meaning of the way words sound as well as the way they look.

If and when the Patent and Trademark Office is satisfied that a trademark is properly registrable, it will be published in a weekly bulletin called the *Official Gazette* for the express purpose of calling it to the attention of others in the industry so that they may disagree if they wish to do so. Anyone who is using a similar mark and believes confusion may result has the right to object to the application, and there will be a small-scale lawsuit right in the Patent and Trademark Office to decide the question. If there is no such opposition, or if there is and the objection is overruled, a trademark registration certificate will be issued by the Commissioner of Patents and Trademarks. The time involved in getting a trademark registration, counting from the date on which the application is filed, ranges from about nine months all the way up to several years.

What Protection Does a Trademark Provide?

The owner of a trademark is protected against the use of the same mark, or a confusingly similar one, by anybody else on similar merchandise or services.

Trademark infringement can be stopped by legal proceedings even if it was unintentional; the test is whether the use of the second mark would probably cause consumers to be mistaken, confused, or deceived. The hypothetical purchaser involved in this situation does not have an opportunity to make a side-by-side comparison, and he is not paying strict attention to his purchase unless the article is very expensive or very technical.

It is obvious from what has been said that the challenged trademark need not be an exact copy in order to infringe. The question of how different it may be and still be subject to a legal injunction depends on several different factors.

If the merchandise from both sources is directly competitive, there can be an infringement even though the trademarks are rather different from one another. For instance, Weather-Match was ruled an infringement of Weathervane when both were used for two-piece lightweight women's suits.

If the two trademarks are identical, there can be an infringement even though the merchandise on which each is used differs markedly from the other. Thus, the maker of Yale locks was able to stop the use of Yale as a trademark for flashlight batteries.

When neither the trademarks nor the goods are identical, the combined effect of the differences is weighed so that the closer the trademarks are to one another, the greater is the range of merchandise that will remain in the area of infringement.

In addition, in many situations the most important factor is the distinctiveness of the trademark whose owner is claiming an infringement. At one end of the scale is the purely arbitrary word coined for use as a trademark, which is called a strong mark. (Kodak is the classic example.) At the other end of the scale is the trademark that merely suggests the general desirability of the product; this typically has been used by many different manufacturers in all sorts of industries and is classed as a weak mark (Acme, Perfection, Excelsior, Royal, Majestic).

The Eastman Kodak Company's trademark can stop another manufacturer from using Kodak even for cigarette lighters, but trademarks like Acme, Excelsior, and Majestic actually have been registered for dozens of different articles by as many different companies. The issue is whether or not the newcomer is trading on the established reputation of the trademark owner; if the consumer is unlikely to infer a connection between the two, there is no infringement.

How Long Does a Trademark Last?

A trademark lasts as long as it continues in use. But if it is registered, separate attention must be paid to the certificate issued by the Commissioner of Patents and Trademarks.

A trademark registration is granted for a period of twenty

years starting with the date on which it is issued. But it will be cancelled automatically after six years unless a sworn statement that the trademark is still in use is filed in the Patent and Trademark Office during the sixth year counting from the date of the certificate. If the registration survives this barrier, it continues in force for the balance of the full twenty-year term without further formalities, and then it may be renewed indefinitely for additional twenty-year terms, provided that it is still in use at the time each application for renewal is made.

Suppose a Trademark Isn't Registered?

Registration of a trademark is entirely optional with the company using it.

The basic rights of a trademark owner are built up through actual use of the mark and consequent public acceptance of it whether or not a registration is obtained, and infringers can be sued even without a certificate of registration. The registration procedure, however, establishes an official record of the trademark and also provides certain additional rights. For one thing, it makes a trademark infringement case easier to prove because the registration is legal notice to everyone and a certified copy is evidence of the proprietor's legal rights; for another, it strengthens the trademark owner's position because the maximum penalties for infringing a registered mark are heavier than if the mark is not registered. Finally, if the trademark has been used continuously for five years following the date of registration, the owner's rights to it become incontestable. This means that, except for certain rare technicalities, a company charged with infringement cannot challenge the validity of the registered trademark in a lawsuit.

How Can Trademark Rights Be Lost?

One way to lose the rights in a trademark is to abandon it.

The law says that a trademark is abandoned when its use is discontinued without the intention of resuming it. Two years of unexplained nonuse constitutes legal evidence of abandonment.

A trademark also can be lost in other ways, some of them devious and technical. For example, if the trademark as the result of widespread use comes to mean the name of the product to the general public instead of just one manufacturer's brand of the product, then the whole industry has the right to use it as such. In a manner of speaking, a trademark can become too successful. If that happens, the trademark passes into the language as a generic word in spite of the manufacturer's desires, and he no longer has the exclusive right to use it as his brand name. This has in fact happened to, among others, aspirin, cellophane, and shredded wheat.

Another way to lose the rights in a trademark is to permit others to use it without retaining control over the quality of their products; a trademark cannot be licensed freely the way a copyright or patent can.

In addition, the trademark registration notice must be watched. The letter R enclosed in a circle means that the trademark has been registered in the United States Patent and Trademark Office. The use of that notice on an unregistered mark or on a mark registered under the law of some state instead of the federal law is a false representation. If a company suing for infringement has been using a false registration notice, the judge may throw the case out of court because of the complaining party's own fraudulent conduct.

No Trademark Rights Without Actual Use

Legal rights in a trademark do not exist unless it is used on a product. So far as the law is concerned, there really is no trademark at all without actual use. No matter how brilliant the concept or how artistic its execution might be, there is no basis for protecting it as a trademark if it is not in use on the goods.

In one case, a manufacturer named Gay Toys, Inc., filed an application in the United States Patent and Trademark Office to register Big Mac as a trademark for toy trucks. McDonald's Corporation opposed this, claiming that public confusion was likely to occur. Big Mac is a registered trademark of McDonald's for carryout foods and for restaurant services, and its licensees also sell some Big Mac toys.

Gay Toys had based its application on use of the trademark since April 1, 1976. In the course of the opposition proceeding, it developed that a salesman had displayed a plaster mock-up of a toy truck at a trade show on that date. The mock-up evidently looked like the real thing, but it was not an actual toy truck. The salesman took orders at the show in April. His company, however, did not get the molds necessary for the production of commercial models in plastic until the end of May.

McDonald's based its legal strategy on the point that Gay Toys could not possibly have used Big Mac as a trademark for toy trucks on April 1, 1976, because none of the trucks had even been manufactured at that date. Gay Toys argued back that there is no legal restriction on what goods must be made of and that plaster surely is an acceptable material.

Chief Judge Howard Markey of the U.S. Court of Customs and Patent Appeals said in his published opinion that this argument just begged the question. The real issue in the case was not what the toy trucks were made of but whether the plaster mock-up was a toy truck. "Visual similarity alone," wrote Judge Markey, "cannot convert a plaster mock-up into a toy truck."

There was no evidence in the case that the plaster mock-up actually was used as a toy or that it even was suitable for use as a toy. The basic requirement that the trademark must be used on the product could not be met because there simply was no product. McDonald's opposition therefore was successful, and the Gay Toys application for registration was denied.

Another case dealt with a different aspect of the trademark use requirement. The operator of a retail store called The

Fashion Factory tried to register that name as a trademark for women's apparel. It turned out that The Fashion Factory logo appeared only on the paper bags that the store supplied so that customers could carry their purchases home.

Ordinarily, using a trademark on a container—a tin can or glass jar, for example—is just as satisfactory from the legal standpoint as using the mark on the goods themselves. But the products sold by The Fashion Factory all carried their own manufacturer's trademarks.

In this case, the Court of Customs and Patent Appeals ruled that using the name of the store on paper bags identified only the store, not the merchandise, and that this is not using a trademark on women's apparel. The application for registration was rejected.

If The Fashion Factory name had appeared on woven labels sewn into the garments or, perhaps, even on printed hang tags, the result might have been different. In that situation, it could have been argued that the trademark was being used on the apparel. There is no rule that prohibits more than one trademark on a given item, so the appearance of the manufacturer's mark on the merchandise would not necessarily have interfered with this approach.

Trademarks also can be registered for services, in which case they are known as service marks. Since a service by its nature is intangible, the use requirements for service marks necessarily differ from those for trademarks. Specifically, use in advertising a service is acceptable, while use only in advertising a product is not.

This insistence on actual use of a trademark on the product before any legal rights can be acquired in it is a peculiarity of U.S. law. In almost every other country around the world, an application for trademark registration can be filed even though the mark has not yet been put into use, although some countries do require a declaration that the applicant intends to start using the trademark commercially at a future date. Under that kind of system, it is possible to find out ahead of time whether legal obstacles exist, such as conflicts with other companies using identical or similar marks.

In the U.S., on the other hand, the trademark applicant has to start using the mark, then apply for a registration, and eventually find out whether or not he can get it registered.

Bills have been introduced into the U.S. Congress to allow a company to file trademark (and service mark) applications on the basis of a good faith intention to use the mark, but our law has not yet been changed.

Adopting the intention-to-use system would bring the U.S. into line with most of the rest of the world and also would remove the major obstacle now preventing us from joining the international Trademark Registration Treaty, which has been stalled for several years.

Unused Trademarks Cannot Be Reserved

One of the basic legal rules about trademarks is that they really have no existence until they are put into use. And "use" for this purpose means that the trademark appears on the label, nameplate, or package of a product shipped for commercial purposes, or, if a service rather than a product is involved, that the mark is used in advertising a service that is in commercial operation.

Anyone who hits upon the idea for a new trademark, therefore, runs the risk that somebody else might independently create the same trademark and wind up with full legal rights to it if he reaches the market first. The first user is the owner of the trademark.

This legal rule was dramatized in a rather unusual context when Wilbur A. Heinemann, Jr., sued General Motors for trademark infringement and unfair competition.

During the spring of 1968, the Pontiac Motor division of General Motors decided to introduce a new, high-performance model in the Tempest GTO line. On July 19, Pontiac's general manager selected "The Judge" as the name for this new model, subject to legal clearance. Admittedly, this choice was inspired by the popularity of the line "Here come de Judge" used on the "Laugh-In" television program.

A trademark search showed no conflicting marks for automobiles, so the proposed name was adopted. The first showing of Pontiac's new car bearing the trademark, "The Judge," took place on September 26, 1968, when the 1969 line was introduced to the public.

On February 17, 1969, General Motors was notified that its use of "The Judge" was claimed to be an infringement on the rights of Wilbur Heinemann. It turned out that Heinemann for a number of years had been modifying old cars, which he exhibited and sometimes raced. He was employed by the Sinclair Oil Company, and his work on these automobiles was a hobby.

Part of the fun of modifying old cars, evidently, is in naming them. For example, in 1961 Heinemann modified a 1951 Ford convertible and called it Saintnic's Slay. In 1964 he modified a 1958 Chevrolet, which he called Brand X. Later in 1964 he bought a 1932 Model A Ford and worked on it intermittently until February of 1968, when the question of finding a name for this automobile became a topic of conversation among Heinemann, his brother, and a friend.

Heinemann originally had planned to call it U.F.O. but dropped the idea when he discovered that someone else already had adopted that name for a racing car. After narrowing the choice down to four possibilities, he finally selected "The Judge." Heinemann also admitted that he picked this name because of the popular line "Here come de Judge" on the "Laugh-In" television show.

"The Judge" was painted on the side of Heinemann's modified 1932 Ford on June 15, 1968, and he displayed the car at a Milwaukee dealer's showroom on July 2. During the next few months, while Pontiac was selecting "The Judge" as its proposed trademark for the new model, getting legal clearance, and putting the automobile into production with that name affixed to it, Heinemann exhibited and raced his car at several events in the Milwaukee area. Neither Heinemann nor General Motors knew of each other's activities at this time.

Heinemann found out about Pontiac's "The Judge" when he attended the first public display of the 1969 line at a local dealer's showroom on September 26, 1968. Shortly afterward he went to see a lawyer.

The following sequence of events then took place: On October 1, 1968, Heinemann filed an application to register "The Judge" as a trademark for "entertainment and advertising" in the state of Wisconsin; the Wisconsin registration was issued on October 3; on February 17, 1969, Heinemann wrote his claim letter to General Motors, asserting that he was the owner of the trademark "The Judge"; on February 19, 1969, Heinemann filed an application in the United States Patent and Trademark Office to register "The Judge" as a service mark for "exhibition automobile racing"; that application was granted, and the registration was issued on July 28, 1970. Meanwhile, settlement negotiations were going on between Heinemann and General Motors, but these were unsuccessful and Heinemann started his lawsuit on December 2, 1970.

For its defense, General Motors relied principally on the legal rule stated at the beginning of this section, specifically, that Heinemann could not show any commercial use of "The Judge" and therefore was not entitled to claim any trademark rights in that expression. Heinemann countered with the statement that he had planned to open an automobile equipment shop that would have capitalized on the name "The Judge." He actually did open a shop in June of 1969 but did not call it "The Judge" because, he asserted, of General Motors' massive advertising campaign associating "The Judge" with the new Pontiac model.

The real judge who decided the case was Judge Bauer of the federal district court in Illinois. After discussing the legal background, Judge Bauer summarized the test that Heinemann would have to meet in order to be successful in his lawsuit: That the term "The Judge" was used in connection with a trade or business at the time of the alleged infringing activity. As Judge Bauer explained, "While the law does not require a nationwide business; an old, established business; or even a profitable business for the acquisition of property interests in trade or service marks, it does require a *presently existing* trade or business for such acquisition."

Judge Bauer ruled that Heinemann was simply racing or displaying his automobile as part of a hobby and that his intention to use the same name on a future business failed to satisfy the legal requirements. The conclusion, therefore, was that Heinemann had no trademark rights in the expression "The Judge"; his registrations were valueless, and the lawsuit was dismissed.

Quoting again from Judge Bauer, what Heinemann "attempted to do was reserve a trade or service mark pending the creation of a trade or business; this the law will not allow him to do."

Actually, U.S. law is almost unique in imposing this requirement, and it frequently has been criticized as inadequate to meet present-day business requirements and for encouraging "token" uses as a kind of subterfuge.

In practically all other countries, a trademark can be registered (or at least applied for) without prior use, although some countries require a statement of bona fide intention to use the mark and others provide for cancellation of the registration if the mark has not been used after a prescribed number of years.

Efforts have been under way for some time to change the U.S. trademark law so that it will be possible to apply for registration of a mark without putting it into actual use. This would indeed be a kind of reservation system, and it would permit potential conflicts to be weeded out before making the investment required to introduce the new mark on a commercial scale.

Trademark Use Must Be Maintained

U.S. law requires that a trademark must be used on a product before any legal protection can be claimed for it. There is no way under the present law (although changes have been proposed in this) for a company to "reserve" an unused trademark, no matter how ingenious and distinctive a creation it may be.

Futhermore, once trademark rights have been acquired, the trademark cannot simply be put away and held for future exploitation. Use must be continued, or the legal rights in the trademark will be lost. If the trademark has been registered in the U.S. Patent and Trademark Office, it is subject to a section in the federal law which states that nonuse for two years or more is considered abandonment of the trademark, unless there is a legally acceptable excuse (which explains why liquor trademarks survived Prohibition).

An abandoned trademark cannot be enforced even against a competitor using the identical mark, and its registration is subject to cancellation by legal proceedings either in the Patent and Trademark Office or the courts. In addition, federal law requires the filing of an affidavit that a mark is still in use during the sixth year after its registration; if that affidavit is not filed, the registration automatically will be canceled by the Patent and Trademark Office.

In order to meet legal requirements and avoid the loss of trademark rights, companies with many brands have been in the practice of setting up trademark maintenance programs under which a minimum sales volume is assured. For example, a friendly distributor may be asked to place a standing order under which one or two cases of goods are shipped every six months, with copies of the invoices going to the corporate trademark department files so that evidence of use will be available if needed. There are many variations, depending in part on the kind of merchandise and the distribution patterns in the particular industry. Some manufacturers simply see to it that a minimum stock is always available and keep records of sales of individual items.

In a decision that affected the marketing practices of many companies, the influential United States Court of Appeals headquartered in New York City invalidated a trademark for perfume because occasional sales in small quantities were not sufficient to meet legal requirements of keeping a trademark in use. Snob is the trademark for a French perfume made by Le Galion and sold in substantial quantities in a number of foreign countries. Le Galion was never able to sell its Snob perfume in the United States, however, because an American corporation named Jean Patou Inc. had registered the identical word as its trademark, based on its own use of Snob on perfume in this country. Conflicts of this sort can arise because any given country's trademark laws stop at its own borders.

In this particular case, Le Galion decided to challenge Patou's rights to the Snob trademark, claiming that Patou never had used it sufficiently to sustain its legal rights. The evidence showed that from 1950 to 1971 Patou had sold only 89 bottles of Snob perfume and that it had never engaged in any advertising or other sales efforts to support the product. Dollar figures were available only for the period between 1951 and 1969; during those 18 years Patou sold 72 bottles, with a total retail value of less than $600, on which it claimed to have made a gross profit of about $100.

The trial judge decided in favor of Patou. Among other things, he ruled that the minimal use of the Snob trademark was sufficient "in light of the customary practice of perfumers to 'reserve' a name and to carry on trademark maintenance programs." The trial judge noted that the difficulty of finding new and attractive brand names for perfumes had caused manufacturers to hold a number of potential names in reserve until the company might decide to begin large-scale distribution. He concluded that minimal bona fide use for the purpose of trademark protection is all that the law requires, and he was satisfied that each of Patou's sales of Snob perfume was in response to an order from a bona fide customer. In other words, the sales program was not a sham, even though it was designed primarily to maintain legal rights in the trademark.

This decision was reversed by the federal Court of Appeals, which ruled that Patou's trademark maintenance program was not sufficient. In his opinion for a unanimous three-member court, Judge Henry J. Friendly laid out the basic principles clearly and concisely.

So far as the initial acquisition of trademark rights is concerned, "adoption and a single use of the mark may be sufficient to entitle the user to register the mark." However, the initial use must be part of a bona fide attempt to begin commercial exploitation. "A company must do more than simply distribute its product in an effort to lay the basis for registration; it must actually put the product on the market before trademark rights will attach."

Although one sale may be enough to justify a valid registration, Judge Friendly wrote, "more is required to sustain the mark against a charge of nonusage." Trademark rights have been upheld in a number of court decisions in spite of modest sales programs, but, in those cases, "the trademark usage, although limited, was part of an ongoing program to exploit the mark commercially." By contrast, as Judge Friendly pointed out, there are other cases where minimal sales have been found insufficient to sustain trademark rights because there was "no present intent . . . to market the trademarked product." To avoid loss of the trademark, the use must have been "deliberate and continuous, not sporadic, casual, or transitory."

From the evidence Judge Friendly concluded that "Patou has never put its product on the market in any meaningful way; . . . the token sales program engaged in here is by its very nature inconsistent with a present plan of commercial exploitation." Specifically, the Court of Appeals did not agree with the trial judge that sales of 89 units in 21 years (Judge Friendly called this "a meager trickle of business") was the kind of bona fide use that justified continued protection of the trademark.

The Court of Appeals was not impressed with the $100 "gross profit" claimed by Patou over an 18-year period. Aside from any other costs, they felt that simply keeping accurate records of the sales of Snob perfume easily would have eaten up the $100. Judge Friendly went on to comment: "Even if it should happen that by some touch of managerial or accounting wizardry Patou has managed to turn a net profit of a few dollars on its sales of 'Snob,' its use of the trademark would still not constitute good faith commercial exploitation."

Where does this leave the conventional trademark maintenance program? The basic reasons for the Court of Appeals' decision can be found in a footnote to Judge Friendly's opinion, in which he explains that: "Determining what constitutes sufficient use for trademark ownership purposes is obviously a case-by-case task. . . . It is important to note expressly that the balance of the equities plays an important role in deciding whether defendant's [Patou's] use is sufficient to warrant trademark protection. . . . The fact that defendant's conduct has barred a foreign competitor from marketing a well-established product in this country, without promoting any compensating public interest, requires close scrutiny of the propriety of defendant's 'use'."

Businessmen like certainty, and lawyers like to be able to give them definite advice. But in the face of Judge Friendly's Solomonic approach to the problem, which requires an indepth study of the facts and a balancing of the equities on both sides, it is obvious that general rules for trademark maintenance programs simply cannot be laid down. For one thing, it is unlikely that anyone would be able to tell in advance who the opposing party will be in some future dispute—if one should ever arise.

A marketing manager knows whether a brand really is being commercially exploited. About all one can say is that anything less raises a risk in light of the Snob decision.

Unused Trademarks Can Be Taken by Another Company

Bristol-Myers Company discontinued the marketing of Ipana brand toothpaste—and specifically abandoned the Ipana trademark—in September 1968. In trademark law abandonment means to discontinue use with the intention not to resume.

But intent is a state of mind that may be difficult to prove, and *tax* law requires a specific date if the trademark owner wants to write off a loss on its investment in the brand. That is why corporations in such a position generally abandon a trademark by formal resolution of the board of directors followed by a public announcement. Bristol-Myers also took the next logical step by requesting the United States Patent and Trademark Office to cancel its registrations of the trademark Ipana, and this was done October 3, 1968.

Since Bristol-Myers had expressly abandoned all rights in the Ipana trademark, that left it up for grabs. The basic rule of "first come first served" applies in this situation just as it does with a completely new trademark. It is essential to bear in mind, however, that "first" requires some commercial use of the trademark, not simply a decision to adopt it or even the filing of an application to register it in the Patent and Trademark Office.

Four separate companies claimed rights to Ipana in the U.S. Patent and Trademark Office after Bristol-Myers abandoned it. Two of these dropped out, presumably because they realized their dates of first use were hopelessly late compared with the two others. This left a contest between La Maur Inc. and an individual named Joseph Block, who was doing business as Ipana Pharmaceuticals Company.

La Maur got into the race by acquiring Ipana Corporation, a new enterprise established to exploit the Ipana trademark after Bristol-Myers had discontinued it. The organizers of this corporation took their first order for Ipana toothpaste on December 3, 1968, although they did not yet have any inventory.

By December 26, however, La Maur had placed a manufacturing order for 53,800 tubes of Ipana toothpaste. The first shipment to an interstate customer (crossing state lines is important in securing a federal trademark registration) took place March 14, 1969.

Ipana Corporation eventually acquired around 900 customers throughout the U.S. It extended the mark to mouthwash. Sales representatives were appointed in 48 of the 50 states. Thousands of tubes of toothpaste and bottles of mouthwash were shipped. Ipana products were advertised in trade publications and sales bulletins.

On March 2, 1970, La Maur acquired all the rights of Ipana Corporation, and put the brand in its House of Style division. Sales and advertising increased under the new ownership. In addition, the Ipana trademark was extended further to a breath freshener, while marketing of the toothpaste and mouthwash continued.

Nevertheless, Joseph Block was ahead of La Maur as far as the Patent and Trademark Office records were concerned. He claimed October 16, 1968 as the date of his Ipana Pharmaceuticals Company's first interstate shipment of Ipana toothpaste.

The Patent and Trademark Office approved Block's application to register Ipana as his trademark, but La Maur contested this, claiming that Block had made no real commercial use of the trademark and, therefore, that La Maur was legally the first user.

The evidence showed that Block had heard about Bristol-Myers' abandonment of the Ipana trademark while he was attending a convention in Puerto Rico in the fall of 1968. He immediately called his attorney in New York, and the report was confirmed. Block returned to New York and bought a quantity of Ipana toothpaste that had been made by Bristol-Myers and was still in the hands of wholesalers.

Then, with the help of his secretary, Block prepared a number of hand-drawn labels marked "New Ipana toothpaste" and "Dist. Ipana Pharmaceuticals Company, New York, N.Y.," which they pasted over the fronts and backs of the Bristol-Myers tubes.

On October 16, 1968, Block shipped one dozen of these sample tubes to a company in Massachusetts and obtained a return receipt for them at his business address, which was rent-free office space furnished to him by his attorney.

Several additional shipments of toothpaste bearing the hand-made labels allegedly were made, but even if some of these shipments did get through, it was not clear that any of the merchandise was resold to the public.

Beginning November 19, 1968, Block ceased all shipments. He testified that he was awaiting a decision about who owned the trademark before making any further capital expenditures.

This created a difficult situation for the Trademark Trial and Appeal Board, the three-member tribunal in the U.S. Patent and Trademark Office that decides questions of the registrability of trademarks. It is a basic principle of trademark law that a single sale or shipment in interstate commerce of a product bearing a trademark is sufficient to acquire rights in the mark when circumstances show an intent to continue the use. On the other hand, it is equally well established that rights cannot be created merely by adopting a mark and, therefore, that a party must use its mark in connection with an existing business in order to acquire rights in it. In other words, as has been stated previously, a trademark cannot simply be reserved for future use.

The Trademark Trial and Appeal Board noted that Block had no office other than the one shared with his attorney on a rent-free basis; had no bank account, ledgers, catalogs, or price lists; and did not even maintain a telephone in his or his company's name. The record did not show what it cost him to buy some of the old stock of Bristol-Myers toothpaste, but aside from this and the telephone calls, Block's only expenditures apparently were $37 for stationery bearing the name of Ipana Pharmaceuticals Company.

The conclusion of the Board was that Block had never used the Ipana trademark "in connection with an existing business in toothpaste or other products, and therefore has created no rights therein." This cleared the way for La Maur to claim full rights in the trademark.

First User Is the Owner of the Trademark

It is not surprising that a manufacturer searching for a new brand name occasionally will come up with one that a competitor has just recently selected. "Great minds run in the same channels," as the saying goes. But it can be very expensive if both companies proceed with their plans and go into production before finding out that a conflict exists.

Unfortunately, our trademark law is not equipped to avoid this problem. In the United States, the first company to put a trademark in use becomes its exclusive owner. It can get a court order, if necessary, to stop its competitor from using the identical trademark even if the competitor was the first to select it.

When a fight over priority occurs in a situation like this, a frequent question is what kind of "use" the law will recognize. The litigation between Farah Manufacturing Company and Blue Bell Inc. over the trademark, Time Out, is an example. The double mental association with sports and leisure made this expression a happy choice for a brand of men's slacks. In the spring of 1973 Farah and Blue Bell both thought it up and decided to use it, within a few weeks of one another.

Farah was first with the conception, on May 16. It received clearance from legal counsel to go ahead with the new trademark because a search of available records did not show anyone else already using it. The fall line was presented to sales personnel on June 5. Tags with the Time Out brand name (and an hourglass logo) were completed on June 27.

Preliminary evaluations of marketing potential for the new line were favorable, so Farah set the stage for claiming trademark rights by shipping 12 pairs of slacks with the Time Out tag attached, one to each of its 12 regional sales managers, on July 3. The sales managers actually paid for the slacks, presumably in accordance with Farah's procedures for establishing commercial use of a new trademark.

Orders were received on the basis of the samples shipped July 3, and Farah went into production. Additional sample garments were shipped to sales personnel on July 11 and 14. Merchandising plans were complete by the end of July. The first shipment to customers, however, did not occur until September.

Blue Bell's project was more ambitious. It was planning a separate division to reach a new segment of the market. Management approved the use of the name Time Out for the new division and as a trademark for the garments on June 18. Blue Bell also received clearance from its legal counsel, since Farah had not yet started production and there was no way any information about Farah's selection of the identical trademark could have gotten into the public records.

The system used by Blue Bell to attempt to nail down its legal trademark rights was different from the one followed by Farah. Blue Bell had several hundred labels made up displaying the Time Out brand name (and a design of a referee's hands forming a "T"). These were attached to some slacks that were already tagged with another Blue Bell trademark, Mr. Hicks. On July 5, several hundred pairs of these slacks were shipped with both tags attached.

Production of Blue Bell's new Time Out line of merchandise began in late August, and the fall designs were presented at a sales meeting early in September. Orders started coming in right away, but it was October before the first shipment of Time Out garments was made.

To give some idea of the financial dimensions of the problem, by the end of October Farah had received orders for 204,403 items of Time Out sportswear, representing a retail sales value of over $2,750,000. Blue Bell had received orders for 154,200 Time Out garments valued at over $900,000 (it is not clear whether this dollar amount was wholesale or retail value). And both companies had started extensive advertising campaigns.

It was at about this point that Blue Bell and Farah discovered they were using the same brand name. Blue Bell started suit against Farah for trademark infringement, and Farah responded by filing a countersuit against Blue Bell for trademark infringement. In other words, each company claimed the trademark for itself and considered the other company an infringer. After a decision by a federal district judge in Texas, the case was taken up to the U.S. Court of Appeals for the fifth circuit.

The three-judge Court of Appeals ruled that both Farah's and Blue Bell's initial shipments failed to meet the legal requirements of "use" for trademark ownership purposes.

Farah's shipment of slacks to its 12 regional managers was merely an internal transaction. The slacks were sold, but not to the public. A trademark exists so that the consumer may identify the merchandise. Since the new trademark was not exposed to the public, it did not matter whether the sample garments were sold or simply shipped free of charge. In order to win a priority contest, the court ruled, a trademark must make an impression on the mind of the purchasing public.

What about Blue Bell's July 5 shipment? The only garments sold were from Blue Bell's established Mr. Hicks line. Customers were ordering Mr. Hicks apparel, not Time Out. When they received the goods, they found (if they noticed it) that a Time Out tag had been attached along with the Mr. Hicks label.

The court recognized the established legal principle that a single article can be identified by more than one trademark (like Nabisco and Ritz on a box of crackers, for example). But there must be good faith use of each mark. Blue Bell's attachment of a secondary label to an older line of goods was not bona fide use, according to the court's opinion, but a bad faith attempt to reserve a trademark for future use. Our law does not countenance the reservation of trademarks, so the court concluded that Blue Bell's attempt was not a "valid use in trade."

With both early shipments knocked out as insufficient to create legal rights in the trademark, the next question was who came first in making real commercial sales. The evidence showed clearly that it was September of 1973 when Farah made its first shipment to the trade of merchandise bearing the Time Out mark. Blue Bell, whose entire Time Out program was about a month behind Farah's, did not ship its Time Out garments to commercial customers until October. Therefore, Farah had priority and owned the Time Out trademark; Blue Bell was ordered to discontinue all use of it.

Why should trying to reserve a trademark be considered an act of bad faith? The answer lies in longstanding traditions, confirmed by the federal trademark statute, that rights in a trademark can be acquired only by putting it into commercial use. Registration, which is optional in any event, cannot take place until *after* the mark is in use.

There is nothing sacrosanct about this law. Indeed, the U.S. is almost the only country that still follows what used to be the old English rule.

In Canada, for example, a company can file an application to register a trademark that it plans to use; the registration will not be issued until after the trademark goes into commercial use, but in the meantime competitors have been put on notice and will not make an investment in an identical mark. Great Britain and most other English-speaking countries have laws that permit the registration of a mark so long as the applicant has a good faith intention of putting it into use. In practically all the rest of the world, a company can go ahead and register a trademark without regard to whether or not it is in use at the time, subject to the possibility of having the registration canceled if use either is not commenced or is discontinued for a specified number of years.

Attempts have been made to change the U.S. law so that it will be more like the Canadian system. An application could be filed based on the company's intention to use the trademark. Competitors who coincidentally came up with the identical mark would not be working in the dark, as under the present U.S. system, because a search of the records would turn up the earlier application.

Both parties in the Time Out case lost something. Blue Bell, of course, had only the gross profit from a limited number of sales to offset the complete loss of its entire project, including the advertising cost. Even Farah, who won the lawsuit, had to live with the uncertainties of the litigation and also had to pay its own legal expenses. Cases like the Time Out decision may provide some impetus for making a change in our law.

A Word of Caution

It should be pointed out that almost everything stated in this chapter has been in relation to the law of the United States of America. The laws of other countries are vastly different. For instance, there are many places where the first one to register a trademark, even though he may never have used it, becomes its absolute owner. But concepts of what constitutes infringement, in terms of creating a likelihood of confusion among the purchasing public, tend to be remarkably similar throughout the world. This book will not attempt to deal comprehensively with the situation in foreign countries, although there is a chapter on foreign problems.

CHAPTER 2

How to Choose a Trademark

Some Basic Do's and Don'ts

The problem of choosing a trademark exists every time an advertiser decides to add a product to his line; if it is new to that particular manufacturer, it will need a brand name even though it may not be new to the world. The solution is an easy one if an existing mark is simply to be extended to the new item—for example, adding Dial shampoo to the Dial soap line—but there are many situations in which that is not suitable. Furthermore, the trend for some time now appears to have been toward a new brand name for every product.

The first criterion for choosing a trademark is an easy one: Don't copy, even innocently. The new mark must not duplicate one already in use by somebody else. Checking services are available, and their use is compulsory as a practical matter—even though none of them is absolutely foolproof, because there is no central registry that contains *all* the marks in use.

Legal requirements, however, are not so easily satisfied. Suppose there is an earlier mark that is similar although not identical? Suppose they don't look alike but do have the same meaning? Suppose the existing mark is registered for a product that is somewhat different from the new one? Questions like these suggest why trademark search reports are best handled through counsel, who can interpret and evaluate the data on the basis of available legal precedents.

The second main criterion is: Don't be obvious. The fellow who thought up Kantleek for a hot water bottle undoubtedly believed he was being creative, but the United States Patent and Trademark Office refused to register the mark because other manufacturers could not be deprived of the right to claim their hot water bottles "can't leak." Just misspelling words doesn't help, especially since they continue to sound the same when pronounced by a retail customer. It is not necessary to invent a brand new word, but it is important that the word finally selected does not simply describe the product. Arrow is a fine trademark for shirts, but it would be no good at all for wooden sticks with points at one end and feathers at the other.

A descriptive mark like Kantleek eventually may come to signify just one particular manufacturer's product in the public mind and thus win the right to registration after all, if no competitor has bothered to use the mark in its descriptive sense and thus upset the claim of exclusivity. But the investment required to bring such an expression to the point of acquiring a "secondary significance" might better have been spent on educating the public through advertising to connect an arbitrary, *distinctive* mark with the product.

The more distinctive the mark, the greater its strength both legally and commercially. Initially it may take greater exposure to establish consumer identification for an arbitrary mark or a coined word, but once the connection has been made, the distinctive quality of the mark will point unmistakably toward a single source. Such a mark will survive periods when advertising campaigns must be reduced or even interrupted completely for business reasons. The distinctive mark not only receives the broadest protection against imitation and infringement, its effectiveness as an advertising device gives additional impact to every use made of it.

Pitfalls to Avoid

Finding a name for a new product is one of the perennial problems in marketing. The task becomes more difficult as the profusion of new consumer goods strains the resources of the language.

Of course, it is always possible to extend the use of an existing brand name to a new product in the line. Ivory, for example, identifies not only bar soap, but also powder and liquid detergent. This method has a great deal to recommend it, for the new product then has a built-in introduction to the buyer. The familiar brand name helps to overcome consumer resistance to a strange item on the shelf, and it may have enough carrying power to launch the new product without a detailed explanatory advertising campaign.

But the trend is against relying upon an established brand name to identify a new product. At the very least, there seems currently to be a need for a new name in conjunction with the old one. Ford Motor Company, for instance, used to get along with Model T and Model A. Then it added a whole Edsel line and also produced a new Ford with its own subsidiary brand name of Thunderbird. More recently, we have become accustomed to such additional Ford cars as the Fairmont, Mustang, Pinto, and LTD.

Any new product, therefore, is likely to require a new name for itself. The first rule in choosing one is to avoid conflict with a brand name already in use by someone else. The legal principle is that there must be no likelihood that a purchaser will be confused, deceived, or mistaken. Note that the law in this field is intensely practical; legal rights are measured by the possibility of confusion in the consumer's mind. In considering this possibility, it is necessary to take into account the methods by which the products are marketed, the care with which they are selected (which frequently bears a direct relationship to the retail price), and the type of individual who normally purchases the article.

Consumers generally do not have an opportunity to make side-by-side comparisons between products bearing similar brand names, so that the fallibility of human memory also must be considered. Finally, the law gives the benefit of the doubt to the first user, so decisions about new brand names must be on the conservative side.

The proposed new name must not be confusingly similar to

an existing one in either sound, appearance, or meaning. It will not do simply to alter the spelling for the obvious reason that some people may only hear the brand name and never see it at all. Similarly, even though you think it ought to be pronounced quite differently, that is not enough if the words look alike because some consumers will rely on the appearance of the name, rather than its sound, and others may pronounce it in their own way. Finally, even duplication of meaning must be avoided if that is likely to cause confusion, so that it would be a mistake, for example, to introduce a Black Cat perfume if a Chat Noir were already on the market.

Suppose the products are directly competitive but the brand names are slightly different from one another, or suppose the brand names are identical but the products are not. In practice, numerous variations in degree occur. All that can be said as a general rule is that the combined effect of the differences between the goods and the differences between the brand names must be considered in determining the likelihood of consumer confusion.

If a brand name is sufficiently distinctive and sufficiently well known, the law will not permit its use by another company even on unrelated products because the consumer might infer a connection. The legal theory throughout is that no company should be allowed to sell its merchandise on the strength of someone else's good will. For instance, the maker of the Rolls-Royce car was able to get a court order prohibiting the use of Rolls-Royce as a brand name for radio tubes. Judge Learned Hand once said that he doubted there could be any confusion between lipsticks and steam shovels, but the Patent and Trademark Office has refused to register Kodak as a trademark for cigarette lighters. On the other hand, a relatively weak expression such as Blue Ribbon, Perfection, or Acme can be used as the brand name for numerous different kinds of goods without creating any confusion, for none of them is sufficiently distinctive to make the consumer think of only a single possible source for the products.

What else ought to be avoided? A brand name should not

simply describe (or misdescribe) the product itself or one of its characteristics. Suppose there is a new type of glue whose chemical composition gives it a green color. The word Green would not be a suitable choice for a brand name for this product because anyone who makes it has the right to use the common name of the characteristic color in describing it.

Further, a brand name should not be a family name. Jones would make a poor brand name for, let us say, shoes, since some other Jones might decide to use his family name in the shoe business as well and would have the right to do so.

Also, a brand name should not be a geographical name, especially if it is the name of a place from which the product actually does or logically might come. Thus, Newcastle would be a particularly poor choice as the name for a new brand of coal.

There are exceptions to these guidelines, such as Ivory soap, Parker pens, and Waltham watches, all of which are perfectly good, legal brand names. The explanation is that each of these names has been used exclusively by a single manufacturer for such a long period of time and with such a wide degree of public acceptance that the consumer now associates the brand name with one particular source for the product. This can happen with new brand names also.

To go back to our first example, the word Green in time might become accepted as an indication of the source of the glue rather than merely a statement of its color. But that is a very risky basis on which to choose a brand name, for some other manufacturer might introduce a competing Green Glue before the first one became definitely established in the consumer's mind. This loss of exclusivity in the marketplace would make it impossible for the first manufacturer ever to acquire protectible legal rights in Green as a brand name because it would not indicate a single source for the product.

On the positive side, what techniques are likely to produce a good brand name? A coined word will be the most distinctive, although it may well take an expensive advertising campaign to get the consumer to remember it. The classic example, of course, is Kodak, deliberately created by George Eastman to be meaningless but easy to pronounce.

One advantage of a coined word is that it can spawn a whole family of related marks, such as Kodalk (photographic chemical), Kodachrome (color slide film), Kodacolor (color negative film), and Kodascope (projector).

A different type of coined word derives from the initials or first syllables of the company's own name. Well-known examples include Nabisco and Texaco, which now have become the corporate names of the former National Biscuit Company and Texas Company.

Another good technique is to choose an ordinary English word that has no significance whatever in association with the product on which it is to be used. Arrow, for instance, is as completely meaningless when applied to wearing apparel as a coined word would be. It therefore makes a fine brand name for men's shirts and, since it is a common word of the English language, Arrow no doubt was easier for the consuming public to learn than a coined word would have been.

Probably the best type of brand name is the word that suggests some desirable quality of the product without actually describing it. That is sometimes a difficult line to draw, but the many successful brand names that fall in this category show that the effort is worthwhile. Think, for instance, of Raid, Sure, and Close-Up; each of them is appropriate for its product, yet each is fanciful and suggestive rather than merely descriptive.

The practical problem of how to avoid conflict with some prior user always remains. Although there is no complete directory of all brand names in use, trademark lawyers have access to various sources of information, including Patent and Trademark Office records, trade directory listings, and others. Reports and opinions can be obtained on the likelihood that a proposed new brand name will be considered confusingly similar to one already in use.

It is an excellent idea to plan on having any new brand name registered as a trademark. If the brand name meets the legal requirements for registration, you can be reasonably sure that you have succeeded in creating a distinctive trademark which, among other things, will stand up in court in case it should be necessary to proceed against an infringer. A trademark registration automatically puts everyone on notice under the law; that is, everyone is considered to have legal knowledge of the trademark even though he may never have bothered to check. Accordingly, there can be no such thing as innocent infringement of a trademark that has been registered.

An application to register a trademark in the United States Patent and Trademark Office cannot be filed until *after* the mark has been put into use, but even having an application on file is worthwhile. Honest competitors normally will check before introducing new brand names and will refrain from copying yours if they find a record of a pending application. For similar reasons, it is wise to list brand names in trade directories or similar publications.

Likelihood of Consumer Confusion Is the Key Test

One of the ways in which a dispute over brand names gets to be public knowledge is a so-called opposition proceeding in the United States Patent and Trademark Office. The company that wants to protect a new brand name ordinarily files an application to register it as a trademark. A competitor who thinks it has a conflicting brand name can oppose the application.

In one case of this type, Colgate-Palmolive opposed Warner-Lambert, claiming that Warner's new trademark, Ultra-Dent, for denture cleanser tablets, would be likely to create consumer confusion with Colgate's established Ultra Brite trademark for toothpaste. The history of Ultra Brite goes back to 1966, while Ultra-Dent had been put into use in December 1970.

The opinion in the case explains the difference between the two basic kinds of toothpaste. The "therapeutic" brands stress and promote cavity prevention, while the "cosmetic" brands stress and promote whiter, brighter teeth. Ultra Brite is an example of the cosmetic type, with its promotion stressing sex appeal as well.

Ultra Brite started in test markets in 1966 and went national in 1967. That year Colgate also registered it as a trademark. Since its introduction, the Ultra Brite brand has received extensive advertising and promotional support. On media advertising alone Colgate spent over $38,000,000 from 1966 through 1971. This included network and spot television, network and spot radio, national magazines, newspapers and newspaper supplements, trade publications, and military publications. The message always was white, bright teeth plus sex appeal.

In addition, during the same six-year period Colgate spent more than $30,000,000 on promotion including sampling. Promotional activities covered such areas as couponing in magazines, cooperative couponing, direct mail, college posters, price-off deals, point-of-sale displays, sweepstakes and other contests, and special promotions to the dental profession. During this period over 120,000,000 free samples of Ultra Brite toothpaste were distributed, by mail and personal distribution, in stores, in colleges, and to people about to get married.

These efforts succeeded in moving Ultra Brite to the No. 3 position among all toothpaste brands in the U.S. From 1966 through 1971, more than 200,000,000 tubes of Ultra Brite toothpaste were sold, producing gross sales revenue of $105,000,000 for Colgate. By the end of 1971, the product had been made available in five sizes in both "regular" and "cool mint" flavors.

Warner-Lambert did not present any evidence about sales or promotion of its Ultra-Dent tablets for cleaning dentures. Probably it had followed the conventional practice of launching the product with the new brand name on a very limited scale, filing a trademark application, and then—after Colgate objected—holding off to see what happened with the legal proceedings.

Warner's defense was based on the assertion that Ultra Brite is a weak kind of trademark whose owner might be able to object to an exact duplication, but is not entitled to a broad scope of protection against similar marks for somewhat different products. In addition to the dictionary meanings of the terms *Ultra* and *Bright* themselves, Warner argued that Ultra is in common use in the cosmetics and toiletries field, pointing out 83 other trademarks containing the term *Ultra*. On closer examination, however, it was revealed that only one of those 83 trademarks was for a dentifrice. That was Ultra Bouquet, registered by Richard Hudnut, which turned out to be a subsidiary of Warner-Lambert. In any event, there was no evidence showing that Ultra Bouquet was in current use, so there was no indication that the brand had any impact on consumer consciousness.

The opinion of the Trademark Trial and Appeal Board said that it might well be true that Ultra Brite initially was a highly suggestive designation for the particular Colgate product, and it could have been argued at the beginning that as a brand name it was on the weak side for this reason. However, the opinion goes on to say, there can be no doubt that, as a result of very extensive advertising and promotion over the years, any weakness that originally may have affected the term Ultra Brite has long since disappeared. What exists today, according to the Board's opinion, is a strong indication of origin for Colgate's dentifrice that is "deserving of protection against the registration of the same or a similar term for goods which purchasers may attribute to opposer [Colgate] in the natural expansion of its business thereunder."

The Board pointed out that a dentifrice and a denture cleanser are closely related goods that serve the same function to the extent that a denture cleanser does for artificial teeth what a toothpaste does for natural teeth. Also, people who have partial dentures may purchase and use both products.

They are sold through the same retail channels and often in the same or nearby sections of the same retail establishments.

Taking into consideration the impact made on the market by Ultra Brite, "with a resultant high consumer recognition factor," and also the absence of any evidence of actual use of any other trademark in the dentifrice field containing the term *Ultra,* the Board found itself unable to go along with Warner-Lambert's contention that purchasers would attribute little or no trademark significance to the Ultra portion of Colgate's trademark. In conclusion, the opinion of the Board stated that the overall resemblances between the two trademarks were such that purchasers might mistakenly assume that Ultra-Dent denture cleanser was another product of the makers of Ultra Brite toothpaste. This is one kind of possible confusion that federal trademark law prohibits, and Warner-Lambert's application to register Ultra-Dent, therefore, was rejected on the basis of Colgate-Palmolive's opposition.

Warner-Lambert chose not to appeal the decision. Although this ruling technically affects only the registrability of the mark (Colgate-Palmolive might have had to bring a lawsuit in a regular court to get an order stopping Warner-Lambert from using Ultra-Dent), the failure to appeal and the absence of evidence of any substantial use of the new brand name by Warner-Lambert indicates that it reached a commercial decision to drop it. The product, of course, could be marketed under a different brand name.

Corporate Identity Program Helps Expand Trademark Rights Against Newcomer

An important marketing decision faced by every conglomerate is whether each of its constituent enterprises should be identified as a member of the same corporate "family" of companies or whether some or all of them should retain a separate identity. The question arises particularly when the conglomerate has been created by a series of acquisitions, as opposed to diversification by internal growth. The trend in corporate identification programs appears to be toward stressing the family resemblance by every available means, including co-ordinated graphics for all subsidiaries and divisions.

Textron, Inc., one of the pioneers in growth by acquisition, adopted the policy some years ago of requiring each of its subsidiaries and divisions to use the phrase "A Textron Company" in association with its own business name. This policy paid a perhaps unexpected dividend when Textron was able to stop the registration of the similar but not identical term Tectron as a trademark for semiconductors because two electronics manufacturers Textron had acquired consistently followed the corporate identification policy—although neither of them used Textron as a trademark for any of its products.

As far back as 1955, the annual report of Textron, Inc., to its stockholders referred to "The Textron Family of Business Enterprises." A more recent summary (adapted from the text of the opinion in the Tectron trademark case) gives some idea of the extent of its diversification. There are four major product groups.

1. Aerospace group: Includes valves, pressure regulators, fluid controls for aircraft and missile fuel systems and similar uses, heat exchange equipment, rocket systems, vertical-lift aircraft, air cushion vehicles, electrohydraulic valves and servo control systems, solar simulators and electro-optics, solar cells and other semiconductor devices.
2. Consumer products group: Includes stationery and writing accessories, sterling silver flatware, grave markers, crystal, chain saws and power lawn mowers, electric golf carts, pumps, lenses and optical machinery, microphones, paints and varnishes, metal buttons, zippers, thread, men's toiletries.
3. Industrial products group: Includes ball and roller bearings, cushioning materials, grey iron castings, grinding wheels, gas meters and regulators, chemicals and agro-chemicals such as linseed oil, poultry, and livestock feeds.

4. Metal products group: Includes staplers and staples, rolling mills, special fasteners, lathes, precision surface grinders, tracer attachments and systems for machine tools.

The Textron corporate identification program has included substantial institutional advertising on television and in such print media as *Business Week, Newsweek,* the *New York Times, Wall Street Journal, Washington Post,* and *Time.* This material explains the association between one or more of its divisions and the parent company, always stressing the name Textron. Examples: "Did you know Textron is also Bell Helicopter?"; "Did you know Textron is also Sheaffer Pen?"; "But did you know Textron is also air cushion vehicles, rocket engines, rolling mills, watch bands . . . ?"; "Products like Bell air cushion vehicles, Homelite chainsaws, Talon zippers, and Spectrolab's solar-power units for outer space. Nine of our divisions make products used in Apollo moonshots."

Because the dispute was about the proposed registration of Tectron as a trademark for semiconductors, Textron naturally emphasized its activities in closely related product lines. Textron has a Heliotek Division that makes interference filters, optical thin films, optical components, and semiconductors such as solar cells, tunnel diodes, silicon-controlled and high-voltage rectifiers, semiconductor resistant units, readout devices, and photo diodes for use in computers, sun sensors, and similar devices.

Textron also has a Spectrolab Division that makes a number of products, including solar cell arrays and panels, solar simulators, and other power system assemblies, which incorporate semiconductor devices.

When they were acquired by Textron, Heliotek and Spectrolab were set up as operating divisions of a subsidiary called Textron Electronics. During that period each of them identified itself as a "Division of Textron Electronics, Inc." on all printed material and in advertising. Later, Textron Electronics was absorbed by Textron, and since that time Heliotek and Spectrolab have followed the prescribed practice of identifying themselves as "A Textron Company." Their products, however, have not been sold under the Textron brand name.

Thor Electronics Corporation was the company that applied for the registration of Tectron as a trademark for products rather broadly described as semiconductors. Textron opposed the application in the United States Patent and Trademark Office, and its objections were sustained by the Trademark Trial and Appeal Board.

The Trademark Board ruled that Textron and Tectron are so nearly alike in sound and appearance that persons aware of Textron's association with its Spectrolab and Heliotek divisions and their products would, upon encountering Thor's semiconductors under the trademark Tectron, mistakenly assume that they were products of Spectrolab or Heliotek or some other enterprise associated with Textron, Inc. And the details of Textron's corporate identification program, as brought out during the proceedings before the Trademark Board, were persuasive evidence that precisely that awareness of Textron's association with its operating divisions had been created in the public mind. Therefore, regardless of the fact that Textron had not been used as a brand name for any of the semiconductor devices made by Spectrolab or Heliotek, a competitor was not permitted to register a similar term as a brand name for its semiconductor products.

CHAPTER 3 Trademark Clearance Procedures

After a new trademark has been selected, the next question is whether it is safe to use it. If the proposed new mark so closely resembles an existing trademark in appearance, sound, or meaning that confusion or mistake is likely to result, it is not legally permissible to put the new mark into use. Confusing similarity depends on a number of elements, including the relationship (or lack of it) between the goods involved and the characteristics of the mark itself.

It is rather obvious that if the new trademark unluckily turns out to be identical to some other company's mark already in use for a directly competitive product, the proposed new mark will have to be dropped. But if the marks are not identical and the goods or services are not the same, somebody must make a judgment about the likelihood of customer confusion. Sometimes it happens that the marks are the same but the products are different or vice versa. Again, questions of judgment arise.

As has been mentioned previously, an important consideration in reaching a conclusion about the availability of a new trademark for use is the degree of distinctiveness it has. The classic examples are a coined word like Kodak on the one hand and a common laudatory term like Blue Ribbon on the other.

Selecting a new trademark can be a major undertaking in itself. Techniques range all the way from programming computers to generate new words with predetermined linguistic characteristics to the more old-fashioned method of the boss asking his wife for suggestions. In between are any number of variations, including the famous occasion when Ford Motor

Company, after retaining the services of a Pulitzer Prize-winning poet to supplement proposals from more conventional sources, discarded the entire list and called the new car Edsel—the first name of the founder's son.

Whatever methods are used, the interim result almost invariably is a list of several terms, perhaps in order of preference, that marketing management would be willing to adopt. This is the point at which trademark clearance procedures must be initiated.

The trademark lawyer may or may not have participated in the preliminary screening process. Many experienced executives find it useful to have a trademark lawyer involved from an early stage. He may be able to stop consideration of a candidate that has an incurable legal defect before someone in management takes a fancy to it and perhaps decides to risk going forward, only to find later that legal difficulties make it necessary to scrap the project after a sizeable investment has been made. Other managers, particularly those who would have to consult outside counsel, feel that bringing a lawyer into the initial screening process is economically wasteful.

Sooner or later, a trademark lawyer is going to have to function on the clearance question because it is basically a legal issue and only an experienced professional with the "feel" of how cases dealing with trademark conflicts are decided can make the informed judgment that is required. However, unless industry security requires absolute secrecy, much can be done with the list of prospective new marks before it is turned over to the trademark lawyer.

Remember that the basic question is confusing similarity with an existing mark. The existing mark need not be well known to create a legal conflict; priority is the test. The people who make up the list of suggestions may be very well informed about their major competitors, but this does not exclude the possibility that someone else unknown to them already is using the same or a closely similar mark.

A series of screening procedures can be used that may save attorneys' time and expenses by eliminating some of the marks on the list before it is sent to counsel for legal clearance. Circulate the list to salespeople, for example, and ask for a written report about the use of any of the marks that is known to them. Get the advertising agency to ask its personnel a similar question. Have a secretary look in trade and telephone directories for similar names. If there is a trade association active in the industry, it may have either a formal or an informal trademark clearance procedure; this can at least be initiated by company personnel. Trade publications in certain industries have indexes of various kinds that can be consulted.

The results of these inquiries may be equivocal because they may reveal similar but not identical marks or identical marks used in different industries. However, any information is better than none.

Now we have reached the point where the trademark lawyer must take over. He should receive the list of proposed new marks, in order of preference, if there is any, and a description of the product or service for which they are intended to be used, together with whatever facts about potential conflicts have been collected by preliminary inquiries of the kind outlined above.

The trademark lawyer starts with this information plus the knowledge that there are over half a million unexpired trademarks registered in the United States Patent and Trademark Office, that hundreds of new ones are registered every week, and that all 50 states have trademark registration systems of their own. He also knows that registration of a trademark is not compulsory and that untold numbers of unregistered trademarks are in use throughout the country, one or more of which may turn out to be a conflict. In addition, a confusingly similar company name also will block a trademark, and people constantly organize new businesses.

How can anyone get the information necessary to give an opinion on the availability of a new trademark? Fortunately, in response to the obvious need, service organizations exist that collect and classify the material and are prepared to supply a "search report" for a modest fee. If the list of proposed new trademarks is long, the trademark lawyer may start with a service that provides rather sketchy reports but charges a correspondingly low fee. This is one way of screening a series of marks quickly and economically. Those that survive the initial culling then will be submitted to one or more other service agencies, depending on how troublesome the situation seems.

Some of these search organizations provide information (for example, state registrations) that others do not. Computerized searches are available from some of them. Some lawyers prefer to rely on personal searches of the actual Patent and Trademark Office records for checking federally registered marks and use the service organizations only for reports based on their libraries of trade publications and directories.

At any rate, whatever source or combination of sources is used, the trademark lawyer eventually receives a list showing identical (if any) and similar marks for the same and related types of goods or services. He may decide that it is necessary to search all types of goods and services if the mark is potentially of great importance or if it is a coined word that might create a problem of the Kodak type mentioned earlier. He probably will check to see whether the trademark appears in the law books as one that was involved in litigation at some prior time.

However, the trademark lawyer is haunted by the knowledge that no search organization can possibly have all the facts because new products constantly are coming on the market that may not be listed anywhere—at least not at the time the report was prepared. He may order reports from more than one searching service if he feels that a cross-check is desirable, but he knows that there always is the possibility of human or computer error.

Perhaps the most frustrating of all, he is conscious of the fact that, if he gives a favorable opinion about a proposed new trademark, someone else nevertheless might be considering the same mark, and might be the first to get it into use—which would mean that the other company had priority and all his work was wasted—and that it is absolutely impossible to guard against this.

The lawyer's job essentially is to review all the reports of arguably similar marks and reach a conclusion about whether or not it is safe to go ahead. If there is a troublesome reference on a search report, he may recommend a commercial investigation to determine whether a conflict is really likely. Sometimes it turns out that a conflicting mark is no longer in use, and it may be possible to ignore it on the theory that it has been abandoned. Sometimes it is feasible to buy another company's rights in a conflicting mark. If the conflict is more apparent than real, the consent of the other company sometimes can be obtained, either as a courtesy or at a price.

The proliferation of trademarks is so great that the clearance procedure may be long and difficult, although there still are rare instances where a search report on a proposed new mark will show nothing even remotely resembling it. Unfortunately, there is no satisfactory international trademark system, so essentially the same procedure must be followed for each foreign country where it is expected the mark will be used, if advance clearance is desired.

There are certain short cuts available in foreign searching, however, and risks frequently are taken because not every new mark will justify the expense of widespread foreign clearance. Efforts have been under way for some time at the diplomatic level to improve the international trademark protection situation with the eventual goal of establishing a method by which multicountry registrations can be obtained by a single application filed in a central intergovernmental office.

CHAPTER 4 Trademark Protection Problems

Mountain King

Some of the fundamental legal rules of trademark infringement have been laid out neatly in a court decision involving, of all things, artificial Christmas trees.

One of the leading brands of artificial Christmas trees is known as Mountain King. These were constructed by hooking prefabricated panels of branches to a center pole to make the lower two-thirds of the tree and adding a prefabricated crest to complete the tree. This method represented an improvement over previous artificial trees, which required attaching each branch to the center pole by a separate hook.

In addition to the basic Mountain King model, the manufacturer offered the Traditional Mountain King and the Giant Mountain King. Sales of this line of artificial Christmas trees increased from $1,500,000 in 1972 to almost $4,000,000 in 1973 and again in 1974, aided by 10 and 30-second TV spots in major marketing areas.

One of Mountain King's principal competitors made an artificial Christmas tree that was put together in a somewhat different way. A hinge device was used instead of hooks to erect the panels that form the lower branches. Also, when disassembled, the Mountain King tree was in several parts, while the competitive item was only in two parts. When both kinds of trees were assembled, however, they looked identical. The competitor selected Alpine King as the trademark for its basic model. In addition, it sold models called Traditional Alpine King and Giant Alpine King.

Mountain King sued Alpine King for trademark infringement. There was no dispute in the lawsuit that the Alpine King manufacturer had full knowledge of what the Mountain King manufacturer was doing. A comparison of the two companies' price lists, catalogs, and posters led the judge who decided the case to conclude that Alpine King had simply adapted some of Mountain King's material for its own use.

What are the basic rules that govern a situation like this? The legal test of infringement actually is a question of marketing psychology. Are potential customers likely to be confused, misled, or deceived by the use of the allegedly infringing mark? This is sometimes a difficult standard to apply. But there are guidelines to help the judge make up his mind.

In the first place, it is not necessary to use the identical words in order to infringe someone else's trademark. Nor does the infringing mark have to be so similar that a person looking at one would be deceived into believing that it was the other. It is sufficient if the allegedly infringing trademark so resembles the other mark in appearance, sound, or meaning that a prospective purchaser is likely to be confused or misled. And the customer is considered to be a person without a very definite or clear recollection of the first trademark.

In this particular case, the word *Alpine* is practically synonymous with Mountain. As the judge wrote in his opinion, "It calls to the mind not only those European mountains known as the Alps, but also a picture of mountains anywhere."

The Alpine King manufacturer had other defenses, however. It argued that the word *King* was not sufficiently distinctive to be entitled to protection or, putting it another way, that the differences between Alpine King and Mountain King were sufficient to avoid the likelihood of confusion because the word *King* also was used by others. As examples, it pointed to King Brand, Green King, Yule King, and Three Kings. But the judge was not persuaded. To him, it was more important that only Mountain King had added Traditional and Giant models to its line until Alpine King duplicated the Traditional and Giant designations for supplemental items in its line.

Alpine King also pointed to the fact that it used the expression Magic Hinge as a second trademark in connection with its artificial Christmas trees. The judge ruled that this was not sufficient to avoid the likelihood of confusion. Magic Hinge referred to a method of construction, while Alpine King referred to the article itself.

The judge therefore concluded that there was sufficient likelihood of customer confusion from the use of Alpine King and Mountain King on directly competitive merchandise to make Alpine King an infringement.

What is the legal consequence of such a ruling? In most cases of this sort, the court will order the infringement discontinued by issuing an injunction against its further use. Although it can be very expensive to have to drop a brand name and substitute a new one, many companies consider an injunction order to be the equivalent of a mere slap on the wrist.

But the judge in the Mountain King case was not satisfied with a simple injunction. Courts have a potent weapon for use against a deliberate infringer, as distinguished from someone who either inadvertently selects a trademark that is confusingly similar or perhaps tries in good faith to come up with an expression that will be somewhat alike but will not confuse the public. The judge in this case found from the evidence that Alpine King had been a wilful infringer and, therefore, in addition to issuing an injunction, he ordered it to pay to the Mountain King manufacturer all the profits made from sales of artificial Christmas trees under the Alpine King trademark.

As the judge said, quoting from an earlier decision, "It is essential to deter companies from wilfully infringing a competitor's mark, and the only way the courts can fashion a strong enough deterrent is to see to it that a company found guilty of wilful infringement shall lose all its profits from its use of the infringing mark."

Comsat

Communications Satellite Corporation, otherwise known as Comsat, succeeded in obtaining a court order prohibiting the use of Comcet as a trademark or corporate name by a computer company. Special difficulties arise when infringement questions are raised in a situation like this, where the trademarks are not identical and the goods or services of the parties are not directly competitive.

Essentially, the judge in such a case must take into account whether prospective purchasers are likely to be confused about the source or sponsorship of the product or services offered under the allegedly infringing mark. In the terms of this case, the question came down to whether prospective purchasers of Comcet's computers might believe there was some form of affiliation between Comcet and Comsat.

The term *Comsat,* of course, was derived from the words "communications satellite." But the fact that a coined word has a known or even an obvious derivation does not weaken it as a trademark. In fact, no one else uses Comsat for any trade purpose whatsoever; it is unique.

In addition, Comsat has spent $1,000,000 in various kinds of promotional activity. Its sales have amounted to many millions of dollars. Its stock, which is listed as Comsat, has been traded on the New York Stock Exchange since 1964. Accordingly, regardless of its obvious source in the ordinary English words "communications" and "satellite," Comsat has become a famous name and a strong trademark. "As such," said Judge Butzner in his opinion for the unanimous three-judge court, "it is entitled to broad protection, for counterfeits more successfully prey on strong marks than on weak."

The defendant in the case was Comcet, Inc., which was organized in 1968, several years after Comsat began its operations. Comcet is affiliated with Comress, Inc. and other related companies whose names are all acronyms. Comress is derived from "computer research systems and software." Another company in the group is Computer Network Corporation, known as Comnet. Still another is Commed, Inc., which derives from "computers" and "medicine." Comcet starts with the syllable com, which was chosen to suggest both "computers" and the corporation's relationship to Comress. The rest of the name comes from the initials of the words "comunications engineering technology."

Comcet had a public offering of its stock, at which point the Securities and Exchange Commission required a statement in the prospectus reading, "Not related to 'Comsat,' Communications Satellite Corp." Presumably this is what brought Comcet to the attention of Comsat. A letter of complaint followed, and when that had no effect, Comsat brought suit.

The court accepted the explanation of how the term Comcet was coined and found no reason to doubt that it was chosen innocently in that there was no deliberate intention to infringe on Comsat's rights. However, in trademark law lack of intent is not a defense. This grows in part from the underlying principle that a court order prohibiting further infringement has for its purpose the protection of the public against confusion as well as the vindication of the trademark owner's rights.

The two trademarks obviously are similar, particularly in sound. However, Comsat is in the business of selling communications services, while Comcet sells communication computers that receive data over telephone and teletype lines, process the information, and relay it to other computers. Even though data transmitted via Comsat's service can originate in a computer or be fed to a computer, it is clear that the two companies are not in a competing business.

On the other hand, Comcet's products, as the court's opinion stated, are closely related to Comsat's services. Specifically, Comcet computers receive data primarily over the facilities of AT&T, which is one of Comsat's customers. In addition, Comcet's computers can be used to receive data transmitted by Comsat's satellites. And many of the companies that are solicited as purchasers of Comcet's computers also are prospective customers of Comsat.

Accordingly, while the two companies are in different industries, those industries are interrelated. As a legal principle, Judge Butzner's opinion comments that "Complementary products or services are particularly vulnerable to confusion." The court concluded that a reasonable person might well believe that Comcet communications computers come from a source related to Comsat's communications services. This statement is the equivalent of ruling that Comcet is an infringement of Comsat.

As a separate ground for upholding Comsat's rights, the Court of Appeals also discussed the incident with the Securities and Exchange Commission at the time that Comcet had its public offering. The court noted that the SEC was quick to detect the possibility of confusion and that Comcet had acquiesced in the requirement that it print a notice on its prospectus disclaiming any connection with Comsat. On this aspect of the case, the court ruled that the likelihood of confusion among investors is an adequate basis for relief by itself.

The final result is that Comcet is prohibited from using its name in any way, including advertising, sales of stock, or as a trademark. The sweeping nature of Comsat's victory is underscored by the fact that its case originally was dismissed by a lower court. The decision discussed here is a complete reversal by the three-judge Court of Appeals.

Continental

Despite its formidable technical vocabulary, the foundation of trademark law rests firmly on marketing psychology. What kind of word or phrase can function as a trademark, whether one company's trademark infringes on the prior rights of another—legal questions like these must be answered by the courts in terms of their appraisal of the most likely consumer reaction under the particular circumstances involved in the case. It is comparatively rare for a judge to give explicit recognition in a published opinion to the influence of advertising on the development of trademark law, but that is what happened in the legal decision discussed here.

Continental Motors Corporation is the largest independent manufacturer of internal combustion engines in the world. It started business in 1902, and its heavily advertised products are sold in every state of the country, as well as abroad. Since 1946 it has operated a subsidiary under the name of Continental Aviation and Engineering Corporation, and approximately 25 percent of Continental's output is used in aircraft.

Continental Aviation Corporation was a service company located at the Opa Locka Airport in Florida. It was not a manufacturer; it overhauled and repaired aircraft engines, instruments, and other devices and sold parts and materials related to these services.

After the usual attempt to settle this dispute by correspondence had proved fruitless, Continental Motors brought suit against Continental Aviation. The complaint claimed, in the language of the federal trademark statute, that the use of the name Continental by the Florida service operation was "likely to cause confusion."

When Continental Motors had completed the presentation of its evidence at the trial, counsel for the defense moved to dismiss the case, and the motion was granted. Florida is in the fifth federal circuit, and the principal reason for this ruling was that the Court of Appeals for that circuit, in a dispute between two insurance companies, had ruled back in 1900 that *Continental* is a geographical adjective that is inherently incapable of being exclusively appropriated as a trademark or trade name. The trial judge felt that this precedent was binding upon him.

Continental Motors appealed to the fifth circuit Court of Appeals and won a reversal. Since the case had not been completed, it was sent back for a new trial. However, no further proceedings were published in the law reports, and the two companies might have reached an out-of-court settlement, especially because the legal argument presented by Continental Motors was sustained. The significant point is that the Court of Appeals formulated a more modern view of the law and gave credit to advertising for influencing the development of trademark concepts.

The nub of the argument presented by Continental Motors

was that a geographic adjective deserves protection on the same basis as any other trademark if, because of association with a particular product or company over a period of time, in the mind of the public the word has come to stand as an identification for that product or firm. As the law books often put it, the geographical term has acquired a "secondary meaning" apart from its original etymological meaning. *Continental*, as a dictionary entry, will always retain its definition as a word meaning pertaining to or relating to a continent. But, when thought of in connection with internal combustion engines, it refers unmistakably to Continental Motors Corporation. At least that is the theory on which Continental Motors was proceeding in the litigation.

In discussing the 1900 Continental Insurance case, Judge Brown of the fifth circuit Court of Appeals wrote that "the continuing vitality of this pronouncement has been substantially, if not entirely, sapped by events of the business world." Later in his opinion the following significant paragraph appears:

> Time, tide, and the relentless movement of the copywriter's pen makes what we once said no longer controlling, not so much from change in the law, but from change in economic facts. Not the least of these is the restless, undulating habits of our air-minded, air-traveling public, many of whom for sport, or pleasure, or business, or an aeronautical combination of them, hop across the nation relying, as they must, on dependable service at airports small and large. And it is here that modern, intense advertising creates the 'image' upon which the public depends."

This is a clear judicial recognition that advertising has the power to take a descriptive term out of the language and convert it into a valuable trademark that the law then will protect against infringement. Moreover, in this decision the court went further and credited advertising with the reversal of an earlier theory of the law, which had held that such a term could not acquire protectible legal status.

Vornado

"The protection of trademarks," wrote Justice Felix Frankfurter, "is the law's recognition of the psychological function of symbols." Although marketing executives sometimes find it difficult to believe, the lawyers and judges who deal with trademark problems are genuinely concerned with consumer psychology.

Any conflict between two trademarks poses the basic question of whether the purchasing public is likely to be confused, mistaken, or deceived. Assuming the customer is familiar with Tornado as a brand name for electrical equipment of various types, will he think that Vornado electrical appliances are products of the same manufacturer? Do the two trademarks so resemble one another in appearance, sound, or meaning that, taking into account the similarity of the merchandise, there is a reasonable likelihood of confusion?

This is a somewhat simplified statement of the issue that actually confronted a court in an appeal from a United States Patent and Trademark Office decision. Registration of Vornado was denied because it was similar to Tornado.

The decision was a close one. Three judges voted against Vornado, while two others disagreed and explained, in separate dissenting opinions, why they would have permitted it to be registered.

The majority opinion recognized that *tornado* is a dictionary word with a well-known meaning, as contrasted with *Vornado,* which is a coined term. However, the significant facts to the majority were that, with the exception of the first letter in each trademark, they are identical, and that there is "striking similarity" between them in sound and appearance.

One dissenting judge felt that the "psychological imagery" evoked by the two marks was "compellingly different." In his view, the marks would produce "distinct and nonconfusing psychological impacts" in the consumer's mind.

The same dissenting opinion also took the position that this was an instance where it is not convincing to test similarity in terms of overall word structure. The judge felt that the single letter difference between the coined word *Vornado* and the dictionary term *tornado* is sufficient to make a consumer attach a very distinct and separate meaning to it. To him it was also significant that the difference occurs in the first letter because "it is this difference which initially stimulates the perception into seeking the meaning for the words as wholes."

The other dissenting judge specifically stated that he was basing his conclusion on the assumption that the general public is entirely familiar with the very common word *tornado*. He said that *Vornado* obviously is not that word, so no one would be likely to think products bearing these trademarks came from the same source. "If the source were the same," he added, "one would expect the marks to be the same, not different, since that is the way marks are used."

This dissenter put Vornado in the class of what he calls "irritating" trademarks, not in any invidious sense, but because they are "just different enough from common words to make one brood about them and their possible origins." To him it was clear that the customer exposed to Vornado as a trademark is not going to confuse it with Tornado because "he knows that word and remembers the difference, which is the first thing to impress itself on his mind."

This decision is unsatisfactory from several points of view. Certainly it must have been a bitter disappointment to Vornado, Inc., to lose the case by a three to two margin, especially since the application for registration had been pending since January of 1961 and the decision did not come until 1968. No doubt, Vornado felt compelled to continue the litigation because the trademark in question also is the distinctive component of its corporate name. Indeed it already owned a registration of Vornado for electric fans that, because of its long standing, remains undisturbed by the court decision.

A more general type of problem raised by this case is how to avoid getting into conflicts that are so difficult to resolve. The ready answer is to use such care in selecting a new trademark that it does not even come close to an existing trademark owned by another company. But this is more easily said than done. There are so many trademarks already in use, both coined words and dictionary words, that finding a new one is increasingly difficult. The typical situation is one in which a trademark lawyer is asked to use his judgment about how safe it would be to proceed, in other words, to attempt to predict what the five judges would say if the case ever got before them. In addition, the background of the Vornado case evidently was that the two companies started out in fields comparatively remote from one another but gradually got closer and closer to the eventual conflict as their product lines expanded. It seems obvious that there is no sure way of avoiding that kind of marketing development and the resulting clash of trademark claims.

Perhaps the most significant point in the Vornado case was made by one of the dissenting judges in the course of his detailed discussion of consumer psychology. "Trademarks are psychological," he wrote, but he noted that the record of the case did not include any tests on "the psychological impact" of Vornado. This appears to be a direct invitation to use experts in psychological market research techniques as aids in the preparation of the evidence for a legal proceeding involving claims of confusing similarity between trademarks. However, since the invitation is found in a dissenting opinion, there is no certain way of knowing how favorably such evidence would be received.

Tylenol

McNeil Laboratories, the Johnson & Johnson subsidiary that markets Tylenol nonaspirin analgesic, obtained a court order stopping American Home Products Corporation from using

Extranol as the brand name for a new extra-strength non-aspirin analgesic.

The legal dispute broke out while Extranol was being tested in the New England market. In January of 1976 McNeil learned that AHP was introducing Extranol and got to court by March 15. On that date a federal judge in New Jersey issued a restraining order halting the use of Extranol. Later, McNeil applied for a preliminary injunction to prevent Extranol from being sold under that name, and the judge granted the injunction after a hearing.

The history of Tylenol is longer than many people realize. McNeil introduced the product in 1955, and Tylenol has been a federally registered trademark since 1956. Several years later, Johnson & Johnson acquired McNeil Laboratories.

At the time of the hearing on the preliminary injunction in 1976, it was estimated that Tylenol accounted for 90 percent of the nonaspirin analgesic market. Each Tylenol tablet contains 325 milligrams of acetaminophen. Extranol tablets contained 486 milligrams of acetaminophen. McNeil already was marketing an extra-strength Tylenol capsule and had plans to introduce an extra-strength Tylenol tablet, both with a slightly greater amount of acetaminophen than Extranol.

As Judge George H. Barlow noted in his written opinion, it is rather unusual for a trademark infringement case to turn on a resemblance in suffixes only. But there are situations where this has been the determining factor.

Two examples discussed by Judge Barlow are the 1959 ruling that Bonamine is an infringement on Dramamine and the 1960 ruling that Valcream infringes on Brylcream. On the other hand, Syrocol was allowed to continue in spite of a claim that it infringed upon Cheracol. (The judge did not discuss the large number of cases in which Seven-Up has had some successes and some failures against other soft drink trademarks ending in Up.) There is no rigid rule about suffixes, or about prefixes for that matter. Each case depends on its own set of circumstances.

In the dispute between McNeil and AHP, Judge Barlow decided that confusion was likely because of the combination of the term "extra" with the suffix "nol." In his view, an uninformed consumer would be very likely to believe that Extranol was an extra-strength version of Tylenol.

The danger of confusion was increased by the fact than an extra-strength version of Tylenol already was on the market in capsule form and a tablet form was about to be launched. To Judge Barlow, it was "not at all inconceivable that a consumer might enter a store to purchase the new extra-strength Tylenol and, instead, buy Extranol"—on the incorrect assumption that this was the new McNeil product.

Judge Barlow made a special point of criticizing AHP's selection of Extranol as a trademark in the light of its consumer survey results. AHP tested five proposed brand names: Di-Exsal, Direxin, Endomil, Saloxium, and Extranol. Fifty-eight percent of the respondents preferred Extranol, and 30 percent of these mentioned that the suffix -nol was similar to the -nol in Tylenol. In the judge's opinion AHP should have taken these test results as a warning that it was coming too close to Tylenol. AHP, he wrote, "was under an obligation to differentiate its trademark from McNeil's."

This portion of the opinion presumably proved to be a useful precedent for marketing management in evaluating the results of consumer surveys on proposed new brand names.

AHP did not take any appeal or continue to fight the case after Judge Barlow issued a preliminary injunction barring the use of Extranol. Packaging changes were made to meet the judge's criticism that Extranol, like Tylenol, was sold in a container with a predominantly red-and-white color scheme, and the AHP product was renamed Extramed.

Spray 'N Vac

The litigation between Glamorene Products Corporation, a subsidiary of Lever Brothers, and Boyle-Midway, a division of

American Home Products, provides a case history of product development as well as trademark problems.

Consumer products for the home cleaning of rugs and carpets originally were dry powders or liquid shampoos that required three steps. The product first was spread on the rug by the housewife; then it had to be rubbed or scrubbed in to do the real cleaning, and finally the residue was removed by vacuuming. Glamorene was the market leader in this field for many years.

When aerosol cans were introduced, it became possible to package liquid rug cleaners so that they could easily be sprayed on a rug. It still was necessary to scrub in the product for cleaning and then remove the residue by vacuuming. The principal developer of the aerosol-type rug cleaner was S. C. Johnson & Son, with its Glory product, which it called a "spray foam."

Other rug-cleaner manufacturers followed with aerosol products, including Glamorene under the Power Foam trademark and the Boyle-Midway division of American Home Products, which extended its established Woolite trademark to an aerosol rug cleaner. It later became significant that Boyle-Midway used the same generic term "spray foam" that S. C. Johnson had introduced for this type of product.

Glamorene apparently was the first company to realize that there would be a significant market for an aerosol rug-cleaning product that would have the advantage of spraying and also would eliminate the need for scrubbing the product into the rug. Based on its marketing research, Glamorene reached the conclusion that a spray rug cleaner that could eliminate the scrubbing step would not only compete with all other rug cleaners, but would develop a new market among a large group of potential customers who were not using home rug cleaners at all.

In 1971 Glamorene's laboratory succeeded in developing a two-step product. This product was capable of penetrating without scrubbing. It lifted the soil to the surface where, after drying, it could be removed by vacuuming.

The next problem was to find a suitable brand name for the new product. Glamorene considered No-Scrub, Amaze and Glamor-Ease. It then added Spray 'N Vac to the list and commissioned an outside marketing research company to test all four proposed trademarks.

A key section of the study reported: "Spray 'N Vac is the one name most frequently associated with a rug cleaner. Nearly all housewives (84 percent) stated that this name made them think of a rug cleaner product." Glamorene therefore selected Spray 'N Vac as the trademark for the new entry. It decided to use the phrase "no scrub rug cleaner" as a generic term.

Spray 'N Vac no-scrub rug cleaner was introduced in test markets late in 1971 and became an instant success. American Home Products stepped up its advertising and promotion in Glamorene's test markets in an attempt to defend its spray foam position, but the new two-step product made substantial inroads.

Glamorene extended its test marketing and followed through with substantial advertising support. In the spring of 1973, the product went national. By the end of 1974, Glamorene had spent $9,762,000 on advertising and promotion for Spray 'N Vac rug cleaner, and total sales had reached approximately $27,000,000.

Boyle-Midway recognized the need to compete with Glamorene's Spray 'N Vac product immediately after its test market success became obvious. Laboratory work began by the middle of January 1972. Boyle-Midway's new product, which operates substantially the same way as Spray 'N Vac, was first marketed in Spetember 1973.

The Boyle-Midway product was called Woolite Spray & Vacuum rug cleaner. The well-known Woolite trademark appeared on the front panel of the can in blue letters and the words *Spray & Vacuum* were in large red letters. Spray & Vacuum took more space than any other word or phrase on the front panel of the new Boyle-Midway product. The words *rug cleaner* also were in red but smaller in size than either Woolite or Spray & Vacuum. This differed markedly from the visual impression of the prior Boyle-Midway spray foam product, where the trademark Woolite and the descriptive terms were all in the same color. The overall effect was that the term *Spray & Vacuum* stood out in an eye-catching and dominant position.

There were two basic legal questions in the lawsuit. First, was Spray 'N Vac just a descriptive term that any manufacturer can use, or was it a valid trademark that identified the Glamorene no-scrub rug cleaner? Second, were the words *Spray & Vacuum* merely descriptive, or was Boyle-Midway using them as the trademark for its competing product?

There is a critical difference in trademark law between a word or phrase that is merely descriptive and one that is suggestive of the product. The judge in this case concluded that Spray 'N Vac did suggest a rug cleaner but was not merely descriptive: "The phrase suggests what can be accomplished with the product and yet is not sufficiently descriptive to preclude its adoption as a trademark."

In the first place, Spray 'N Vac does not really describe the product or how it is used. The individual words that make up the expression may describe in very terse, abbreviated form two aspects of the way the product can be used. When these words are combined, however, the whole expression is suggestive rather than descriptive.

Whether it is Glamorene using Spray 'N Vac or Boyle-Midway using Spray & Vacuum, it is also necessary to use additional words such as *no-scrub rug cleaner* to describe what the product is and how it functions. Without reading the directions on the container, the consumer would not know that the terms *Spray 'N Vac* and *Spray & Vacuum* relate to a two-step product. They do not themselves connote the fact that the scrubbing step has been eliminated. Both terms do suggest a rug-cleaning product because that is the natural association that has grown up with the word "vacuum." As the judge said, "A suggestive term can function as a valid trademark."

The second question was answered largely in terms of the appearance of the Boyle-Midway container. The dominant positioning of *Spray & Vacuum* on the label indicated an intent to create a visual impact and attract the consumer by those words. Boyle-Midway also found it necessary to include the words "without scrubbing" on the label so that the consumer would have sufficient information to understand the use of the product. All of this added up to the conclusion that Boyle-Midway was using the words *Spray & Vacuum* as a trademark.

The ultimate legal issue in a trademark infringement case is whether the public is likely to be confused. As the judge wrote, "The term Spray & Vacuum is essentially the same in appearance, sound and meaning as Spray 'N Vac." With directly competitive products and almost identical trademarks, the answer was rather obvious. However, Glamorene also introduced some evidence of actual confusion to support its claim of infringement.

Both consumers and retail clerks were confused because of the similarity between the two marks. Retailers advertising the Boyle-Midway product abbreviated Spray & Vacuum to Spray & Vac, and wholesalers did the same thing in their price lists. Retailers sent to Glamorene substantial numbers of Boyle-Midway coupons for redemption. In addition, surveys showed consumer confusion.

The judge made the important point that the test for likelihood of confusion is not a side-by-side comparison of the products involved. "It is the general overall impression created in the mind of the consumer who may have an imperfect recall of the complaining party's trademark." By this test, Boyle-Midway had infringed on Glamorene's trademark.

Nevertheless, *spray* and *vacuum* are ordinary words in the language, and Boyle-Midway cannot be prevented from using them altogether just because Glamorene established Spray 'N Vac as its trademark. The judgment in the lawsuit prohibited the use by Boyle-Midway of Spray & Vacuum, or any equivalent expression, as a trademark. It could, however, use the words *spray* and *vacuum* in copy on labels and in advertisments as part of the directions for use, provided that those words (1) were in letters no larger than the letters in surrounding copy;

(2) that they were in the same type as the words in contiguous copy; (3) that they were in the same color as the words in contiguous copy; and (4) that they appeared in contiguous copy of not less than ten words in length. All of these restrictions were for the purpose of limiting Boyle-Midway to true descriptive uses of the words, as distinguished from using them as a symbol to attract public attention.

Uncola

The Seven-Up Company established "The Uncola" as its trademark over the objections of Coca-Cola, which had argued that no one company should be allowed exclusive rights to a term that was nothing more than the equivalent of *noncola*.

Later, Seven-Up sued No-Cal for calling a diet lemon-lime drink Shape-Up and for using the expression "The Unsugar" in advertising it. Seven-Up claimed this would give consumers the misleading impression that Shape-Up is the diet version of 7Up.

The federal district court in Brooklyn, New York, ruled in favor of No-Cal. The judge was convinced that No-Cal was just trying to contrast its product with Seven-Up's and was not confusing the public. He therefore dismissed the case, but only after a thorough discussion that included some pertinent details about the marketing history of both products.

In 1968 Seven-Up launched its Uncola advertising campaign in an effort to reposition itself in the soft drink field. The purpose of the campaign was to change the image of 7Up from a "special occasion" drink to a general soft drink, like the leading colas. Seven-Up was particularly anxious to increase its share of the teen age market, which accounts for a substantial percentage of the consumption of all carbonated soft drinks.

The term *Uncola* was used to symbolize the concept that 7Up was different from the colas, but at the same time that it was an all-purpose soft drink like a cola. Whatever the impression on the public might have been, the campaign's success is a matter of history.

No-Cal is a privately owned company which specializes in sugar-free carbonated drinks. It had plans years ago for a lemon-lime drink to be called Shape-Up, but the introduction of the product was delayed by the government ban on the use of cyclamates in the fall of 1969. Cyclamates were the sweeteners used in all No-Cal drinks, so its entire line had to be reformulated. Shape-Up was finally introduced in 1973.

No-Cal's agency was Solow Wexton (which later went bankrupt), and it was their idea to use the term Unsugar. Incidentally, Seven-Up did not have a sugar-free product at the time. (Its Diet 7Up contained sugar and therefore did contain some calories.) Also, Seven-Up used The Uncola only in connection with its regular 7Up product. Diet 7Up, whether sugar-added or in its later sugar-free formula, was not advertised as The Uncola.

The judge accepted Seven-Up's theory that its use of "un" in The Uncola was what prompted No-Cal's use of "un" in The Unsugar. "But," he wrote, "such idea stimulation does not make for infringement." He noted that the dictionaries list over a thousand "un" words in which the prefix simply means the negative.

The judge seems to have been influenced by the fact that The Uncola was never used except in association with the Seven-Up trademark, while Shape-Up was never used except in association with the brand name No-Cal. The opinion reviewed various earlier lawsuits in which Seven-Up sometimes won and sometimes lost trademark infringement claims against other lemon-lime drink manufacturers who used the word "up" as a suffix for their trademarks. The judge felt there was no likelihood of consumer confusion in this case because Shape-Up has associations of its own in the English language, which would cause the consumer automatically to differentiate it from 7Up.

The court's opinion also contains some observations about comparative advertising. The judge wrote:

Competition in the American marketplace is vigorous, and advertising practices reflect this fact. Comparative advertising has become increasingly prevalent, with products openly comparing themselves with those of their competitors. [Seven-Up's] use of language or image is not sacrosanct or immune from being employed as a basis of comparison by a competitor. [Seven-Up] itself made use of such a basis for comparison when it adopted the "Uncola" campaign in an effort to join the popular "cola" group, not by similarity (only except insofar as its product was also a soft drink), but by differentiation.

After the formal judgment was filed dismissing the lawsuit, Seven-Up took an appeal to a higher court. However, the case later was settled and the appeal withdrawn. Under the terms of the settlement, No-Cal must not use the word Unsugar (which it had already dropped), and its use of Shape-Up was restricted to situations where the No-Cal name also was conspicuously displayed.

Arm & Hammer

Church & Dwight Company, which extended its long-established Arm & Hammer trademark to underarm deodorants in 1975, won a preliminary injunction against the use of Arm in Arm by Helene Curtis as a trademark for underarm deodorants. N W Ayer ABH, Curtis' advertising agency, also was named a defendant in the lawsuit.

Baking soda has been sold under the Arm & Hammer trademark for over a century. Church & Dwight owns several federal registrations for the words themselves and for the associated label designs.

As the evidence showed, baking soda has a variety of applications in cleaning and deodorizing as well as baking. Church & Dwight advertised and promoted baking soda for use as an antacid, as a dentifrice, and as an ingredient in various other health and beauty care preparations. In particular, files going back more than 50 years included advertisements promoting the use of Arm & Hammer baking soda as a deodorant.

The Arm & Hammer line already had been extended to various consumer products, such as laundry detergent, washing soda, borax, and oven cleaner. A further extension to underarm deodorants was a logical step, and Church & Dwight started research in baking soda in aerosol spray containers in 1973. After marketing research tests that continued into the early part of 1975, Church & Dwight put its Arm & Hammer deodorant into national distribution in late June and early July of 1975.

Meanwhile, in August of 1974 Helene Curtis began considering a personal deodorant containing baking soda. The evidence showed that this idea derived from TV commercials promoting the deodorizing properties of Arm & Hammer.

In October of 1974 representatives of Helene Curtis met with Church & Dwight to get some technical information about the use of baking soda in the toiletries and cosmetics field. Along with the history of baking soda and its manufacture, Helene Curtis was given information about its use as a deodorizer in various applications, including consumer reports of underarm deodorant efficiency.

Helene Curtis decided to go forward with an aerosol deodorant containing baking soda. To select a trademark for the new product, Helene Curtis and N W Ayer reviewed 95 prospective brand names. They selected Arm in Arm, which was the only one on the list that resembled Arm & Hammer.

In a November 1974 marketing research test of Arm in Arm as a brand name, over half the respondents who thought the name was appropriate said they associated it with baking soda. Other tests took place in February 1975, leading Helene Curtis to conclude that Arm in Arm was a very acceptable brand name for the new product, in part because it produced an image of Arm & Hammer baking soda.

Helene Curtis also chose a color scheme for its Arm in Arm deodorant container that resembled the appearance of the

Arm & Hammer baking soda box. This was selected over two other designs because it suggested baking soda, and Helene Curtis stayed with it even though some of its research showed that respondents were reminded of the Arm & Hammer package.

The Arm in Arm product went into limited test markets on April 28, 1975, and advertising commenced on May 12, 1975. Church & Dwight complained to Helene Curtis on May 8 and again on May 12, objecting both to the Arm in Arm brand name and to the yellow and red color combination of the package design. Suit was started on May 16.

The litigation was delayed in its early stages for various reasons, including a successful move by Helene Curtis to transfer the case from Rochester, New York, to Chicago, Illinois, the location of its headquarters. Meanwhile, both products went into national distribution and were advertised extensively. Again, Helene Curtis' own research turned up damaging evidence. In a study of consumer reaction to three Arm in Arm TV commercials, more respondents believed the product was made by Arm & Hammer than believed it was made by Helene Curtis.

The test of trademark infringement is the likelihood that consumers will be confused by resemblances in the brand names of the respective products. Actual confusion is the best proof that confusion is likely, but evidence of actual confusion generally is hard to find. In this case, however, Church & Dwight was able to produce letters it had received from consumers complaining about problems with Arm in Arm, advertisements for Arm in Arm submitted incorrectly by retailers requesting cooperative advertising allowances, and a report from its redemption agency showing numerous submissions of Arm in Arm coupons for credit.

Church & Dwight's application for a preliminary injunction eventually came before Judge Frank J. McGarr of the United States Court in Chicago. He ruled that "Curtis purposefully chose a confusingly similar and infringing trademark for the reason that Arm in Arm readily produces in consumers' minds the image of Arm & Hammer baking soda." Judge McGarr pointed out that there was nothing to keep Helene Curtis from competing with Arm & Hammer personal deodorants under a nondeceptive trademark. He issued the preliminary injunction requested by Church & Dwight, ordering Helene Curtis to discontinue the Arm in Arm trademark until final conclusion of the case.

Helene Curtis took an appeal from this decision and succeeded in getting the Court of Appeals to grant a stay, which kept Judge McGarr's order from going into effect while the appeal was pending. After a hearing, however, the Court of Appeals unanimously affirmed the decision granting Church & Dwight a preliminary injunction against the use of Arm in Arm.

Breath Savers

With various sources questioning advertising's usefulness and its credibility, there is reason for additional concern when sarcastic comments about advertising are made by the judiciary. And such sarcastic remarks have been made—in an opinion by a highly regarded judge in the important federal district court that sits in Manhattan, the home of Madison Avenue.

The occasion for the judge's unflattering remarks was a dispute between Beech-Nut and Warner-Lambert over their respective new entries in the product subcategory known as breath mints. Warner-Lambert asserted that it held 98 percent of this market with its Certs and Clorets products. Beech-Nut, which had a solid position in a closely related field with Life Savers, introduced a new product under the brand name Breath Savers in 1971 for the specific purpose of taking a share of the breath mints market. Warner-Lambert then came out with a new item called Breath Pleasers.

Beech-Nut complained about the similarity of names and also charged unfair competition in the packaging of the new Warner-Lambert entry. Specifically, the same colors (although in different shades) were used for the same flavors; Warner-Lambert used stars where Beech-Nut had snowflakes; and there were other points of resemblance that, in Beech-Nut's view, were intended to confuse the trade and the public.

Reviewing the crowded condition of the market in this product field, the judge found that there were enough differences to offset the similarities in the consumer's mind. He listed ten other brand names for similar products, all of which contain the word *breath.* Commenting on this, the judge wrote in his opinion: "As the poets of Madison Avenue have drawn inspiration from things related to 'breath,' they have left a variety of marks less than utterly unique."

From this and other facts, he concluded that there were sufficient distinctions between the Breath Pleasers and Breath Savers brand names and package designs to avoid confusion in the marketplace. Summing up the legal position, he said, "In a well-trodden field like this, especially where the key word is free as air, small variations are likely to make enough of a difference to ward off charges of infringement."

The judge reserved his most sarcastic comments for what he called the "instructive legend" on the Breath Pleasers package that says, "Formula KG40," and the "comparably illuminating thing" on the Breath Savers package that reads, "Activated with MH2." On this aspect of the case, the judge wrote:

> The use of scientific-sounding numbers and letters to describe ingredients is a dispiritingly common device in a species of communication that does not have as a paramount aim the imparting of useful information.

This decision refused to grant a preliminary injunction and left both parties free to continue their marketing and their lawsuit. Nothing further appears in the law books, however, so the case apparently was dropped.

Scrabble

One of the most successful products of the Selchow & Righter Company is the word game sold under the registered trademark Scrabble. When Selchow & Righter found out that the

McGraw-Hill Book Company was planning to publish "The Complete Scrabble Dictionary" with an on-sale date of October 24, 1977, it rushed into court. A preliminary hearing was held before United States District Judge Kevin Thomas Duffy in New York on October 14, and on October 21 Judge Duffy issued a decision ordering McGraw-Hill not to publish the book until there was an opportunity for a full trial.

Selchow & Righter claimed that the proposed McGraw-Hill Scrabble dictionary would infringe its trademark and that the term *Scrabble* would lose its distinctive quality if it were used, as McGraw-Hill proposed, without any indication that it was a registered trademark. In addition, Selchow & Righter had an "Official Scrabble Player's Dictionary" scheduled for publication in the fall of 1978, so that it arguably faced loss of its dictionary sales as well as injury to its trademark.

The possibility that the distinctive quality of the trademark might be destroyed by its appearance in the title of McGraw-Hill's dictionary posed a serious commercial threat to Selchow & Righter. Aspirin, cellophane, escalator, and thermos are just a few examples of former trademarks that have passed into the language as generic terms and now are available for anyone in the industry to use. It is the legal obligation of the trademark owner to protect his rights in order to prevent the trademark from becoming generic; that presumably explains the tough position taken by Selchow & Righter in the lawsuit.

McGraw-Hill put forward several defenses. It claimed that Scrabble had lost its trademark significance already and that it was not entitled to protection when used on products, such as dictionaries, different from those for which it was registered, that is, board games and accessories. McGraw-Hill also argued that it was simply using the term *Scrabble* to describe a word game and not as a trademark.

Judge Duffy reviewed the various publications introduced as evidence by McGraw-Hill and found them not sufficient to support the claim that *Scrabble* had become a descriptive term for a particular kind of word game and that it was no longer recognized as a trademark for Selchow & Righter products. Five of the seven publications relied on by McGraw-Hill, according to Judge Duffy's written opinion, described Scrabble as a trademarked game. He also noted that, although *Scrabble* appears in Webster's New World College Dictionary, it is defined there as a trademark for a word game.

Selchow & Righter proved that it had vigorously policed its trademark, but it had to overcome the negative effect of a decision just a year earlier in which it failed in its attempt to obtain a preliminary injunction against the Book-of-the-Month Club's publication of "The Scrabble Book." One main difference between the two cases was that the BOMC publication used the circle-R registration symbol in conjunction with the term *Scrabble,* thus acknowledging its trademark status.

McGraw-Hill offered to put an insert in its dictionary giving credit to Selchow & Righter as the owner of the registered trademark and stating that it was used without permission. The proposed insert, however, also contained language that suggested Scrabble was simply the name of the game. This was not acceptable to Selchow & Righter, and Judge Duffy agreed that the insert did not go far enough to solve the legal problem.

It is clear from the opinion that Judge Duffy felt very strongly about the presence of the registration symbol in the title of BOMC's "The Scrabble® Book" as compared with its absence from the title of McGraw-Hill's "The Complete Scrabble Dictionary." Without the trademark designation, Judge Duffy wrote, "it is likely that the trademark 'Scrabble' will lose its valuable federal protection." For authority, he referred to the case involving thermos, where, as Judge Duffy said, "improper policing of the trademark contributed to rendering that term generic."

This decision was affirmed by the federal Court of Appeals in New York City on June 19, 1978. Of significance was the following statement: "While the English word 'Scrabble' may once have had currency in contexts distinct from the word game at issue in this case, its use as the name of a game is sufficiently fanciful to render it fit for employment as a [trade]mark."

Bionic

The word *bionic* has been in the unabridged dictionary for quite some time, but it is fair to say that it was unknown to the general public until the success of the TV series "Six Million Dollar Man" and its spinoff "Bionic Woman."

The TV programs are produced by Universal City Studios, which has a natural interest in licensing the merchandising rights to its popular titles and characters. A sister company of Universal, called Merchandising Corporation of America (both are subsidiaries of MCA, Inc.), is in charge of those activities.

In the fall of 1975 American Footwear Corporation and its affiliates spent approximately $50,000 in developing a hiking and mountain climbing boot with some novel features. American called a session of its staff in January 1976 to brainstorm a brand name for the new boot. "Six Million Dollar Man" already was on the air at that time, and "Bionic Woman" premiered during the same month. The brainstorming session chose Bionic as the new trademark.

American's Bionic boot was displayed for the first time at the New York Shoe Fair early in February of 1976. Orders began to come in immediately; American placed a manufacturing order with its supplier, and the first shipment to customers was made on July 2, 1976. *Footwear News* featured the Bionic boot in a supplement to its issue of April 26, 1976.

Meanwhile, General Footwear Company, a Canadian manufacturer located in Montreal, was negotiating with Merchandising Corporation of America for a license from Universal which it hoped would increase the market share for its products in the United States. Although these discussions started in December 1975, and a basic agreement was apparently reached the following March, the contract was not completed until October of 1976.

General's license covered the titles "Six Million Dollar Man" and "Bionic Woman" and the names and likenesses of the two principal characters in each series. The license did not deal with Bionic as a separate trademark. Moreover, it was limited to girls' casual footwear composed of canvas, leather, or rubber, and it specifically excluded boots.

Someone at General saw the April 26, 1976, supplement to *Footwear News* and complained to Merchandising Corporation of America in May. On June 25, Merchandising sent a letter to American charging it with trademark infringement. Merchandising also arranged for the publication of a "Buyers Beware" article in the July 26, 1976, issue of *Footwear News*, claiming that Universal had the exclusive right to use Bionic as a trademark and that anyone who did so without its permission was an infringer.

American Footwear fired the first legal shot by bringing suit against General Footwear on July 30, 1976. General countered with a separate lawsuit against American on September 20. Universal then intervened in both cases, and they were combined into a single action.

The basic positions of the parties can be summed up as follows: American claimed trademark rights on Bionic for its boots. Universal claimed the exclusive use of Bionic on all commercial products, including boots and shoes, and the right to stop anyone who was not licensed by the Merchandising Corporation of America. General, as Universal's licensee, claimed the exclusive right to use the trademark Bionic on footwear.

The trial was held before Judge Robert L. Carter of the federal district court in New York City. His May 31, 1978, decision was in favor of American and against both Universal and General.

Judge Carter dealt first with the source of the Bionic trademark. It was clear to him that Universal's TV series "Six Million Dollar Man" gave American the inspiration to adopt Bionic as a trademark. He ruled, however, that this fact alone would not substantiate a charge of trademark infringement.

According to Judge Carter it was entirely permissible for American to capitalize on the public acceptance of a concept, idea, or word that Universal had been responsible for creating or popularizing. The only limitation was that a party like American who takes advantage of the atmosphere created by someone else may not "achieve a competitive boost" by confusing the public into buying his products in the mistaken belief that they are associated with the other party. In this area American was innocent; it made no effort of any kind to connect the boot with the TV series or with any of the characters in the programs.

A second major point in Judge Carter's opinion was that Universal itself never used or licensed Bionic alone. The license agreements all referred to the full titles of the programs, and the likenesses of the TV stars who appeared in them were the principal commercial tie-ins used by licensed manufacturers. As Judge Carter pointed out, the word *bionic* is used only in a descriptive sense in the programs: Bionic man, bionic boy, bionic dog, bionic woman.

According to Judge Carter the real issue in the entire case was whether Universal, through its TV series, had foreclosed the use of *bionic* by others in the marketing of goods. That claim, Judge Carter ruled, was simply too broad.

The judge therefore decided that American was entitled to an injunction against Universal and also against General to prevent them from using Bionic on footwear or interfering with American's use of that trademark. Judge Carter added, however, that the injunction to be issued should in no way interfere with Universal's rights in its TV shows or in licensing its merchandise.

The scope of the merchandising rights created by a successful entertainment program can be difficult to determine, as this case illustrates. Judge Carter's opinion contains a number of useful hints for any company trying to establish the broadest possible coverage in such a situation.

CHAPTER 5 Family of Trademarks

Macro

One of the valuable attributes of a trademark is that it creates an exclusive marketing field extending beyond the specific product on which the trademark is used. Competitors must not only avoid using the same trademark on the same kind of product, they must also avoid using the same trademark on other products that the consumer might think came from the same manufacturing source.

For example, a deodorant manufacturer could hardly expect to get away with selecting a trademark already in use by another company for toilet soap. The basic rule is to avoid the likelihood of consumer confusion or mistake, and this includes the use of similar trademarks as well as identical ones.

The breadth of the marketing field beyond the specific product on which the trademark is used depends on many factors. Perhaps the most important is the distinctive character of the trademark, or lack of it.

Even a rather ordinary trademark can get a broader scope of protection if it is used in various combinations on several products in a way that creates a "family" of trademarks. The likelihood of consumer confusion then can be viewed in terms of a family resemblance. The result is to expand the exclusive marketing field of the basic trademark because competitors must avoid creating the mistaken impression that their products are members of the same trademark family.

A demonstration of this principle took place in a dispute

over the registrability of Macroguard as a trademark for chemical resistant coatings, more specifically listed as protective, decorative, corrosion-resistant, and skid-resistant paints for exposed surfaces, particularly metal and concrete surfaces. The application was opposed in the United States Patent and Trademark Office by MacDermid, Inc., a manufacturer of chemical products for the coating, plating, and surface treatment of metals.

MacDermid's principal trademark for this product line is Macro. However, it uses that trademark in many different combinations. For example, Macro Brite, Macro Drab, Macro Bronze, and Macro Polish identify different chromate conversion coatings for application to such metals as zinc and cadmium. MacDermid also produces related products under similar trademarks, including Macro Wet, an additive for chrome coating solutions to reduce surface tension; Macro Leach, a powder for removing chrome; Macro Color, a dye for mixture with a chromate coating; and Macro Seal, a liquid sealer for use on metal or chromate coating. In addition, MacDermid uses the term Macromates in its literature to refer to its line of chromate conversion coatings.

Against this family of Macro trademarks, the applicant for registration of Macroguard put forward a series of fruitless arguments. One point was that the products are specifically different in various respects. However, their basic end use is for application to metals and to protect them against corrosion, which is sufficient to make them related products in the consumer's mind. Another point was that MacDermid sells through technically trained salesmen. But this would not rule out the likelihood of confusing a consumer who saw the Macroguard product advertised or on sale.

It also was argued that *macro* is a dictionary term meaning large or big, that it is used as a prefix by numerous manufacturers for various types of goods, and that it should be entitled only to a limited degree of protection for those reasons. The evidence showed, however, that none of these other manufacturers used *macro* in connection with coating products. Moreover, the concept of size has no significance with regard either to the MacDermid line or the Macroguard product.

The final sentence of the Patent and Trademark Office opinion emphasizes the significance of the trademark family concept. In view of the fact that MacDermid always uses another term immediately following Macro, the opinion states, "confusion seems all the more likely," since purchasers "might readily assume" that Macroguard coatings are another item in the already established line of Macro products.

While this particular decision deals with products that, by their nature, have limited distribution and probably are purchased for the most part by industrial users, the same legal principles apply to ordinary consumer products. Indeed, the average purchaser of a household product is likely to be a less careful observer than the purchaser of coatings for metal surfaces, so the family effect could provide an even broader field of exclusive marketing protection when used for products in mass distribution.

CHAPTER 6 Initials and Acronyms

AO

Initials can make troublesome trademarks. As a hypothetical example, Amalgamated Biscuit Company, American Bread Company, and Allied Bakeries Corporation might very easily exist in the same industry. They could use the first parts of their names, Amalgamated, American, and Allied, as trademarks for their competing products without running into any conflict with one another. But if they all should succumb to the common temptation to use their initials, there would be almost inevitable confusion at the consumer level.

In the absence of unusual circumstances, the first of these companies to put ABC into use as a trademark for bakery products would be able by legal action to stop the others from using their initials.

A case in point is the Patent and Trademark Office decision dismissing a claim by American Optical Corporation whose corporate logo for many years has consisted of the letters "AO" in one form or another. American Optical Corporation charged that customers were likely to be confused by the use of the letter A enclosed in a circle as the trademark of Autotrol Corporation.

American Optical argued that customers would consider the circle around the "A" to be an "O," so there would be a direct conflict with its well known "AO" symbol.

The decision of the Trademark Trial and Appeal Board reminds us that, in spite of its seeming complexity, trademark law depends fundamentally upon the psychological impression that symbols make on the consumer's mind in the context of actual marketing situations.

The Board's opinion stated that it did not believe the average person encountering Autotrol's trademark would characterize it as an "AO" design. It is quite true, the opinion went on to say, that under some circumstances a circle and the letter O could be considered to be the same, but that would depend on the context in which the circle appeared.

In this analysis, it is especially important to consider the manner in which the circle is used when letters also are included in the total design.

It is possible for a circle and other lettering to be presented in the same style and with equal emphasis. In such a case, the logo probably would create a single impression and, by association with the other elements in the design, the circle would be perceived as a letter O, along with the other letters included in the logo.

On the other hand, if the circle is presented in a style less distinctive than the enclosed letter, it serves primarily as a background design for the letter it surrounds. Under such circumstances, the circle would be recognized as a circular background and not as the letter O.

The trademark tribunal's opinion points out that this is essentially a test of the initial impression the logo is likely to make on a prospective purchaser. The average person does not stop to analyze the various portions of a trademark to determine what they could or should be. The commercial impression on the customer's mind is made by the logo at the time of first impact.

Looking at the specific design that Autotrol had applied to register, the Trademark Trial and Appeal Board unanimously concluded that it would suggest the letter A within a circle and not the letters "AO" as used by American Optical Corporation. Thus, there is no conflict in the legal sense; Autotrol was entitled to get its certificate of registration.

American Optical also lost the case on another ground. "The

question to be resolved," the Board's opinion stated, "is whether or not the marketing of the respective products of the parties under their particular marks is likely to cause purchasers to ascribe them to the same, albeit anonymous, source." This would require an analysis of the two companies' product lines even if their logos were considered to be identical. Autotrol's trademark is used on controls for water-treating equipment. American Optical, although known primarily in the ophthalmic field, also makes a long line of scientific apparatus for use in different industries. All of these products are marked with the "AO" logo, which also is used consistently as a corporate identification symbol in advertisements and on all technical literature, promotional materials, and packaging.

American Optical's advertising expenditures were running at the annual rate of $1,500,000 in the early seventies, when the detailed facts were introduced into evidence in the Patent and Trademark Office proceeding. And the evidence also showed that American Optical's sales volume had shot up from $50 million in 1959 to $190 million in 1968 and to over $200 million in 1970. The marketing impact of the "AO" logo was undeniable.

Naturally, American Optical tried to develop as close a connection as possible between some of its technical products and the water-treating equipment that used Autotrol's products.

The Trademark Trial and Appeal Board agreed that American Optical had a protectable interest in its "AO" logo that extended beyond the precise items in its line to cover any product that might reasonably be expected to come from it in the natural expansion of its business.

But, as the Board pointed out, it is incumbent on a party like American Optical, which complains about a possible trademark conflict, to show that its goods are related in some positive manner to those of the other party. If that cannot be done, the party must at least show that the normal marketing conditions applicable to the goods of both parties are such that they would be encountered by the same customers or prospective purchasers in an environment where a conflict between the marks would be likely to give rise to confusion about the source of the products.

Putting it another way, the Board's opinion emphasized that American Optical, despite the widespread use and recognition of its "AO" trademark, could not prevent the registration even of the identical letters for any and all products.

As a matter of hard facts, American Optical was unable to convince the Board that there was any commercial relationship between its products and the control equipment sold by Autotrol. Evidence was introduced about various types of pumps and controls included in certain of American Optical's products, but the Board was not persuaded that they were related in any significant way to water-treatment equipment.

The Trademark Trial and Appeal Board therefore concluded that American Optical had not succeeded in establishing that there were conditions and circumstances conducive to a marketing environment where confusion in trade was likely to arise.

Since the likelihood of confusion among purchasers about the source of the products is the key question, the Board also ruled against American Optical on this line of argument. Even if the Autotrol symbol were considered to be "AO" rather than the letter A enclosed in a circle, American Optical still would not be entitled to foreclose registration of that symbol as a trademark for the unrelated product line of controls for water-treatment equipment.

AMP

One kind of disappointment that can result from the choice of a corporation's initials as a trademark is that the initials may form an acronym that is identical to a term in common use in the industry.

In 1941 a company was organized under the name of Aircraft Marine Products. It followed the familiar routine of building a trademark on its initials and, beginning in 1944, obtained 17 registrations of AMP for different types of electrical components. Continuing in the path of numerous other enterprises, in 1956 Aircraft Marine Products changed its business name legally to AMP, Inc.

AMP is a substantial manufacturer of electrical components for aircraft, boats, home appliances, and other electrical apparatus. It is listed on the New York Stock Exchange under the symbol AMP. Its annual sales for the years 1969 through 1973 averaged over $250,000,000. It has installations in 14 foreign countries as well as numerous plants and offices in the United States. It advertises AMP products in various trade publications and also in *Forbes, Fortune,* and *Business Week.* In 1973 it spent approximately $8,000,000 on advertising, which represented 2 percent of its operating budget.

Zeroing in on the state of North Carolina, AMP, Inc. has places of business in seven different cities there, including a manufacturing plant in Charlotte. When it discovered that a man named Foy had gone into the electrical repair and contracting business in Charlotte as the Amp Electric Company, corporate feathers were ruffled, and a lawsuit for trademark infringement was filed.

In the course of the trial, the history of Amp Electric Company came out in some detail. Foy had been in business with his brother under another trade name, but they separated. In searching for a new name for his individual operation, he tried to find one that would put his company near the front of the telephone directory listings and came up with Amp. Foy acknowledged that he had seen the name AMP, Inc., on the sign on that company's building in Charlotte before he made his name selection, but there was no evidence that he intended to trade on the larger company's reputation.

The federal judge in Charlotte acknowledged that, despite the David and Goliath aspects of the situation, AMP, Inc., was entitled to have its rights protected against the local Amp Electric Company even though the damage might be inconsequential. But the key legal question is the likelihood of confusion among customers, and Judge McMillan ruled that this element was lacking. Foy therefore was allowed to continue to use the term *Amp* in his company name in spite of the trademark registrations owned by AMP, Inc.

Because *amp* is a commonly used abbreviation for the word *ampere*, the judge explained, it cannot *uniquely* identify AMP, Inc., or its products. In other words, there is room for more than one AMP in the electrical industry provided there is no direct conflict of goods or services.

Since AMP, Inc., manufactures components for the industrial market, while the Amp Electric Company deals directly with the consumer (generally a householder who requires repair or installation service), the judge concluded that there is no likelihood of confusion between the two.

Judge McMillan went into considerable detail in his discussion of the evidence on the common meaning of *amp*, noting that it is an everyday word in the jargon of electrical suppliers, sellers, buyers, and users. He even permitted himself the whimsy of proving how well known an expression it is by quoting from a collection of limericks:

> A lady removing her scanties
> Heard them crackle electrical chanties;
> Said her husband, "My dear,
> I very much fear
> You suffer from amps in your panties."

AMP, Inc., expressed particular concern about the use of the name Amp Electric Company even in the limited field of Foy's repair and contracting business, because it planned to begin the manufacture of switches and receptacles for home wiring. The judge was not persuaded that this made any significant difference in the likelihood of confusion.

AMP, Inc., appealed this ruling, and the Court of Appeals sent the case back for reconsideration on the ground that Judge McMillan had used too restrictive a standard in determining that there was no likelihood of confusion. Nothing further appears in the law books, so the case apparently was either settled out of court or simply dropped.

Using this lawsuit as an object lesson, we can see that a company whose initials happened to form a word commonly used in the industry got into a situation where it felt it was necessary to go to court to enforce its rights. At a minimum it ended up with a substantial investment in litigation expenses.

The AMP case demonstrates that there are at least some circumstances when a careful look at the possible consequences of selecting the obvious acronym could be worthwhile in terms of avoiding future problems.

CHAPTER 7 Protection for Slogans and Themes

Underneath It All

The Vassarette division of Munsingwear had been using the slogan "Underneath It All . . . A Vassarette" for some 40 years, and it had been a United States registered trademark for women's undergarments since 1958. Early in June 1977 Munsingwear learned that Maidenform, a major competitor, was planning to use "Underneath It All" with the phrase "I'm A Maidenform Woman" as a slogan in its upcoming fall advertising campaign.

Munsingwear tried to persuade Maidenform that its proposed advertising would be an infringement of Munsingwear's legal rights in the slogan. Maidenform refused to settle and instead filed suit against Munsingwear, asking the court to declare that its intended use of "Underneath It All" would be legal. Munsingwear retaliated with a countersuit in which it demanded that Maidenform's prospective infringement be stopped by court order.

Litigation often is painfully slow, but sometimes it can move swiftly. This case was started on June 27, 1977, in the federal district court in New York City. On July 15 Munsingwear filed a motion for a preliminary injunction to stop Maidenform from using the disputed slogan while the lawsuit was pending and until preparation could be made for a full trial. The motion was argued by lawyers for both sides on July 19, before Judge Charles S. Haight Jr. On July 29 Judge Haight issued his decision, ruling that Munsingwear had exclusive rights to use "Underneath It All" and ordering Maidenform not to include those words in its advertising. By that time, Maidenform had committed over $1,000,000 for advertising space.

The case originally was assigned to Judge Constance Baker Motley, one of the few women on the federal bench. As luck would have it, Judge Motley was away on vacation when Munsingwear moved for a preliminary injunction, and Judge Haight took over. This gave Judge Haight an opportunity to include in his published opinion a male-oriented quip about the subject matter of the lawsuit: "It is fair to assume that the ultimate purchasers of this merchandise are women, who—except for those who have become affected by the spirit of the Age of Aquarius—share a common anatomical need for bras and other types of under apparel."

Judge Haight had a serious purpose in mind: to show the likelihood of confusion among purchasers—which is the legal test for trademark infringement—if both parties were allowed to use the same slogan. He also pointed out that the products are sold in the same retail outlets at a similarly modest price and that, unlike the purchase of a luxury item, the selection of a particular brand of undergarment does not require a great deal of care and consideration. This led him to the conclusion that there would be "a substantial likelihood for confusion among the buying public, since identification with the words 'Underneath It All' would no longer distinguish the products of Munsingwear from other competing manufacturers."

Because the products of both parties compete directly for the same customers and the slogans are identical, there could not have been much doubt about the conclusion that confusion was likely to occur. Maidenform's main defense was that the words "Underneath It All" are simply descriptive in connection with underwear and therefore that any manufacturer should be able to use them. Judge Haight thus was faced with a frequent problem in trademark disputes: drawing the line between a descriptive term, which everybody has the right to use, and a suggestive term, that can be the valid and exclusive trademark of one particular manufacturer.

Judge Haight ruled that the words "Underneath It All" do more than convey an immediate idea of the ingredients, qualities, or characteristics of the products. On the contrary, it requires imagination, thought, and perception to reach a conclusion about the nature of the goods from those three words. The slogan, therefore, is suggestive rather than descriptive, and Vassarette's trademark rights are valid.

Judge Haight recognized that the phrase is descriptive to the extent that it states correctly that undergarments are worn underneath outer garments. But he had no difficulty in concluding that Munsingwear's use of the phrase reflected sufficient additional creative and imaginative elements to make it suggestive, rather than descriptive, according to the legal tests. It suggests, according to Judge Haight, that Vassarette products are "the very foundation of beauty; that the art of hairdresser, cosmetician, and dressmaker alike come to nothing if a Vassarette is lacking underneath."

For future reference in creating slogans, a key point made by Judge Haight in sustaining Munsingwear's exclusive legal rights to "Underneath It All" is that this slogan is "an imaginative and suggestive arrangement of words not previously joined together in common usage."

Judge Haight also felt that Munsingwear faced the risk of serious dilution of its trademark as the result of customers buying Maidenform products in reliance on the slogan "Underneath It All," with accompanying loss of sales and damage to Munsingwear's reputation. He therefore ordered Maidenform not to use "Underneath It All" in any manner, either alone or in combination with other words.

Maidenform could have taken an appeal from this order to a higher court, or it could have waited for the case to come to trial and hoped to win a different result after a full-dress presentation of witnesses and other evidence not available in the proceedings for the preliminary injunction. Instead, the case was terminated by an agreement under which both the original complaint and Munsingwear's counterclaim were dropped. Judge Haight's opinion remains as a legal precedent, and Munsingwear's exclusive rights to the slogan have been confirmed.

Where There's Life . . . There's Bud

When a floor wax manufacturer introduced an insecticide-containing product and started to advertise it with the slogan, "Where there's life . . . there's bugs," Anheuser-Busch heard echoes of its well-established slogan "Where there's life . . . there's Bud" and started lawsuits against both the manufacturer and the company that produced its television commercials.

Who could have imagined a more unlikely situation than a brewer suing a manufacturer of floor wax for infringement of an advertising slogan? As one judge phrased it, "The goods are obviously noncompetitive." Nobody could possibly confuse the insecticide-containing floor wax with Budweiser beer.

Nor is this a case where the complaining party is concerned about the poor quality of the alleged infringer's product and a resulting loss of good will among consumers who might mistakenly associate the two. No question was raised about the quality of the bug-killing wax.

And the slogan Anheuser-Busch was suing to protect is made up mostly of just plain English words: "Where there's life . . . there's Bud." The defendant didn't copy the trademark nickname "Bud"; it merely used the plain words that are part of the language and therefore cannot be monopolized by anyone—or can they?

As a matter of fact, the words *bugs* and *Bud* are so obviously different that nobody really could get the two slogans mixed up either. But Anheuser-Busch nevertheless obtained restraining orders against both Chemical Corporation of America, the manufacturer of the wax, and Fred A. Niles Productions, Inc., producer of the commercials containing the "bugs" slogan.

Some reading between the lines is necessary in order to

analyze just what the courts have done here. One definite point is that there has been a clear recognition of the role of advertising in creating legally protectable rights in a trade slogan. The Chicago judge who issued the order against Niles Productions referred to "the favorable image Plaintiff [Anheuser-Busch] has created in the mind of the public." The Florida judge who issued a similar order against Chemical Corporation of America spoke of the "imprint upon the mind of the purchasing public."

In the ordinary case of unfair competition, the basis for complaint is that the consumer probably would not have bought the infringing product in the absence of the trademark or other distinguishing features that suggested a connection with the plaintiff's "favorable image." The damage is done because the purchaser either thought he was buying the plaintiff's product or was motivated to buy someone else's product because of a favorable feeling induced by similarity to the plaintiff's familiar brand. The Anheuser-Busch situation is unusual because the damage is indirect.

The consumer who sees or hears "Where there's life . . . there's bugs" presumably reacts by remembering the long-familiar "Where there's life . . . there's Bud." This may not induce a purchase of insecticide-containing floor wax, but the mental association has been made.

The real problem that concerned Anheuser-Busch is the next stage: The consumer now sees or hears "Where there's life . . . there's Bud" and reacts by remembering the "bugs" slogan. The possibility of damage to Anheuser-Busch lies in the extremely unfavorable effect of an association between bugs (or insecticide) and beer that could be made in the consumer's mind.

Although not fully expressed in either opinion, this seems to be what the judges had in mind when ordering a halt to the use of "Where there's life . . . there's bugs." One opinion uses the words "impair" to "a substantial degree" the rights of Anheuser-Busch in its slogan; the other opinion says that the good will associated with Anheuser-Busch's slogan "will be disparaged and degraded." In other words, the harm lies not in the fact that consumers will tend to buy more of Chemical Corporation of America's bug-killing floor wax but that they will tend to buy less Budweiser beer. Unlike the ordinary case, this one does not rest on the complaint that the alleged infringer is capitalizing unfairly on the plaintiff's trademark or slogan; Anheuser-Busch brought suit to prevent direct damage to its good will.

This is a rare example of an infringement case where the claim of legal injury does not depend on any confusion or mistake in the purchaser's mind. What we have instead is what might be called a threatened erosion, or dilution, of the good will of a product because of an unpleasant psychological association. While this can be particularly serious when the product is food or drink, the same principle also could be applied in other fields.

The case against the floor wax manufacturer eventually reached the United States Court of Appeals, where the decision in favor of Anheuser-Busch was affirmed.

Enjoy Coca-Cola

Quietly and rapidly, the publication of decorative posters has become a substantial business. One variety of poster might be called the "spoof," and several of these humorous posters have attracted claims of infringement.

In 1972 the federal court in Brooklyn, New York, had to deal with an exact blown-up reproduction of the "Enjoy Coca-Cola" display, in the usual white script lettering on a red background—except that the letters "ine" were substituted for "-Cola" so that the poster read, "Enjoy Cocaine."

The judge said in his opinion that "one would have to be a visitor from another planet not to recognize immediately the familiar 'Coca' in its stylized script and accompanying words, colors, and design." The poster publisher, a company imaginatively named Gemini Rising, Inc., did not deny that it was deliberately imitating the Coca-Cola trademark; it defended the infringement claim on the ground that "the poster was intended to be a spoof, satirical, funny, and to have a meaning exactly the opposite of the word content."

This, of course, was not the usual type of trademark infringement case, in which competitive products bear similar brand names and the issue is whether the public is likely to be confused. Nevertheless, there was an element of business competition involved because both parties, in the words of the opinion, "are seeking to attract public attention and patronage for their respective products by the graphic display of a distinctive and widely known trademark."

As the judge said, however, the real thrust of Coca-Cola's complaint was that, unless the unauthorized use of its trademark and format was stopped by court order, its good will and business reputation would suffer in the eyes of those who, believing it responsible for the "Enjoy Cocaine" poster, would refuse to deal with a company that would seek commercial advantage by treating a dangerous drug in such jocular fashion.

According to the judge's analysis, the situation was especially serious because the soft drink industry is highly competitive, with many substitute products available, so that even the slightest negative connotation concerning a particular beverage might well affect a consumer's purchase decision.

In his opinion the judge wrote: "To associate such a noxious substance as cocaine with plaintiff's wholesome beverage as symbolized by its Coca-Cola trademark and format would clearly have a tendency to impugn that product and injure plaintiff's business reputation." Putting the same point somewhat differently, the judge also commented: "In this day of growing consumer resistance to advertising gimmicks, a strong probability exists that some patrons of Coca-Cola will be 'turned off' rather than 'turned on' by defendant's so-called 'spoof'." And this could have resulted in an immeasurable loss to Coca-Cola.

The real turning point in the case evidently was the submission of sworn statements showing that some members of the public actually attributed the poster to Coca-Cola. One housewife complained to the local Coca-Cola bottler. In the Pittsburgh area a group boycott of Coca-Cola was threatened. With this proof of actual confusion among consumers to support his theoretical analysis of the effect the spoof might have, the judge ruled that Coca-Cola was entitled to a preliminary injunction halting distribution of the "Enjoy Cocaine" poster.

In 1969 the Girl Scouts of America brought a somewhat similar case against a different poster publisher. The poster in question showed a young girl wearing the well-known green uniform of the Girl Scouts with her hands clasped over her protruding, clearly pregnant, abdomen. The slogan "Be Prepared" was displayed next to her hands.

The Girl Scouts organization was seriously concerned that members of the public would believe the poster was disseminated by the Girl Scouts themselves. The judge in this case felt that, even if some viewers might believe that the subject of the poster actually was a pregnant Girl Scout, "it is highly doubtful that any such impression would be more than momentary or that any viewer would conclude that the Girl Scouts had printed or distributed the poster."

In contrast to the Coca-Cola case, there was no proof of any damage to the Girl Scouts. No evidence was presented to show that contributions had fallen off, that members had resigned, that recruits had failed to join, that sales of authorized Girl Scouts posters or other items had decreased, or that volunteer workers had declined to support the organization.

So this judge concluded: "Those who may be amused at the poster presumably never viewed the reputation of the plaintiff as being inviolable. Those who are indignant obviously continue to respect it. Perhaps it is because the reputation of the plaintiff is so secure against the wry assault of the defendant that no such damage has been demonstrated."

The Girl Scouts thus were effectively laughed out of court. Their plea for a preliminary injunction prohibiting further distribution of the poster was denied. Despite the similarities between the two cases, there were important differences in the facts to account for the apparently contradictory results. One particularly significant distinction, pointed out by the judge in the Coca-Cola case, is that the Girl Scouts are a noncommercial organization not engaged in any trade.

Still another poster case involved the 1968 "Presidential campaign" of comedian Pat Paulsen. This poster displayed a photograph of Paulsen in one of his humorous costumes, with a "1968" sash across his chest. The publisher had added the words "For President" at the bottom of the photograph. Paulsen moved for an injunction against the poster manufacturer.

Here there could be no question of any trademark infringement, as in the "Enjoy Cocaine" case. Nor was there any injury to reputation, as claimed in the pregnant Girl Scout case, for the comedian himself had initiated the "Paulsen for President" campaign. The principal legal theory in this case was invasion of the right of privacy. Specifically, a New York law prohibits the unauthorized use of an individual's name or picture for "advertising purposes" or "the purposes of trade."

In order to put sensible limits on this law, the New York courts have interpreted it in such a way as to exempt the dissemination of news or information concerning matters of public interest of so-called "public figures." Indeed, failure to provide such an exemption might make the right of privacy law unconstitutional as an unwarranted restriction on the freedom of the press.

The spoof in this case came from Paulsen himself rather than from the poster publisher. Paulsen argued that he wasn't truly a public figure (as a real Presidential candidate clearly would be) because he was "only kidding" and the whole campaign was merely a publicity stunt. Nevertheless, the judge ruled that Paulsen had forfeited his right of privacy. "When a well-known entertainer enters the Presidential ring, tongue in cheek or otherwise, it is clearly newsworthy and of public interest."

Therefore, as in the pregnant Girl Scout case, but for an entirely different reason, Paulsen's motion for a preliminary injunction was denied.

Another type of legal problem was created by the posters showing Lucy, the little girl from the Peanuts comic strip, in a very pregnant condition. The caption read: "Damn you, Charlie Brown."

Several publishers have issued posters of this type. United Features Syndicate, which controls the rights to the Peanuts strip, has been able to stop as many of these as it has been able to find, without court orders, simply by making its legal position known.

The difference between the pregnant Lucy poster and the others discussed above is that the cartoon characters in the Peanuts comic strip are protected by copyright. And nobody could produce a recognizable version of Lucy without copying, and thus infringing the copyright.

These four "funny" posters, from the legal viewpoint, are similar only in a very superficial way. Their case histories are presented together here, not to justify, but to illustrate the vagaries of the law in the field of protecting commercial values in various kinds of symbols and themes.

The Greatest Show on Earth

Chandris America Lines specializes in Caribbean cruises during the October-April season. On June 21, 1970, a full-page advertisement prepared by Albert Frank–Guenther Law for Chandris appeared in the *New York Times* Sunday magazine section. The illustration was a photograph of a model dressed in a spangled and feathered costume suggestive of a night club chorus girl. The headline read, "THE GREATEST SHOW ON EARTH ISN'T," and the following is the text of the body copy:

> Take a great show out to sea, and it becomes something else. Maybe it's the sea air, or Caribbean moon, or just the congenial Amerikanis atmosphere, or "zestasia," but something special happens. Singers, dancers, comedians,

every act is a show stopper. (No matter, you have all the time in the world to enjoy them.) But shows are just one reason the rhms Amerikanis is called the last word in luxury. You stay in a luxurious stateroom with twin beds, wall-to-wall carpeting, piped-in music, tapestried walls, TV, private bathrooms and telephone. You have space galore in cozy lounges designed for twice the number of passengers we'd dream of carrying. Haute cuisine, three orchestras, a discotheque, cinema, swimming pools, a sauna, air-conditioning, acres of deck, plus some of the most exotic destinations anywhere, put Chandris America cruises in a world of their own. Call your travel agent or Chandris America—before we're SRO. You'll see why Chandris America makes getting there very different.

Counsel for Ringling Brothers–Barnum & Bailey Combined Shows complained almost immediately. In a telegram to Chandris dated June 23, 1970, the lawyers said, among other things:

Your shocking full-page advertisement in the *New York Times* Magazine on June 21, 1970, has just been brought to our attention. Not only does that ad infringe upon our client's servicemark, and dilute the value thereof, and confuse the public; it directly disparages our client's name and reputation.

Settlement negotiations followed, but they were unsuccessful. Even though the challenged advertisement had been scheduled for only a single insertion, Chandris and Albert Frank–Guenther Law for some reason (unexplained in the published report of the legal proceedings) decided not to give in to Ringling's demands, and Ringling then brought suit against both advertiser and agency.

The principal basis for the lawsuit was a claim that the advertisement was likely to cause confusion among the public in one of two ways. The average reader, Ringling Brothers argued, would believe either that it had gone into the business of performing its circus at sea or that it had gone into the business of sponsoring Chandris' cruises. As part of this argument, Ringling Brothers took the position that the model in the advertisement was wearing a costume similar to that used by the girls in a parade that is part of their circus program. Another basis for the lawsuit was Ringling Brothers' claim that the advertisement was a wilful and malicious disparagement of its business.

Ringling Brothers sought a court order restraining Chandris and Albert Frank–Guenther Law from using the slogan "The Greatest Show on Earth." The defendants responded with a countermove, asking the court to dismiss the case on the ground that it was obvious on the face of the advertisement that no infringement upon the legal rights of Ringling Brothers had occurred.

There was no question about the facts that Ringling Brothers–Barnum & Bailey was celebrating its 100th anniversary, that it had used the slogan "The Greatest Show on Earth" for many years, and that the slogan had been registered in the United States Patent and Trademark Office as a service mark (i.e., a trademark used for services rather than products). Similarly, on the key legal issue, it was quite clear that infringement turns on whether or not it is likely that the public will be confused, mistaken, or deceived about the source of the services and that confusion, mistake, or deception can occur not only when the parties are direct competitors, but even when they are promoting different kinds of services.

The case came before Judge Mansfield of the federal district court in New York City. He noted that Ringling Brothers had been active in protecting its rights to the slogan by complaining whenever an apparent infringement came to its attention.

Judge Mansfield found nothing invalid or imperfect in Ringling's legal rights to its registered slogan. However, he ruled that there could not be any confusion and, therefore, that there was no infringement because of the use of the word "Isn't" in the headline of the challenged advertisement. Infer-

entially complimenting Albert Frank–Guenther Law, the
judge wrote that the addition of the word "Isn't" created "the
eye-catching ambiguity which marks good advertising headlines." At the same time, that word "destroys any rational basis
for believing that defendants' cruise has any connection with
plaintiff or its circus."

Going on to the charge of wilful and malicious disparagement, Judge Mansfield pointed out that Ringling itself had
suggested various theories of what the public might think the
advertisement meant. Assuming for the sake of argument,
however, that it could be construed as a claim that Chandris'
shows are better than Ringling's, the judge ruled that this was
"a legitimate trade comparison, falling well within the limits of
ordinary trade puffing." Therefore, it is not the kind of disparagement that can give rise to any legal liability. Judge
Mansfield accordingly ordered the lawsuit dismissed, and
there is no record of any appeal to a higher court.

CHAPTER 8 Protection for Titles

Introduction to the Subject

It once was reported that a prominent motion picture producer paid $25,000 for the right to use the title of a book called "Napoleon." While this story probably is either a joke or a press agent's invention, it does make two valid points: Titles are worth money, and there is much misunderstanding about legal rights in titles.

To begin with, the copyright law does not protect titles. A title by itself is not considered a literary work and will not be accepted by the United States Copyright Office. And copyrighting a literary work protects the contents but not the title. The same rule applies to music, plays, motion pictures, and anything else that can be copyrighted.

This rule is a practical necessity. Titles tend to be short, and there are only a limited number of usable combinations of common words. A glance at one of the volumes in which the U.S. Copyright Office indexes new works will show numerous duplications and close resemblances among titles. Many of these works are complete failures; some of them are copyrighted in manuscript form and never achieve publication. An intolerable situation would be created if someone could claim copyright infringement merely on the basis of priority in the use of a title.

The law of trademarks does not protect titles either. A title cannot be registered in the U.S. Patent and Trademark Office as a trademark because it is simply the name of the book, play, or other property to which it is attached. The trademark law treats a title like the name of a product, not a brand name. There is an important exception to this rule when the title identifies a series rather than a single item. The title of a magazine therefore (if it meets other legal requirements) can be registered as a trademark. So can the title of a radio or television program series, although technically that is a service mark rather than a trademark because it applies to entertainment services rather than some kind of goods.

Series titles should be registered whenever possible. The federal trademark law provides definite advantages for registered marks which are very helpful if it is ever necessary to bring suit for infringement.

Apart from these special cases of series titles that are registered in the U.S. Patent and Trademark Office, the branch of the law under which titles must seek protection is known as unfair competition. There is no federal law of unfair competition, so the results may vary from place to place and from time to time depending on the views of individual judges and the legal precedents in their particular states. The law in general has grown more liberal, however, and there are some basic principles that are recognized fairly uniformly, although there may be differences of opinion about how they are to be applied to a given set of facts.

First, a purely descriptive title will not be protected at all. There is no need to pay anyone for the right to use "Napoleon" as the title of a motion picture based on Napoleon's life story. The same would be true of "How to Play Contract Bridge," "The History of Advertising," "A Trip to the Moon," or any other title that simply describes what the work is about.

Second, even a distinctive title will not be protected unless it has some current significance for the general public. Merely creating a title is not enough; it must be promoted so that the public will associate it with some particular book, program, song, or picture. If the public never finds out about the title, or if a once-known title is forgotten, others are free to duplicate it.

If there is a borderline case between descriptiveness and

distinctiveness, promotional effort will swing the balance. A highly publicized title can acquire distinctiveness through public exposure, even though it consists of commonplace words.

Some examples from the law books will give a more concrete idea of what happens in title piracy cases.

The owner of the rights to a magazine story entitled "Broken Doll" complained about the use of the same title for a motion picture 15 years later. Result: No protection.

A radio program was on the air for six months. Three and one-half years afterward, someone else produced a program under a similar title. Result: No protection.

"That's Right, You're Wrong" was the title of a motion picture. Twenty years earlier, an unsuccessful play had been produced under the same title. Result: No protection; any impact the play might have made on the public was dissipated as the result of the passage of time.

"Slightly Scandalous" was an unsuccessful stage play. However, it did try out in Philadelphia and open on Broadway; it also was publicized in Hollywood. Not long after it closed, a motion picture based on an entirely different story was released under the same title. Result: The play title was protected; there had been a recent prior use accompanied by substantial publicity. The California Supreme Court affirmed an award of $17,500, taking the practical view that even a flop attracts public attention and noting that other titles had been sold for more.

Some courts have been reluctant to protect a title against unauthorized use in a different field. It once was ruled, for example, that a motion picture could not be confused with a song, so a song title was denied protection against use of a similar title on a motion picture. Other courts have recognized the commercial value of a successful title in another field, and even the title of a poem, "The Ballad of Yukon Jake," was protected against unauthorized use of "Yukon Jake" on a motion picture. This is the more modern view. The change in legal perspective is dramatized by the fact that a court in 1913 denied protection to the book title "Nick Carter" when it was used for a motion picture, while a court in 1934 granted protection to the book title "Frank Merriwell" when that name turned up on a motion picture.

The title of a work that is in the public domain is in a special category. Anyone is free to use the work itself after its copyright expires, and the user automatically has the legal right to call it by its proper title. Walt Disney thus was unable to stop the release of a competitive version of "Alice in Wonderland" even though Disney had spend substantial sums in publicizing his forthcoming film of the same name. If there had been some fraud involved—such as advertisements conveying the false impression that the rival version was the Disney picture—the court presumably would have reached a different result.

Playboy

It is an unfortunate fact of commercial life that some of our best known and most successful trademarks are in frequent need of protection against imitators and coattail-riders of various sorts. Playboy is one of those that has made frequent court appearances. One success was against a dune buggy manufacturer who also operated a group of related businesses in the automotive field around San Mateo, California.

HMH Publishing Company is the owner of the Playboy and Bunny trademarks. It publishes *Playboy* magazine and also has been involved with a number of different business activities, including a model agency, television program production, film production, book publishing, and a products division that sells a variety of merchandise such as keys, key chains, wallets, jewelry, and clothing. Through a franchising arrangement, the Playboy and Bunny marks also are used in the operation of night clubs and hotels.

The other party in this particular lawsuit was Victor Brincat, the owner of Playboy Auto Manufacturing Company and four other businesses, each using the Playboy name in its title. In

addition to making dune buggies, he sold automobile uphol-
stery and dune buggy bodies and accessories, and he operated
a repair shop and a towing service. In what turned out to be a
crucial detail, the evidence revealed that Brincat also used the
trademark Bunny in connection with some of his Playboy business activities.

There are three significant points in this case. First, the
owner of a trademark that is also a word with a well-known
connotation in the language cannot expect a complete
monopoly that would prevent all other uses of the same word
as someone else's trademark.

Second, even that kind of a trademark will be protected
against use by another if the public is likely to think that the
trademark owner sponsored the other use.

Third, in what might otherwise be a doubtful situation, the
fact that the alleged infringer acted with knowledge of the
trademark's prior use and intended to cause confusion will
weigh heavily against him.

Some trademarks are completely arbitrary with relation to
the products on which they are used, either because they are
coined words with no meaning whatever, or because they are
meaningless in the context of their use. Playboy is not in that
category.

The opinion of the United States Court of Appeals in California, which decided the case, points out that the word "playboy" was firmly established in the English language before
HMH selected it as a trademark. It carries a strong connotation of wealth, urbanity, and sophistication, and accordingly
has a natural attraction for any enterprise catering to the interests of men.

This does not mean that the word is ineligible for trademark
protection. It does mean, however, that the trademark owner
will not be able to secure complete exclusivity over others who
may also want to use the word as a trademark for some other
product or service.

The court's opinion referred as an example to a 1957 decision in which the publisher of *Esquire* magazine failed in its

attempt to stop the use of Esquire as a trademark for men's slippers. Also, the court suggested that the word "playboy" probably would be a valid trademark for whisky, provided that the whisky label did not simulate the Playboy logotype used by HMH.

But even a trademark of this general nature will be protected in related fields where it can be assumed that the public would be confused into thinking that HMH must have authorized the use of its trademark for the other product or service. This kind of trademark infringement is known as "confusion of sponsorship."

In order to show that confusion of sponsorship was likely in this particular situation, HMH introduced evidence of all its connections with the automotive field. This included statistics on the amount of automobile advertising that ran in *Playboy* magazine and the quantity of editorial material related to automobiles that had appeared in the magazine over the years. There also was evidence that some of these advertisers had on occasion hired Playboy Bunnies to make personal appearances at automobile dealerships in order to promote their products.

The Court of Appeals was not particularly impressed with the fact that both the advertising and editorial content of *Playboy* magazine included numerous references to automobiles. The promotional tie-ins with dealers were more persuasive in indicating a likelihood that the consumer would infer some sort of connection between Brincat's enterprises and *Playboy* magazine. But the Court said flatly that, in the absence of other considerations, it would not have been inclined to rule in favor of HMH on the issue of confusion of sponsorship.

What became the decisive aspect of the case was the third point, the knowledge and intent of Brincat when he chose Playboy as the distinguishing part of his five businesses' names. Ordinarily the intent of the accused party is of no concern in a trademark infringement case. The fundamental issue always is whether the consuming public is likely to be confused. This can happen even if the alleged infringer acted in complete good faith and even without any knowledge of the existence of the trademark he is charged with having infringed. Ignorance is no excuse in such a lawsuit.

But the converse does not follow. If the accused party deliberately copied someone else's trademark, intending to ride on his coattails and profit from the likelihood that the public would infer a connection between the two enterprises, it will be assumed that there is a real chance of confusion. Otherwise, the defendant presumably would not have gone out of his way to choose that particular trademark.

The evidence showed that Brincat had read *Playboy* magazine and visited Playboy clubs before he started his businesses. It also appeared that he had consulted an attorney, who had advised him against using Playboy as a trademark. Finally, there was evidence that Brincat used the word *bunny* together with Playboy, and this was a unique combination that nobody other than HMH ever had attempted.

It was this final detail that most impressed the Court of Appeals. It showed not only knowledge of HMH's activities, but an expectation that the public would come to the erroneous conclusion that Brincat's business had some authorized connection with HMH. Confusion of sponsorship thus had been established. The injunction prohibiting Brincat from using HMH's trademarks, which had been issued some time previously by the trial judge, therefore was affirmed by the Court of Appeals.

Penthouse

When you have to select a new trademark, try to avoid using the title of an established magazine that might have even a faint connection with it in the consumer's mind. That is the moral of a long series of legal battles won by magazine publishers. An example is the objection raised by Penthouse to an attempt by Dyn Electronics, Inc., to register the word *Penthouse* as a trademark for radio receivers and tape playback units.

Penthouse, as many will remember, started in England. Successful exports to the United States beginning in 1967 led to the organization of a New York company to publish an American edition. The first issue produced in this country was dated September 1969.

Average monthly paid circulation of *Penthouse* during fiscal 1971 was 125,000 copies, according to the Audit Bureau of Circulation. By 1974 monthly sales had reached 4,000,000 and were still increasing. The total readership of a magazine, of course, is considerably higher than the number of copies sold because of pass-on readers. The estimated average monthly readership of *Penthouse* in the final quarter of 1974 was over 8,500,000.

Major advertising categories in *Penthouse* were tobacco products, hi-fi and audiovisual equipment, alcoholic beverages, and grooming aids. Hi-fi equipment is the subject of one-tenth to one-sixth of the advertisements in a typical issue of *Penthouse*. It advertised itself as the "fastest growing magazine aimed at the prime hi-fi buying audience." A readership survey showed that a large segment of the *Penthouse* audience owned a tape player unit, a radio receiver, or both. It also was established that the *Penthouse* readership was composed primarily of 18 to 35-year-old males and that this group was a substantial market for radios and tape playback units.

The Penthouse brand name appeared on other products in addition to the magazine, including leather goods, jewelry, cigarette lighters, posters, puzzles, and books. Penthouse also had sold phonograph records and prerecorded tapes through advertisements in its magazine, although none of those items actually carried the Penthouse trademark.

In an effort to bring itself closer to Dyn's hi-fi electronics field, Penthouse took the unusual step of relying on the track record of its great rival *Playboy*. The evidence showed that Playboy label records and tapes were sold by a subsidiary company belonging to the publisher of *Playboy* and also that Playboy radios were on the market. Penthouse claimed these facts about *Playboy* proved that radios and tape playback units would be a natural business expansion for *Penthouse* magazine, which would bring it into direct conflict with Dyn's Penthouse brand.

Dyn Electronics, an importer of various kinds of auto equipment, was organized several years before Penthouse introduced its magazine in the United States. By 1974 Dyn's total sales volume had reached $15,000,000 per year. Only a tiny fraction of these sales, however, were of products that carried the Penthouse trademark.

In December 1972 Dyn conceived the idea of using Penthouse as the brand name for a new bubble-top audio product. This was intended to be Dyn's top-of-the-line unit, and Dyn claimed it had chosen the name Penthouse because it suggested the top of something. By this time *Penthouse* already was a registered trademark for magazines, and Dyn's witnesses admitted they knew of the publication.

Only limited sales of a few radios and tape units were made to test the new Penthouse trademark. When the publisher of *Penthouse* magazine protested, Dyn held up full-scale commercial introduction of merchandise under this name until the dispute over trademark rights could be decided.

Dyn Electronics had filed applications in the U.S. Patent and Trademark Office to register Penthouse as its trademark, and that is what *Penthouse* magazine tried to stop. This kind of case comes before the Trademark Trial and Appeal Board.

In a long opinion, the Board analyzed in detail the history of *Penthouse* and its related business ventures, as well as the history of Dyn Electronics. Following the lead of *Penthouse,* the Board also analyzed the business of *Playboy* and the use of its title as a trademark for various products and services.

The basic issue in a case like this is the psychological question of whether a prospective purchaser of Penthouse radios or tape playback units would be likely to think there was some connection between them and *Penthouse* magazine. The Board's discussion gives considerable insight into how this question is decided, which means that it contains helpful hints for anyone to use when selecting a new trademark.

As a starting point, the Board noted that *penthouse* is a word of the English language with a well-known dictionary meaning. However, it has no particular significance with respect to magazines or to hi-fi equipment. In other words, it is basically a good trademark because it does not tell the consuming public anything about the product but functions only as a symbol.

As the evidence showed, *Penthouse* had become extremely well known to the public as the title of a magazine. But that does not mean its owner can block the registration of the identical word as a trademark for *every* conceivable item. Dyn's electronic products were distinctly different from either a magazine or any of the other products on which the publisher used Penthouse as a trademark. So *Penthouse* had the task of persuading the Board that purchasers familiar with its publication, if they came across radios or tape players imported by Dyn and bearing the Penthouse brand name, would be likely to believe that they originated with, or were in some way endorsed by or affiliated with, the publisher of the magazine.

On the strength of the kind of evidence already summarized here, including the expansion of *Playboy* into records, tapes, and radios under its trademark, and the substantial amount of hi-fi advertising carried in *Penthouse,* the Board ruled in favor of the publisher and rejected Dyn's application.Although Dyn had made only a limited investment in the Penthouse trademark, it appealed this decision. The appellate court, however, affirmed the Board's ruling in a one-paragraph (unpublished) opinion.

The following is a list of other magazine titles and a variety of different conflicting goods and services involved in some earlier decisions that illustrate the same point:

Ebony .... Radio broadcasting services
Esquire .... Restaurant
Life ....Television sets
Look.......................................Cosmetics
Playboy ....Dune buggies
Seventeen .... Dresses
Seventeen .... Girdles
Seventeen .... Luggage
Vogue .... Ladies' hats
Vogue .... Modeling school

CHAPTER 9   Characters— Real and Imaginary

Dracula

The legal principles that control merchandising rights in a celebrity's name or picture are still in the process of development. There is no specific legislation on the subject, so the rules have to be worked out on a case-by-case basis as disputes reach the courts. Besides, this is the kind of situation in which each of the 50 states has the right to make up its own mind. Under the circumstances, it is not surprising to find that there is a certain amount of confusion in this field.

One example is the lawsuit brought by the surviving widow and son of Bela Lugosi who objected to the merchandising licenses issued by Universal Pictures to various manufacturers under which they, for a royalty, were granted the right to reproduce the character Count Dracula as portrayed by Lugosi in motion pictures produced by Universal. Since 1960, Universal had made a number of lucrative merchandising contracts permitting the exploitation on shirts, games, cards, masks, and other items of several different "monsters" featured in its horror films, including Wolf Man, The Mummy, The Phantom, Mr. Hyde, Frankenstein's Monster, and, of course, Dracula.

In a 40-page opinion that discussed a variety of legal arguments (many of which will be ignored here for the sake of simplicity), Judge Jefferson of the California Superior Court ruled in favor of the heirs. His decision basically was that Bela Lugosi's appearance in the role of Count Dracula constituted a property right that became an asset of his estate upon his

117

death. His heirs, therefore, were entitled to collect damages from Universal for the granting of unauthorized merchandising licenses—but only back to 1964, the cut-off date under the applicable statute of limitations.

The first thing to be noted about this decision is that it depended on the terms of the employment contract made by Lugosi with Universal when he was engaged to play the title role in "Dracula" in 1930. That contract granted to Universal the right to use the actor's performance and appearance "in connection with the said photoplay" (i.e., "Dracula") and "in connection with the advertising and exploitation of said photoplay." Nowhere was there any mention of merchandising rights. The contracts for sequels evidently added nothing on this point.

Much time and attention were given by both sides to the proper interpretation of the 1930 employment contract. Judge Jefferson concluded that the issuance of the merchandising licenses could not properly be considered advertising or exploitation of the motion pictures themselves and accordingly that Lugosi had not granted Universal the right to do what it had been doing.

By way of contrast, the opinion discussed an unsuccessful suit by Gene Autry against Republic Pictures some years ago. Autry objected to the use of his films on television without any additional compensation to him and to the fact that each film was cut to 53 minutes to allow time for commercials in a one-hour broadcast period. But Autry's employment contract had granted Republic the right to use all or any part of his performances and appearances "in such manner as the producer may desire." Autry accordingly lost that case.

It is apparent, therefore, that the value of the Dracula decision as a precedent for other cases involving allegedly unauthorized commercial uses of an actor's appearance depends on the terms of the particular contract.

If merchandising rights were granted specifically, or if the producer acquired the right to use the actor's appearance in any manner it wished, then neither the actor (if still alive) nor his heirs would have any legal ground for objection. That kind of contract does not permit the producer to issue merchandising licenses; the only question would be whether some other clause in the contract required the producer to compensate the actor for the additional uses, perhaps by a percentage of the receipts from licensees.

The second major point to be considered is the nature of the legal right that is being protected. In most situations the name or likeness of an individual is protected under the "right of privacy." This is the legal right that, for instance, requires a written release from a model or actor before a still picture or a film can be used for advertising purposes.

There is no federal law on this subject; it is a question that each state is free to decide for itself. And practically every state recognizing the right of privacy considers it such a personal thing that it can be enforced only by the individual himself. It does not survive, so in these states the heirs of a deceased person have no legal right to complain about the unauthorized use of his name or likeness.

The issue has been tested in a number of different states. For example, Judge Jefferson discussed the Illinois case in which Al Capone's widow and son joined with the administrator of his estate in suing Desilu Productions for an unauthorized and fictionalized biographical film. The suit was dismissed because Illinois does not recognize a property right in a name, likeness, or story that survives the death of the individual.

Other states have reached similar conclusions. One additional example mentioned in Judge Jefferson's opinion involved a one-liner on the once-popular television program "That Was The Week That Was." The statement made on the air was the following: "Mrs. Katherine Young of Syracuse, New York, who died at 99, leaving five sons, five daughters, 67 grandchildren, 72 great-grandchildren—gets our First Annual Booby Prize in the Birth Control Sweepstakes." Two of her sons brought suit for invasion of their mother's right of privacy. The court ruled that relatives have no right of action under Ohio law for the invasion of the privacy of a deceased person.

Some states, however, recognize a variation on this kind of

personality right. When a celebrity is involved, so that his name and likeness have commercial values that he can exploit, these states drop the "right of privacy" label. A New York case involving baseball cards, for example, called it a "right of publicity."

Other cases in different states, most of which also happen to deal with athletes, have reached similar conclusions about the existence of a property right. Up to the time of the Dracula decision, however, none of these lawsuits seems to have presented the question of whether this commercial right survives the death of the individual so that it can be enforced by his heirs.

Judge Jefferson found that he was free to make up his own mind because there was no California appellate court decision on the point. He concluded that it was preferable as a matter of sound reason to recognize the commercial values in a celebrity's name or likeness as a form of property right, distinct from the very personal right of privacy. As Judge Jefferson viewed the situation, it followed logically from this that the right of commercial exploitation survives the death of the celebrity and becomes an asset of his estate that descends to his heirs.

This is a novel doctrine, and it would be too much to expect it to gain widespread acceptance immediately, even in California. Those states already committed to the opposite view about the nonsurvival of what they classify as a personal rather than a property right are not likely to rush to change their positions—although that is not outside the realm of possibility. And even those states that recognize a property right for celebrities might be wary about going along with the idea that the right survives and can be inherited.

In the Dracula case itself, the situation was manageable because only two heirs survived and both of them had joined in the lawsuit. But suppose one of Ludwig van Beethoven's heirs brought suit to collect damages for the unauthorized use of the great composer's likeness on sweatshirts. What is the court to do then? It might be necessary to get all the heirs into the case. Or could each heir sue separately and collect his proportionate share? Perhaps the complaining party would have to satisfy the court that there weren't any heirs who had consented to the use of Beethoven's picture on sweatshirts because it wouldn't be fair to the manufacturer to make him pay unless all of the heirs objected.

This obviously is a fanciful situation. And yet something very much like it could arise. Policy considerations similar to those that led some courts to deny heirs the right to enforce a right of privacy might then be used to justify a similar denial of the right to enforce the commercial property right. Perhaps it will be ruled eventually that this right also dies with the individual, simply to keep from cluttering up the courts with disputes like the imaginary one above about Beethoven's heirs. Five years later, the California Court of Appeals reversed Judge Jefferson's decision and ruled in favor of Universal.

The appeal court judges found a different way to analyze the problem. To them the important point was that Lugosi never had exploited himself in the Dracula character by means of merchandise licenses. Since the right was not exercised during his lifetime, there was nothing to survive. This decision then was upheld by the California Supreme Court after a further appeal.

It is not entirely clear from the opinion whether the heirs would have any surviving rights if Lugosi had exploited himself as Dracula by merchandising licenses while he was alive. This branch of the law is still in the process of development, and other test cases will have to wind their way through the courts before a definite answer can be given. Another point to bear in mind is that, as noted by one of the California Supreme Court judges, Lugosi's own personality was not involved; he was only portraying a role created by the author of the original story.

Laurel and Hardy

A decision in New York attacked the problem of conflicting claims to the merchandising rights in the names and likenesses of the comedians Laurel and Hardy. The legal situation was further complicated by the fact that both individuals had been dead for some time.

Stanley Laurel and Oliver Hardy made a number of motion pictures for Hal Roach Studios under a series of employment contracts starting in 1923. In 1939 these contracts came to an end, and Laurel and Hardy worked for other producers, including a company they organized for themselves. The pictures made under the contracts were copyrighted by Roach, and no question was raised about the fact that these pictures continued to be Roach's property.

The original Hal Roach Studio went into bankruptcy in 1967, at which time its name and other assets, including the Laurel and Hardy films, were acquired by another corporation also called Hal Roach Studios. In 1971 there was another reorganization, in the course of which a third corporation named Hal Roach Studios took over the rights. Meanwhile, in 1969 Roach had issued a Laurel and Hardy merchandising license to a man named Feiner. He in turn had sublicensed all rights outside the United States to Overseas Programming Companies, Ltd.

Previously, in 1961, when Laurel was still alive, the exclusive merchandising rights in the names and likenesses of Laurel and Hardy had been granted to Larry Harmon Pictures Corporation by Laurel and by Hardy's widow.

Although the opinion in the lawsuit does not go into detail on how the dispute came to light, apparently Harmon was just making plans to get into various projects utilizing the Laurel and Hardy names and likenesses when it discovered that Laurel and Hardy sweatshirts and other items were already on the market under licenses granted by Feiner. It doesn't make much business sense for a manufacturer to take on an item of this sort unless he can get an exclusive right in his field. With two groups claiming each could grant exclusive licenses, litigation was inevitable.

Harmon was joined by the widows of Laurel and Hardy, who are the sole beneficiaries of their husbands' estates under their wills. They sued Roach, Feiner, and Overseas, along with Feiner's corporation and Roach's executive vice-president. The defendants responded with a counterclaim asking that they be declared the owners of the rights.

Roach and the others relied primarily on certain clauses in the employment contracts with Laurel and Hardy. It was true that the contracts typically gave Roach the right to use each actor's name, voice, and likeness "for advertising, commercial and/or publicity purposes." But the judge reviewed each contract and each variation in language carefully and came to the conclusion that these rights were granted to Roach only for the period of the contracts, i.e., while Roach still had Laurel and Hardy in its employ as actors. Other clauses also gave Roach certain rights in perpetuity, but the judge ruled that these applied only to the motion pictures made during the period the employment contracts were still in effect. As already noted, no challenge to Roach's continued ownership of the films was made by Harmon or by the widows of Laurel and Hardy.

Two important questions still remained. Did Laurel and Hardy themselves have exclusive merchandising rights in their names and likenesses, or was anyone free to use them? And, if Laurel and Hardy did have those rights legally, did the rights die with the individuals, or did they pass to the widows as sole beneficiaries under their husbands' wills?

This is the point at which the judge drew a sharp distinction between the comparatively familiar "right of privacy," which protects an individual against the unauthorized use of his name or picture for commercial purposes, and the relatively unfamiliar "right of publicity," which, according to some court decisions, is the proper legal basis for the commercial exploitation of the name or picture of a celebrity.

Judge Stewart wrote in his opinion that "much confusion is generated by the notion that the right of publicity emanates from the classic right of privacy." To him, "the two rights are clearly separable."

The judge went on to explain that:

> The protection from intrusion upon an individual's privacy, on the one hand, and protection from appropriation of some element of an individual's personality for commercial exploitation, on the other hand, are different in theory and in scope.

The right of privacy is something truly personal. Its original purpose was to protect an individual against an injury to his feelings. That kind of right does not survive. But the right of publicity is purely commercial in nature. It is treated as a kind of property that can be sold or licensed. Judge Stewart said, "There appears to be no logical reason to terminate this right upon death of the person protected."

Judge Stewart ruled that Laurel and Hardy did have a right of publicity in their own names and likenesses and that this right descended to their heirs. Each deceased comedian left only one heir, which avoided a possible problem of multiple descendants.

Judge Stewart concluded that Roach did not have the merchandising rights it purported to grant to Feiner and that Harmon's contract for exclusive merchandising rights was valid. As a result, he issued an injunction preventing Roach, Feiner, and Overseas from attempting to exercise merchandising rights in the names or likenesses of Laurel and Hardy, or even from claiming them. He also directed that a separate hearing be held to determine the amount of damages to be awarded to Harmon as the result of the improper issuance of merchandising licenses under the purported authority of Roach.

Joe Namath

The "model release" that is such a common feature of the advertising business is a written promise by the individual concerned not to sue anybody for the use of his picture. The reason everyone involved in the transaction insists on getting a release signed by the model is that most states have a law prohibiting the use of an individual's name or likeness for commercial purposes without his written consent. Failure to observe this legal requirement is known as a violation of the person's "right of privacy."

In New York, to choose a typical and important example,

the law says that the name or likeness cannot be used "for advertising purposes or for the purposes of trade." It would be almost impossible to apply those words literally because even magazines and newspapers are operated "for the purposes of trade," in other words, to make money, and they could not function if every name and picture they used had to be covered by a written release. So news photos and other editorial material have been recognized for a long time as exceptions to the strict language of the statute. Indeed, a series of decisions makes it clear that it would be an unconstitutional interference with the freedom of the press (First Amendment) if a state law did require written consent from the subject of every picture used in a newspaper or magazine.

This exception applies to the editorial content of the publication. It does not relieve anyone from the necessity of obtaining a signed release when a picture is used in an advertisement.

Joe Namath had an in-between kind of problem. Some of the many photographs of Namath that appeared editorially in *Sports Illustrated* over the years were reused in a series of ten promotional advertisements in other magazines for *Sports Illustrated* itself. These insertions carried subscription applications for *Sports Illustrated* along with promotional copy, a picture of Namath, and headlines like "How to Get Close to Joe Namath" and "The Man You Love Loves Joe Namath," depending on whether the publication was oriented toward male or female readership.

Namath brought suit for a total of $2,250,000 in compensatory and punitive damages. In 1972, the year that the *Sports Illustrated* advertisements were published, Namath claims to have received "in excess of several hundred thousand dollars" from commercial endorsements. His complaint, as the judge said in the published opinion, really was not that his privacy was being interfered with; he wanted compensation for the commercial exploitation of his name and picture.

The original use of the photographs obviously needed no release. The reuse clearly was for advertising purposes, but does it make a difference that the commodity being advertised is itself a news medium? Curiously enough, there is an almost exact precedent that was decided by a New York court several years ago. *Holiday* magazine had published an article about a resort in the West Indies, illustrated with photographs of famous, guests. Among them was Shirley Booth, the well-known actress. This picture of her was republished six months later as part of an advertisement for *Holiday*.

The ruling in the Booth case was in favor of the publisher. The use of the previously published picture, in the court's opinion, was merely "incidental advertising of the news medium itself." In effect, *Holiday* simply was quoting from its own pages in the advertisement, whose purpose was to establish the type and quality of the magazine. So the New York right of privacy law was not violated either by the original use of Shirley Booth's picture in a fair presentation of news, or by the incidental reuse of the picture in an advertisement for the news medium in which she was properly presented.

There are obvious resemblances between the Booth and Namath cases. Namath argued, however, that his situation was closer to that of a man named Flores, who had been successful in a still earlier suit against the Mosler Safe Company for using in one of its advertisements a reproduction of a newspaper story in which Flores was mentioned. Judge Baer, who ruled on the Namath lawsuit, noted a significant distinction. Mosler was advertising an ordinary commercial product for sale; *Sports Illustrated,* on the other hand, is a magazine, and the fact that it is published and sold for profit does not prevent it from being "a form of expression whose liberty is safeguarded by the First Amendment."

Judge Baer said it was understandable that Namath wanted to be paid for the use of his name and picture in advertisements for periodicals in which he appeared as a newsworthy character, just as he was paid for his endorsements of commercial products. However, the judge continued, this was something he could not accomplish under existing state and federal law. "Athletic prowess is much admired and well paid in this country," Judge Baer noted. But, he concluded, "It is commendable that freedom of speech and the press under the First Amendment transcends the right to privacy."

Howard Hughes

Howard Hughes, sometimes called "the bashful billionaire," was involved in more than one lawsuit attempting to protect his privacy against invasion by commercial interests. The same basic legal principles apply to the use of any celebrity's name, whether he has a passion for privacy like Hughes, or a passion for publicity, as is more often the situation.

In one celebrated litigation just a few years before his death, Hughes tried to stop the publication of an unauthorized biography, claiming that it was an invasion of his privacy. He had taken the unusual step of transferring to a corporation, Rosemont Enterprises, the exclusive commercial rights to exploit his name and life story, so that Rosemont also asserted a legal claim against the book publisher. It was decided that, despite Hughes' desire to preserve his privacy, he was in fact a public figure. He, therefore, was fair game for any biographer able to accumulate enough material about him for a book.

Also, since he was a public figure, he did not really own the exclusive rights to his own life story; it was public property just like a news event. Because of this, Rosemont's supposedly "exclusive" contract did not give it any legal position to complain about the publication of the unauthorized biography.

Subsequently, Hughes, again joined by Rosemont Enterprises, challenged a so-called adult educational game that, without authorization, was called "The Howard Hughes Game" and used biographical data about Hughes' career as the basic material for the game. This time, Hughes was successful in stopping the unauthorized activity. It is natural to wonder about the differences between the two cases and why the courts (both in New York) came to what may seem to be opposite results.

The crucial distinction is that the biography is basically in the same category as news, while the game is an article of merchandise exploiting the commercial values in the Hughes name and life story. This is not an easy line to draw. Book publishing also is a commercial business operation. But in the case involving the biography, Hughes essentially was complaining about the public display of his private life, while in the case involving the game, he was complaining about the appropriation of the property rights in his name and career.

A public figure gives up the rights of privacy enjoyed by the ordinary citizen simply because he is a public figure. But a public figure, even more so than the ordinary citizen, has commercial rights in his personality that the law will protect against unauthorized use for the very reason that they are worth money. The public figure, whether Howard Hughes, an athlete, an actress, or perhaps even a criminal, may be able to collect royalties for such commercial rights as the manufacture of a game using his name and based on his career; it is up to him to decide whether or not he wishes to allow commercial uses of this kind.

As the opinion in the Hughes game case states, "There is no question but that a celebrity has a legitimate proprietary interest in his public personality. He must be considered as having invested years of practice and competition in a public personality, which eventually may reach marketable status."

From the standpoint of the advertiser or agency that wishes to know what it may or may not do without violating someone else's rights, it is unfortunate that there are no specific rules. New York Supreme Court Justice Birdie Amsterdam said in the Hughes game opinion: "Each case must be decided by weighing conflicting policies; the public interest in the free dissemination of information against the interest in the preservation of inviolate personality and property rights."

A further complication was introduced when the game manufacturer appealed to a higher court. The basic legal decision was affirmed, but the appeals court limited the territorial scope of the injunction to the state of New York. This points up the fact that privacy and publicity problems are for each individual state to decide; there is no federal law on the subject. The commercial importance of New York as a market is so great, however, that a legal prohibition against advertising or selling in New York can have the same business impact as if it were nationwide in scope.

The principles of law involved in the Hughes cases are the same as those that require a signature on a model release before the name or picture of an individual can be used in advertising. In spite of the uncertainty noted by Justice Amsterdam, there are many situations where the answer is reasonably clear and many others in which simply recognizing the dimensions of the problem may have great practical value in reaching a business decision about whether or not to take the risk of going ahead without authorization.

Paladin

Victor DeCosta, a mechanic from the town of Cranston, Rhode Island, claims to be the original Paladin. He brought suit against CBS for producing "Have Gun Will Travel," and this case went on long after the TV series went off the air. During its successful run it grossed in excess of $14,000,000.

DeCosta lived in the West during the Depression and worked for a while as a Texas range hand. After his return to Rhode Island in 1947, he maintained his western interests by participating in rodeos, horse shows, and similar activities. For his costume he selected a black shirt, black pants, and a black flat-crowned hat. A St. Mary's medal was attached to the hat.

During one of his appearances, a spectator yelled at him a phrase in Italian containing the word "paladino." He looked in the dictionary, found that paladin meant "champion of knights" and encouraged people to call him by that name. He also bought a chess knight to use as his symbol and eventually had a silver chess knight attached to his holster.

DeCosta used to put on an act involving a derringer that he concealed in his sleeve, in addition to the revolver he carried in his holster. One day, while he was getting ready to mount his horse, somebody shouted, "Have gun will travel." This phrase was picked up by a group of children who were hanging around, and DeCosta started to use it himself.

The final step in the entire conception was the preparation of a business card, which carried a reproduction of the chess knight and the words "Have Gun Will Travel, Wire Paladin, N. Court St., Cranston, R.I." DeCosta distributed photographs of himself in costume and many copies of his business card— approximately 250,000 of them.

He did all this just for the pleasure and personal satisfaction he got out of it. One of the court opinions (there have been several) summed it up: "This was perhaps one of the purest promotions ever staged, for plaintiff [DeCosta] did not seek anything but the entertainment of others. He sold no product, services, or institution, charged no fees, and exploited only himself."

In 1957 the TV series "Have Gun Will Travel" premiered on CBS. The star, Richard Boone, wore a black costume, a flat-crowned black hat with an oval silver decoration, and a silver chess knight on his holster. He announced himself with a calling card carrying a reproduction of the chess knight and the words "Have Gun Will Travel, Wire Paladin, San Francisco." The TV Paladin also used a hidden derringer. To put the finishing touches on the resemblance, both Boone and DeCosta had black moustaches.

DeCosta filed a lawsuit charging that CBS has misappropriated the idea and character of Paladin from him; he also charged infringement and unfair competition under different legal theories. The first round in the courtoom battle was a trial before a jury, limited to the misappropriation charge only.

CBS called a number of witnesses to the stand, including the two writers of the TV scripts and the original producer of the show. They all testified that they had never before seen DeCosta or any of his cards. They said that the TV series was an independent creation with no relationship to DeCosta's Paladin character except coincidence.

The jury obviously disbelieved this testimony, since it brought in a verdict in favor of DeCosta for $150,000. When the case was appealed, the court said that it thought the jury was "amply justified" in its reaction to the testimony. But the Court of Appeals threw out the verdict on technical legal grounds, so that DeCosta merely, to quote the Court's opinion again, "had the satisfaction of proving the defendants pirates."

The Court of Appeals ruled that there was no proper legal basis for any verdict in DeCosta's favor. The entire conception of the Paladin character was "fully conveyed" by his calling cards. These cards could be considered "writings" within the meaning of the section of the United States Constitution that deals with copyrights. DeCosta had failed to take any steps to protect the cards by copyright—instead, he had given them away in large quantities without any restriction. The result, according to the Court of Appeals, was that anyone was free to copy the character, the name, the slogan, and the symbol. Paladin, as created by DeCosta, was in the public domain. Even if CBS did take the idea from DeCosta, there was no legal liability for having done so.

Eventually the case went back down to the trial court level, where DeCosta pursued the other two theories. On this second round, he took the position that the name Paladin and the other attributes of the character were the legal equivalent of his trademark ("service mark," actually, since it was entertainment services rather than products that were involved). That was the second theory; the third was labeled unfair competition, but this did not differ significantly from the claim of service mark infringement.

This time DeCosta won what presumably would have amounted to even a larger sum of money. The ruling was that DeCosta had a valid service mark, that CBS had infringed it, and that DeCosta, therefore, was entitled to receive an amount equal to the entire profit that CBS had made from its infringements.

But, once again, the ruling in DeCosta's favor was thrown out on appeal. The Court of Appeals doubted that DeCosta had anything that could be protected by the law of service marks or unfair competition because he was not engaged in any trade, business, or profession. The protectible interest that the law recognizes is "good will," and the court thought that there could be no good will in this context unless it had been subjected "to the acid test of the willingness of people to pay for goods or services." Since DeCosta charged nothing for his performances, he had not developed any commercial good will that could be protected.

The court did not stop its analysis at this point. Even assuming that DeCosta possessed something legally protectible, it was incumbent upon him to show that CBS had caused a likelihood of confusion or deception among the public. DeCosta produced a few witnesses who testified that they thought he was the TV character when they first saw the show on the air, but the court found this unconvincing in view of the tremendous exposure of the TV series.

Again the Court of Appeals had some kind words for De-Costa, but no money. The opinion says: "We recognize that plaintiff [DeCosta] has lost something of value to him. . . . While he was not injured financially, there can be no doubt that he has felt deprived." But, as the Court went on to point out, they could not grant him any financial relief without a legal basis for liability. Since there was insufficient evidence of a likelihood of confusion, the claims of service mark infringement and unfair competition could not be sustained.

DeCosta tried for a second time to persuade the U.S. Supreme Court to review his case, but the request was turned down and the litigation finally came to an end after more than ten years in the courts.

The Human Cannonball

Hugo Zacchini, the "human cannonball," climbs into an outsize cannon and is shot into a net 200 feet away. The entire performance lasts 15 seconds.

Zacchini was performing at a county fair not far from Cleveland when a free lance reporter for WEWS-TV, the Scripps-Howard station in Cleveland, went to the fair carrying a small motion-picture camera. Zacchini noticed the camera and asked the reporter not to film the performance.

The reporter came back the next day and videotaped the entire act. The full 15-second performance was shown on the 11 o'clock news that night.

Zacchini sued Scripps-Howard for damages, claiming an "unlawful appropriation" of his "professional property." Previous decisions in Ohio had recognized a "right of publicity," which permits an individual to control the commercial exploitation of his name or likeness.

The Ohio courts agreed that Zacchini had this right of publicity and that it covered the "human cannonball" act he performed. But, when the case got to the Supreme Court of Ohio, Scripps-Howard won with the argument that the act also was a news event—which it had the right to broadcast under the "freedom of the press" clause of the First Amendment.

The United States Supreme Court took the case for final review because of the important constitutional question. The Supreme Court ruled that there was a distinction between a news report of a performance and a broadcast of a performer's entire act.

Freedom of the press is a basic principle that would permit the TV station to report the newsworthy facts about Zacchini's performance. But, said the Supreme Court, the media are not immunized when they use a complete act without the performer's consent.

The Supreme Court decided that Ohio was not required to defer to the First Amendment "freedom of the press" clause when enforcing its "right of publicity." So the case was sent back to the Ohio courts for reconsideration.

The vote in the Supreme Court was close, five to four. The principal dissenting opinion (joined by three justices) expressed concern about using the concept of an "entire act" as the ground of distinction between what is privileged news reporting and what may be the basis for an award of damages. The dissenting judges felt that a 15-second item included in an ordinary daily news program should be protected by the "freedom of the press" clause even if it did contain Zacchini's complete performance.

According to the dissenting opinion, whenever a television news editor is unsure whether certain film footage received from a camera crew could be an "entire act," he might feel obligated to cut the segment out or substitute "watered-down verbal reporting, perhaps with an occasional still picture." The public then would be the loser.

Even though Zacchini won the legal principle, he may have difficulty proving that he suffered any financial loss. The significance of the case, overriding any question of possible monetary damages, is the Supreme Court's approval of an individual state's theory of a "right of publicity" that can be superior to the media's constitutional right to report newsworthy events.

Hazel

Shirley Booth played "Hazel" in a successful television series that ran from 1961 to 1966 and has been in syndication since then. "Hazel" began as a cartoon character, created by Ted Key. The TV series was produced under a license from him, as the owner of the copyright.

In January 1971 Colgate launched a series of commercials for its Burst product. These featured a cartoon "Hazel," also under a proper license from Ted Key. The voice of the cartoon character was provided by an actress named Ruth Holden (but unidentified on the commercial), who imitated the voice of Shirley Booth in her characterization of Hazel in the TV series. Miss Booth promptly started a lawsuit against Colgate-Palmolive and its agency, Ted Bates and Company, claiming substantial damages. As the argument appears from the opinion written by Judge Bonsal of the federal district court in New

York City, Miss Booth asserted that her voice in the Hazel character was so distinctive that the public would be deceived into thinking that she was the one who gave the performance in the Burst commercial. She complained, in support of this, that concealing the identity of the performer who imitated her voice contributed to the public deception and that this must have been what Colgate and Bates intended.

On this theory, Miss Booth could have been damaged in at least two ways. If she was right, the advertiser got what amounted to the benefit of her services without paying for them. And the exposure of the Hazel voice in the Burst commercial might have lessened the opportunities for Miss Booth to obtain commercial assignments at a suitable fee.

Although he did not do so, Judge Bonsal might have gone into the history of mimicry as a component part of burlesque and satire. To imitate someone's mannerisms, including his voice, is not only standard comedy routine, it is also frequently used as social and political criticism. This, of course, can be done without legal liability. It would be intolerable if an impersonator appearing, for example, on the "Tonight" show, had to get a license every time he wanted to do a take-off on President Nixon, Henry Kissinger, or—for that matter—Shirley Booth.

There is a clear distinction between that kind of impersonation, whose only commercial purpose is to earn the entertainer his fee, and the kind of activity which may have a competitive effect on the person who is imitated, such as the use of a distinctive voice to sell a product—which might be called commercial mimicry.

A strong federal legal policy favors the imitation of anything that is not protected by a patent or a copyright, based on the idea that imitation promotes competition and that this is the most desirable system for our economy. A tone of voice cannot be patented or copyrighted. Judge Bonsal's principal ground of decision was that this federal policy favoring imitation was more important than the private interests of Miss Booth, even assuming that her voice as Hazel was so distinctive that the public could recognize it on the air. The lawsuit, therefore, was dismissed by the court.

Within the past few years there have been several other cases that are strikingly similar. Nancy Sinatra, whose recording made such a hit out of "These Boots Are Made for Walkin'," sued Goodyear Tire & Rubber Company and Young & Rubicam for a series of "Wide Boots" TV commercials. An unidentified voice imitated Miss Sinatra singing "These Boots Are Made for Walkin'." But the federal Court of Appeals in California spoke of the importance of free competition in unpatented and uncopyrighted ideas and threw the case out.

Also in California, a group called the Fifth Dimension sued TWA and Foote, Cone & Belding over the "Up, Up and Away" commercials. The lyrics of the original song were modified to relate to TWA, but unidentified performers imitated the sound of the recording by the Fifth Dimension. The ruling? Imitation alone is not a basis for legal complaint.

One case that pointed in the other direction was a lawsuit by Bert Lahr against Adell Chemical Company involving a cartoon duck character advertising Lestoil. The actor who did the duck voice was alleged to be a specialist in imitating Lahr's vocal style. Lahr, like Booth, put forth a number of legal theories. With respect to unfair competition, he complained that the Lestoil commercial had greater value because the audience believed it was listening to him.

The Lahr case was decided on what must be called a technicality. The federal appeals court in Massachusetts ruled that he ought to have a chance to prove his contentions, including the claim that his voice really was unique and recognizable, at a trial. But Adell Chemical was out of business by the time the appeal was decided, and there is no indication in the law books that the case was ever pursued.

From the legal viewpoint, the Lahr decision is getting a little old to be used as a precedent. Specifically, it was decided in 1962, two years before a pair of extremely significant U.S. Supreme Court decisions that emphasized the "imitation" policy mentioned above. These were relied upon by the courts who decided against Shirley Booth, Nancy Sinatra, and the Fifth Dimension.

Actually there is another important difference between Lahr and the other three cases. Booth, Sinatra, and the Fifth Dimension all were working with someone else's copyrighted material. Each of them was performing under license from the copyright proprietor. And, in each of those three cases, the advertiser and agency also were operating under copyright licenses. Lahr was the only one who claimed a truly independent right in his own vocal mannerisms. On this analysis, the Lahr case may still be a useful precedent—if the complaining party has a really distinctive voice, as contrasted with simply a distinctive performance of copyrighted material belonging to somebody else.

Why shouldn't voices be protected against imitation? As a matter of fact, the law recognizes sounds as a variety of trademark. Almost everyone remembers the squeaking door effect that introduced the old "Inner Sanctum" radio series. The NBC chimes also have been registered as a trademark, and so has Screen Gems' electronic fanfare.

It is extremely important from the technical legal viewpoint to realize that trademark infringement is a kind of unfair competition. Trademarks are entirely different from copyrights or patents, and there is no federal legal policy that encourages the imitation of other people's trademarks.

But most of the courts haven't seen the commercial mimicry situation that way, as the cases discussed here demonstrate. There is a federal unfair competition bill before Congress, however, and perhaps that will change things in this area.

The pending bill lists various kinds of unfair practices and ends with a catchall provision prohibiting any activity that "otherwise constitutes unfair competition by misrepresentation or misappropriation." Peculiarly enough, there is a somewhat similar law in California, which was invoked in the Sinatra case. It prohibits any "unlawful, unfair, or fraudulent business practice." But the court decisions construing the California law limit its application to situations in which the parties

are competitors, and the judge hardly needed to point out that
Nancy Sinatra was not competing with Goodyear in the tire
business.

On the other hand, the proposed new federal law specifically states that it is unnecessary to prove competition between
the parties in order to obtain relief against unfair acts. In other
words, there can be "unfair competition" without any actual
competition in the usual business sense; the emphasis is on the
"unfair" part of it.

Cases like the one Shirley Booth lost will be brought again if
the federal unfair competition bill becomes law. Of course it is
possible that even the broad language of that bill might be
construed by the courts in such a way as to deny protection to
imitated voices. If that happens, performers will continue to
feel enraged about commercial mimicry, and eventually they
may try to get a special law passed to take care of the situation.

CHAPTER 10 Nicknames

Bug

Volkswagen has been successful in protecting its trade symbols against use by unauthorized sales and service businesses. By 1971, Volkswagen had reached the point where the courts recognized its exclusive rights, not only to the name Volkswagen and the encircled VW monogram, but also to the blue-and-white color scheme and the Memphis Bold type face that were used consistently in displaying these trademarks.

Volkswagen later went even further: a decision in a series of trademark enforcement lawsuits granted protection for the nickname "Bug" and also for the design that is a stylized silhouette of the best-known Volkswagen model.

The case was filed against two individuals who operated a company in Dallas under the trade name "The Bug Shop." Over 90 percent of this company's business consisted of servicing Volkswagen cars. Most of the remainder was the sale of parts and accessories that fit Volkswagen automobiles but were acquired from independent distributors representing various foreign manufacturers. The Bug Shop also sold some used Volkswagen cars and rebuilt parts and accessories for Volkswagen cars.

There is nothing illegal about unauthorized automobile companies announcing (if it is true) that they sell used Volkswagen cars or repair Volkswagen products. The problem arises out of creating the misleading impression that the shop in question is part of the *authorized* Volkswagen-franchised sales and service organization.

Volkswagen, the German manufacturer, and Volkswagen of

America, its exclusive United States importer, have gone to great lengths to set up a carefully supervised organization of authorized dealerships under a network of regional distributors.

The Volkswagen companies and their distributors try to make certain that the services performed by authorized dealers are done properly and that the dealers have the facilities, parts, equipment, technical information, and trained personnel needed to do a good job. Authorized dealers are required to send their service employees to schools run by Volkswagen distributors in accordance with standards established by the parent company. These dealers also are provided regularly with up-to-date technical data about servicing Volkswagen automobiles. And they are obligated to stock a minimum inventory of replacement parts and accessories.

The Volkswagen organization in the U.S. includes over 1,100 independent retailers. More than 50 of these are in Texas, and six are located in Dallas County, where The Bug Shop was established. The authorized dealers are required by contract to use the Volkswagen trademarks to identify the products and services they sell, which must be done in the manner specified by Volkswagen—this includes using the blue-and-white color scheme and the Memphis Bold type face.

Volkswagen has backed this organization with substantial advertising expenditures. Specifically, in 1970, the last complete year covered by the evidence in the lawsuit, over $32,000,000 was spent nationally, more than $400,000 in Texas media, and over $100,000 in local Dallas–Fort Worth media.

This advertising featured the name Volkswagen, the initials VW, and the emblem consisting of an encircled VW, all of which are registered trademarks. In addition, evidence was introduced in the federal district court in Dallas to show that the word *bug* and the silhouette design, though not registered in the U.S. Patent and Trademark Office, have achieved widespread public recognition as symbols identifying Volkswagen products.

For its part, the company that was the target of the lawsuit not only called its business The Bug Shop, but it took other steps to associate itself with the Volkswagen organization in the public mind. Its principal means of advertising was to insert classified notices under the column heading "Volkswagen" in local newspapers. The silhouette design appeared in numerous newspaper advertisements and also in promotional mailings. The color blue was used on a white background on stationery and business cards.

Quantities of The Bug Shop's advertising material referred to "Volkswagen parts," "VW parts," "new Volkswagen parts," "rebuilt Volkswagen parts," "Volkswagen accessories," and "VW accessories." Their business cards and printed forms used the terms "Volkswagen service" and "Volkswagen parts and service." "VW service" and "VW servicing" appeared in newspaper advertising. "Volkswagen repair center" and "complete Volkswagen repair service" were used in a classified telephone directory advertisement. And a sign at their place of business read "Volkswagen parts & service."

On the basis of detailed evidence of these activities, the federal judge in Dallas concluded that the owners of The Bug Shop had intended to confuse customers and potential customers into believing that their business was authorized by Volkswagen or otherwise operated with the sponsorship, approval, or consent of Volkswagen. He ruled that this was trademark infringement and unfair competition. It is noteworthy that the word *bug* and the silhouette design were both protected as Volkswagen trademarks, despite the fact that they have not be registered. The Bug Shop was ordered to delete the word *bug* from its name and to stop using any of the Volkswagen symbols as trademarks.

However, as stated earlier, an unauthorized shop may service Volkswagen automobiles and advertise the fact so long as it does not mislead the public into thinking that it is part of the Volkswagen system of franchised dealers. The court order, therefore, permits the Dallas company to use factual phrases such as "We service Volkswagen cars," "parts for VW autos," or even "rebuilt parts for bug cars."

But these statements must be used only in specifically limited ways, in order to protect Volkswagen against the possibility that customers might believe that they were dealing with an authorized outlet. For example, the order of the court requires that when the word Volkswagen, the abbreviation VW, or the word *bug* is used, it may not be set out alone; it must be placed on the same line as the other words in the factual phrase of which it forms a part.

Also, the trademark must appear in "the same type, lettering, print, color, mounting, spacing, illumination, size, format, and material" as those other words. In addition, use of the type face Memphis Bold or the color blue is prohibited in connection with any factual phrase containing one of the Volkswagen trademarks. The Volkswagen silhouette and the encircled VW emblem may not be used at all.

Finally, in more general terms, the court ordered that none of the Volkswagen trademarks could be used as a dominant feature of the Dallas company's advertising, or as a dominant feature of signs at its place of business.

There was an appeal, but the appellate court agreed with the legal conclusions of the Dallas judge. The Court of Appeals thought he had been too strict in some of his requirements, however, and eliminated a few details from the court order. For example, the absolute prohibition against using the color blue was relaxed, and so was the requirement of placing the VW trademarks on the same line as the rest of the phrase—many harmless descriptive sentences, the appellate court pointed out, would simply be too long to fit on a single line.

Bug is by no means the first nickname that has been protected as a trademark. The Coca-Cola Company for years tried to discourage people from using the nickname Coke, but when a competing cola product appeared under the phonetically identical designation "Koke" the Coca-Cola Company brought suit for infringement and won. It then changed its corporate policy and began to use "Coke" itself. Coke now is a separately registered trademark of the Coca-Cola Company. So is Pepsi for Pepsi-Cola. Bud for Budweiser is another example of a nickname that has been granted legal protection against imitation.

CHAPTER 11 Loss of Trademark Rights: The Generic Problem

Introduction to the Subject

In the search for new brand names, tastes and trends vary from the complex to the simple. A coined word—Kodak is always the classic example—will be the safest choice, especially if strong legal protection against possible imitations is an important goal. Marketing management frequently resists terms like this on the ground that it costs too much to teach the consumer what products they identify. It is much more common to swing to the opposite extreme and choose a word that describes the product in some way. This kind of brand name can cause serious trouble because a competitor, accidentally or on purpose, may come up with the same or a very similar term and then neither company will be able to establish exclusive trademark rights in the brand name.

Even a descriptive word can be made into a good legal trademark if it is used and advertised by a single manufacturer so extensively that it becomes recognized as the designation for that particular company's product. This is what the lawyers call acquiring a "secondary meaning." Obviously, that cannot happen unless *exclusive* use of the brand name is maintained, so there is a little bit of luck involved in any such situation. If a competitor should start using the same descriptive term as its brand name, the required element of exclusivity has been lost and the law will not recognize either party as the owner.

There are some words that are even poorer choices for
brand names than ordinary descriptive terms. Certain words
simply cannot be taken out of the language and monopolized
as any single company's trademark. A number of Patent and
Trademark Office decisions illustrate this important principle
and demonstrate why it is useless to try to protect such a word
by registering it as a trademark.

One such case involved an attempt to register Kelly Spinner
for a swivel drive used for oil well drilling rigs. Although the
Patent and Trademark Office examiner was satisfied with this
application, it was opposed by a competitor who established
the fact that in this industry a *kelly* is a piece of apparatus.
Specifically, it is defined as a "grief stem," which is further
explained as a "tube or rod of square cross section fitted into a
square hole in the rotary-drill table and forming the top section of the rotary-drill shaft in an oil well." The particular
device manufactured by the company seeking a trademark
registration was a spinner, used to spin a kelly. Therefore,
Kelly Spinner—distinctive as it might sound to the outsider—
actually is just the name of the product, and accordingly, the
application for registration of this term as a trademark eventually was denied.

Another example from the Patent and Trademark Office
records is an application for the registration of Nuclide for
laboratory analysis apparatus, such as mass spectrometers and
spectrographs. It turns out that the word *nuclide* is the scientific name for a species of atom distinguished by the particular
constitution of its nucleus. "Nuclide analysis apparatus" thus
sounds to the potential purchaser in this sophisticated industry
like a line of products intended for use in the study and analysis of nuclides—which, of course, is the simple fact. As such,
the word *nuclide* cannot function as a trademark; it is merely
descriptive when applied to this manufacturer's goods. Any
competitor has an equal right to use it.

Similar cases have involved such terms as Sudsy for ammonia—the type that makes suds when it is diluted for household
use—and Pasteurized for Helena Rubinstein's face cream—

which actually is pasteurized. Also denied registration as a trademark was Shampoo Plus Egg, which Helene Curtis attempted to register as a trademark for—you guessed it— shampoo plus egg.

The basic reason for all these decisions is that the function of a trademark is to identify products and distinguish them from similar products manufactured by others. A term that is simply the generic name of a product or describes some essential characteristic of it cannot perform that function. It therefore cannot be taken out of the language and used as any single manufacturer's trademark for his product.

Moreover, brand names can be oversold. If your product is way ahead of all its competitors, this may be the time to look around for danger signals and take preventive action if necessary. When a product is so successful that the public adopts the brand name as the name of the product itself—as distinguished from one particular manufacturer's version of the product—the brand name has passed into the language and the manufacturer who originated it no longer has the exclusive right to use it.

Some horrible examples of valuable brand names actually lost in this way are: aspirin, cellophane, linoleum, milk of magnesia, and shredded wheat. Each of these once represented the product of a single manufacturer who obviously invested substantial sums in building up the brand. Each of them reached the point where it came to mean the product rather than merely a source for the product, and competitors won the right to use the name for their own versions of it. Technically the brand name had become a generic term for the product, and generic terms are incapable of functioning as trademarks.

There are ways of guarding against this result. Explanatory footnotes in advertising are a common technique for putting the public on notice that the manufacturer claims trademark rights in his brand name and that it is not just the name of the product itself. Du Pont, for example, has used this: " 'Orlon' is Du Pont's registered trademark for its acrylic fiber." RCA Victor footnoted Victrola with the legend: "RCA Trademark for record players." Slogans can perform a similar function, perhaps even more effectively. The Eastman Kodak Company from time to time used: "If it isn't an Eastman, it isn't a Kodak." At a later period its advertisements carried, underneath the Kodak logo, a line reading: "—a trade-mark since 1888." Another typical footnote reads: "TABASCO is the registered trademark for the brand of pepper sauce made by McIlhenny Co."

Some companies place advertisements devoted specifically to education for proper trademark usage in consumer and trade publications. Minnesota Mining (for Scotch tape), Du Pont (for Orlon), and the Technicolor Corporation have used such campaigns; Du Pont also issues instruction booklets on the correct manner of using its registered marks.

The appearance of a company's brand name editorially in lower case type is a specific danger signal. Many manufacturers react by sending a form letter to the editor pointing out the unfavorable implication that the brand name has become just a word in the language and requesting initial caps and quotation marks in all future uses.

The problem is particularly acute when a new product is to be introduced. Care must be taken that the brand name coined for the new item is used in such a way that it identifies the source of the product and that it does not become the name by which the public identifies the product itself. This can be done by using the words "brand" or "trademark" to show the manufacturer's intention. But that is only a beginning, because the purchasing public may not keep such a fine point in mind.

A superior method is to use the brand name in association with the name of the general type of product involved. For example, the family medicine cabinet displays "BISODOL Antacid Tablets" and "CORICIDIN Cold Relief Tablets." Legal commentators are fond of suggesting that if the Bayer Company had marked its famous product "ASPIRIN brand of acetylsalicylic acid" or even just "ASPIRIN headache pills"— instead of "BAYER ASPIRIN"—it probably never would have lost its trademark rights. Q-Tips, Inc., which was forced to defend its trademark in court and did so successfully against the claim that it had become generic, labels its packages "Q-TIPS Cotton Swabs."

Another way to guard against public misuse or misunderstanding of a brand name is to apply it to more than a single item. Johnson & Johnson, for example, has a whole line of Band-Aid products. And Vaseline is a well-known brand of skin lotion as well as the trademark for various types of petroleum jelly.

One type of fallacious reasoning must be frankly discussed. Some sales and advertising executives hold the view that it is desirable for the public to become confused into thinking that their particular brand name is the name for the product. They figure that the sales clerk in the retail store will always know the difference and push their product across the counter even though the customer may not have had any particular manufacturer's product in mind.

Let us make up an example. Suppose there were no such thing as glue. Then a chemist invented it and sold the rights in this new type of adhesive substance to the X Manufacturing Corporation, which introduced the product under the name of Stickum. Of course, it was an immediate success, and competitors soon succeeded in producing similar formulas, which were put on the market as A adhesive, B adhesive, and C adhesive. The argument then might go that a customer interested in gluing some things together would think Stickum simply meant an adhesive of this new type; he would say to the clerk, "I want some Stickum, please," and the clerk would hand him the X Manufacturing Corporation's brand of adhesive even though the customer did not have X specifically in mind and would have been perfectly satisfied with Brand A, B, or C.

Undoubtedly, occurrences like that do take place in various fields. However, this is precisely the kind of public misunderstanding of the significance of the brand name that led to the complete loss of trademark rights in the valuable brands mentioned at the beginning of this chapter. What happens typically is that the usage becomes so loose that a competing manufacturer or a retailer starts to advertise someone else's product, using your trademark as if it were the name of the product itself. The next step is a lawsuit, and if the public actually has adopted the brand name as the name of the product, the suit will be lost. That means that the entire industry is privileged to use what was once an exclusive trademark that belonged to a single manufacturer. Encouraging this kind of public confusion may bring short-term sales results, but it is a big step along the road to disaster.

A special aspect of this question is the patented product. The existence of a patent means that the manufacturer has a legal monopoly for seventeen years; nobody else can make the product without his consent. If that manufacturer exercises his monopoly, his planning should include both a brand name for the product and some additional word or words by which the public can identify it. Otherwise, the brand name will be the only designation the product has; when the patent expires and competitors become free to make the product, they will automatically acquire the right to use the brand name too. That is precisely what happened in the case of shredded wheat, among others. The reason for this rule of law is that the original manufacturer would be able to get the effect of an illegal extension of his patent monopoly unless competitors were free to call the product by its name—otherwise they would be unable to identify it in the way the public had learned to call for it.

Thermos

One of the most important trademark opinions in recent years was written by Judge Robert P. Anderson of the United States District Court in New Haven, Connecticut, in the litigation between American Thermos Products Company and Aladdin Industries, Inc. Judge Anderson ruled that the word *thermos,* although registered as a trademark many years ago, had passed into the English language as a generic term for a vac-uum-insulated container. The use of *thermos* in that sense by a competitor, therefore, is not an infringement of the registered trademark. This decision subsequently was affirmed by the U.S. Court of Appeals. Judge Anderson's opinion stands as a case history of what can go wrong with a successful trademark.

The story of the American Thermos Products Company goes back to 1907, when a predecessor company took over the U.S. business of a German concern, Thermos-Gesellschaft m.b.H., which had introduced the vacuum bottle as a com-mercial product for general use. (It was an adaptation of the vacuum flask developed about 1893 by Sir James Dewar for laboratory purposes.) Sales of vacuum ware in this country have grown steadily. Back in 1907, according to the statistics included in Judge Anderson's opinion, the American Ther-mos Products Company's predecessor had net sales of $114,987. By 1910, sales had risen to $381,184; in 1923, they were $1,405,677; in 1936, $2,536,112; in 1945, $5,315,053; and in 1961, $13,280,164. Aladdin Industries makes a variety of different products; it introduced a line of vacuum ware in 1945 and in that year had sales of $560,128. By 1960 Aladdin's net sales of vacuum ware had increased to $6,805,283.

The lawsuit was filed in 1958, charging Aladdin with threat-ening to sell vacuum ware under the name *thermos*. Aladdin acknowledged in its answer to the complaint that it intended to sell vacuum-insulated containers as "thermos bottles" and pleaded as its defense that the word had passed into the lan-guage as a generic term. Reading between the lines, it appears that Aladdin must have made it known to the trade that it was planning to use thermos as the descriptive name for the prod-uct, after years of seeing thermos used in a generic sense by its own customers. In other words, Aladdin apparently was satis-fied that the word *thermos* had become generic so that trade-mark rights in it were no longer enforceable.

The evidence introduced at the trial showed the critical im-portance of the trademark owner's advertising program and its policing of improper uses. From the standpoint of preservation of trademark rights, the history of the American Thermos Products Company, as analyzed by Judge Anderson, falls into three distinct periods. The first was from 1907 to 1923, the second from 1923 to the early 1950s, and the third from then to the time of the trial in February, March, and April of 1962.

When the predecessor company started in 1907, such generic terms as *vacuum bottle, vacuum-insulated vessel,* and *vacuum jacketed bottle* already were in use in the industry. From the beginning, however, the Thermos Company's advertising was directed at popularizing the expression "Thermos bottle." Its 1910 catalog contained the statement "Thermos is a household word." As Judge Anderson noted, this kind of advertising, intentionally or not, was "an encouragement for generic use as a synonym for 'vacuum insulated'."

During that early period, the Thermos Company was aware of what it later described as "careless" uses of the trademark by the purchasing public in a generic or descriptive sense. At the time it was considered to be advantageous free advertising. The Thermos Company estimated for its dealers in 1917 that this was the equivalent of three to four million dollars' worth of advertising expense.

Summarizing the first period, Judge Anderson wrote, "The course of conduct of the plaintiff [American Thermos] from 1907 to 1923 in its advertising and educational campaigns tended to make 'thermos' a generic term descriptive of the product rather than its origin."

The second period commenced in 1923 after the Thermos Company had received a rude shock in a trademark infringement action brought against the W. T. Grant Company. Although American Thermos was successful, the federal judge who decided the case indicated in his opinion he thought Thermos might have become a descriptive term and therefore invalid as a trademark. However, he dismissed a defense based on this theory for the technical reason that it had not been raised at the proper time by W. T. Grant.

Almost immediately after this case was concluded, American

Thermos changed its advertising and labeling to include the term *vacuum* or *vacuum bottle* in association with the Thermos trademark, although it was not always consistent in this practice. It also began to complain to others about generic uses of the word thermos, including dictionary listings. Judge Anderson emphasized the fact that no affirmative action was taken to seek out these generic uses; American Thermos protested only those that happened to come to its attention. Furthermore, if a publication or a writer after receiving a protest letter failed to comply, the Thermos Company did nothing further about it.

Judge Anderson found that the number of protests by American Thermos during the period from 1923 to the early 1950s was "infinitesimal" in comparison with the large numbers of generic uses of thermos in publications of all sorts, which were introduced as evidence by Aladdin Industries. He concluded that American Thermos had "failed to use reasonable diligence to rescue 'thermos' from being or becoming a descriptive or generic term."

The third period, covering the years from about 1954 to the time of the trial in 1962, was when American Thermos put on a determined campaign to educate the public to the trademark significance of Thermos. One method used was to change the name of the corporation to the American Thermos Products Company and diversify its line. Such items as tents, camp stoves, lanterns, and bottle openers were manufactured, all labeled as Thermos brand products to get away from the idea that Thermos meant "vacuum-insulated."

The policing activities against improper uses of the term were intensified during this third period. According to the opinion, 178 letters of protest were written in 1957, 270 in 1958, 1109 in 1959, 950 in 1960, and 1171 in 1961. The jump in 1959 coincides with the extension of the Thermos Company's clipping service to include editorial and literary references to Thermos; prior to that year the clipping service had been limited to appearances of Thermos in paid advertising.

Judge Anderson's comments on the activities of American Thermos during the third period are:

The plaintiff's extraordinary efforts commencing in the middle of the 1950s and carried on into the time of the trial came too late to keep the word 'thermos' from falling into the public domain; rather it was an effort to pull it back from the public domain—something it could not and did not accomplish.

Finally, Judge Anderson attempted a Solomonic decision. He permitted Aladdin Industries to use thermos in lower case only, and always preceded by "Aladdin's" or by Aladdin's plus another brand name (for example, Aladdin's Huckleberry Hound thermos bottle). The registered trademarks of American Thermos, including the logotype version of Thermos, were declared to be still valid. However, use by Aladdin of thermos in the restricted manner outlined by Judge Anderson will not infringe upon any of these registrations.

As noted above, this decision was affirmed on appeal. Subsequently, some modifications were made in the restrictions that had been imposed on Aladdin. For example, Aladdin was permitted to spell *thermos* with a capital "T" when the rules of grammar require it, so it now can use the word at the beginning of a sentence.

Both parties commented so much on the court decision in their advertising, publicity, and correspondence with alleged infringers that the court entered a special "policing order" limiting the way in which the case could be described by either of them. Any departure from these rules subjects the violator to a penalty of $25,000. These unique provisions indicate the enormous importance of the case in this field of the law.

Yo-Yo

A long and expensive campaign by Donald F. Duncan, Inc., to hold on to the term Yo-Yo as its exclusive trademark for the familiar spinning top on a string came to an end early in 1965 when the federal Court of Appeals in Chicago ruled the trademark invalid because it is simply the name of the toy. Putting it another way, yo-yo is in the public domain, and any manufacturer of this kind of toy may use it freely to describe his product.

The facts revealed in the court's opinion indicate that Duncan's attempt to monopolize yo-yo by claiming it as a brand name was doomed to failure from the beginning. In addition, the court pinpointed the mistakes it found in Duncan's advertising program that contributed to the failure. The opinion therefore is a valuable case history of what *not* to do in selecting and preserving a trademark.

Duncan started manufacturing in 1929 and shortly thereafter applied to the United States Patent and Trademark Office for the registration of Genuine Duncan Yo-Yo as a trademark for a kind of toy described in the application as "bandalore type spinning tops." The registration was granted in 1932, and in the following year Duncan obtained a second registration covering the term Yo-Yo by itself, also for bandalore type spinning tops.

Duncan's trademark problems started early. Its first application for registration was delayed because a registration of Flores Yo-Yo already had been issued to another manufacturer. The Patent and Trademark Office records show that Duncan acquired the rights to the Flores Yo-Yo registration, and it was only after this transaction that its own registrations for Genuine Duncan Yo-Yo and subsequently Yo-Yo alone were granted.

The opinion does not detail all the difficulties Duncan had in trying to stop other toy manufacturers from using yo-yo as the descriptive name for competing products, but evidently two major incidents were settled in 1948 and 1955 when Duncan issued licenses permitting others to use the Yo-Yo trademark. These settlements, of course, avoided any court test of the validity of Duncan's claim to exclusive rights in Yo-Yo.

In 1955 Duncan apparently became concerned that its trademark rights were in danger because of the various ways in which the corporation itself had used yo-yo in a generic sense rather than as a brand name. It began a widespread campaign to educate the public to refer to the toy itself by the generic term "return top" so that a Yo-Yo return top could be distinguished from competitive products bearing different brand names of other manufacturers. The technique of associating a generic term with a trademark in order to assure the continued recognition of the trademark as such—and not just as the name of the product—is recommended highly and practiced widely. In this instance, however, the court found that yo-yo already was too far gone to be resuscitated as a trademark. The court also found that Duncan had made a mistake in selecting "return top" as the generic term to be publicized because it never had been used as a name for this type of toy before and the public simply failed to accept it.

In the years before 1955, Duncan had used Yo-Yo interchangeably with and without initial caps and frequently had treated it generically rather than as a trademark for a particular brand of toy. One promotional piece, for example, contained this sentence: "In case you do not know what a yo-yo is, it's that gaily colored little spool on a string, that in the hands of almost any youngster becomes a thing alive and performs hundreds of fascinating tricks." Duncan also had fallen into the trap of using the slogan, "If It Isn't a Duncan, It Isn't a Yo-Yo." Superficially, this might appear to build up the desired exclusive association between Yo-Yo and the Duncan company, but a grammatical analysis of the sentence reveals that yo-yo is being used as the generic name for the product and the constant repetition of the slogan therefore helped to destroy the trademark by perpetuating generic usage.

In 1962 and 1963 Duncan's advertising budget reached $1,000,000 per year, with considerable emphasis on the use of "return top" as the generic name for the toy. It then instituted the lawsuit for trademark infringement that led to the decision in Chicago.

Royal Tops Manufacturing Company, the defendant in the case, introduced a flood of evidence to show that yo-yo does not function as a trademark in the consumer's mind and also proved that Duncan never was entitled to claim it as a trademark in the first instance. Although it was contended that Donald F. Duncan, Sr., coined the term yo-yo when he began manufacturing the product in 1929, it turned out that this type of toy has been known in the Philippine Islands for hundreds of years—always under the generic name of yo-yo.

The president of Royal Tops was himself of Filipino extraction; he was born in the Philippines in 1909 and lived there until after his graduation from high school. He testified from his own personal experience that the yo-yo was a traditional Filipino toy and that it never was called anything but a yo-yo. This testimony was corroborated by, among other things, an article published by the *Scientific American* in 1961, entitled "Filipino Toys," that describes and illustrates the yo-yo, using that term in its generic sense as the name of the toy.

An expert witness with high academic qualifications testified that yo-yo is a Malayo-Polynesian word of Philippine origin, that the toy itself originally came from the Orient, and that yo-yo was the name given to it in the Philippine Islands when the toy became known there. Numerous documentary references supported this expert testimony, including a Chicago newspaper article of March 5, 1933, which quotes the assistant director of the Philippine National Library as saying that the word yo-yo is descriptive of the movement and sound of the toy and that it is known by that name in the various Filipino languages throughout the entire archipelago.

Duncan's claim to exclusive trademark rights therefore was improper from the beginning. Similar situations have arisen before—for example, with the Indian game known as Parcheesi—and the established legal rule is that, "The one who first introduces a foreign game or article under its true name cannot monopolize either the game or the article or the name thereof." In more general terms, another legal precedent quoted in the Duncan decision reads: "A word commonly used in other countries to identify a kind of product and existing there in the public domain as a descriptive or generic name may not be appropriated here as a trademark on that product, even

though the person claiming the word was the one who introduced the product here and the word then had no significance
to our people generally."

Teflon

In 1936 Du Pont figured in a famous lawsuit that led to the loss
of its exclusive rights to the Cellophane trademark. Du Pont
had charged another company with trademark infringement
because it was using Cellophane as a designation for transparent cellulose film made by a competitor. The defense
turned out to be a counterattack; it was claimed that Cellophane, even though registered as a trademark, had changed
its meaning for the consuming public and had become simply
a generic term for a particular type of transparent wrapping
material.

Much of the evidence came from Du Pont's own publications
and advertising. The court was convinced that cellophane was
the name of the product itself rather than a Du Pont trademark. Du Pont had used the word with a lower-case "c" in
house organ articles and elsewhere and advertised "Du Pont
Cellophane," which seemed to imply that Du Pont was just one
brand of a product called cellophane. In other words, Du Pont
itself treated the term as a generic rather than as a proprietary
brand name.

A primitive form of survey was used in an attempt to save
the trademark. Du Pont arranged with four magazines to have
letters sent to a total of 17,000 of their subscribers, asking
whether "cellophane" was a trademark. Of those who replied,
72 percent answered in the affirmative. The court did not
comment on the biasing effect of the manner in which the
question was phrased, but it did point out that the answers
were induced by flattering letters from the magazines and
offers of prizes for prompt replies. On that ground, the court
declined to give any weight to the survey.

A similar pattern can be seen in a lawsuit decided in 1975,

but this time the result went the other way. Du Pont had learned its lesson from the Cellophane case, and an attack on the status of the trademark Teflon failed.

In this case, Du Pont sued a Japanese manufacturer known as YKK and its United States subsidiary for using the trademark Eflon on zippers. Du Pont contended that Eflon was sufficiently close to Teflon to create a likelihood of consumer confusion. In this connection, Du Pont pointed to advertisements for the Eflon zipper as "slippery, slide-y" and the zipper that "runs smoothly." The judge agreed that these were characteristics that had some degree of association with the widely advertised "no stick" attributes of Teflon, the Du Pont product.

Teflon is a trademark coined by Du Pont to identify a group of resins whose most familiar use is in the form of nonstick finishes for cookware. Du Pont does not make the cookware or any similar consumer products itself; it sells the Teflon resin to manufacturers. Nevertheless, Du Pont has put substantial advertising support behind the Teflon trademark, amounting to around $3,000,000 per year for the ten years before the lawsuit.

The care with which Du Pont has treated Teflon contrasts sharply with the disregard of legal requirements that characterized its treatment of Cellophane. Du Pont's task of protecting its legal rights in Teflon was made more difficult by the fact that the material is used as an ingredient by industrial customers who in turn advertise its presence in their products to the consuming public. The details of what the judge described as "a vigilant trademark education and protection program" came out in the course of the lawsuit.

Du Pont supplies guidance to industrial buyers of Teflon resins on correct trademark usage for advertising and displays, and information on making references to Teflon in business correspondence. Salespeople and other Du Pont personnel who deal with buyers of Teflon products are instructed concerning trademark matters. Du Pont has published a booklet on the proper usage of the Teflon trademark that has been widely distributed among its customers.

Du Pont's trademark protection program also includes extensive surveillance efforts by its own legal and advertising departments and by its advertising agency, N W Ayer. When misuse of the mark is detected, it is promptly called to the offending party's attention. Ayer has maintained a continuous watch over the usage of the Teflon trademark in cookware advertising. Protective trademark advertising prepared by Ayer, designed to convey the understanding that Teflon symbolizes only Du Pont's nonstick finish, has appeared from time to time in retailer-oriented publications such as *Women's Wear Daily, Home Furnishings Daily,* and *Discount Store News.*

It was obvious that Du Pont had been following a sophisticated pattern of trademark vigilance for the purpose of maintaining its legal rights in Teflon and preventing it from falling into the public domain as a generic term. The Japanese zipper manufacturer, nevertheless, claimed that Teflon had become generic and that therefore there was no valid trademark for it to have infringed. This presented the judge with the very pertinent question of whether Du Pont's educational efforts had succeeded.

The court that decided the Cellophane case had explained that it makes no difference how much money or effort is expended by a company to persuade the public that a particular term is a trademark, symbolizing its products alone. If the effort failed—if Du Pont "did not succeed in actually converting the world to its gospel"—the trademark would have become generic and therefore unenforceable no matter how much money and effort had been invested in the campaign.

This aspect of the Teflon case turned out to be a battle of surveys. Again, that is reminiscent of the Cellophane case, although the techniques used were quite different, as might be expected after 40 years.

YKK introduced the results of two surveys of adult women, one geared to awareness of kitchen utensils coated with a chemical substance to keep grease or food from sticking to them and the other to the awareness of substances that manufacturers apply to the surfaces of products in order to prevent things from sticking to them. The respondents who expressed awareness were then asked, "What is the name or names of these pots and pans?" or, in the second survey, "What name or names are these substances called?"

There was a very high percentage of "Teflon" responses to these questions. However, the survey results were easily exploded by pointing out that the word "name" is ambiguous in this context. The respondent might have thought that a generic name was being called for, but she also might have understood "name" as equivalent to "brand name," i.e., a trademark. The judge decided that these surveys failed to prove that Teflon had degenerated into a generic term.

In addition to attacking the methodology of the opposing party's surveys, Du Pont commissioned surveys of its own. One of these asked for a "brand name or trademark" for protective coatings applied by manufacturers to the inside of household utensils in order to prevent food and grease from sticking. This questionnaire was attacked for introducing another kind of bias.

Du Pont's second effort turned out to be the key survey. This one really concentrated on the crucial issue. By using the example of "Chevrolet/automobile," the interviewer first explained the difference between a brand name (trademark) and a common name (generic term). He then asked whether each of eight names, including Teflon, was a brand name or a common name. The results were that 68 percent of the respondents identified Teflon as a brand name and 31 percent as a common name.

The complete tabulation is interesting in many ways. It is reproduced at the top of the next page, as quoted in a footnote to the judge's opinion.

Thermos was declared a generic term after a court battle in 1963, yet a slim majority of respondents still considered it a proprietary brand name in 1975. Aspirin still had 13 percent believing it to be a trademark in spite of the fact that a court declared it had fallen into the public domain and become a generic term all the way back in 1921. A scattering of respondents even thought that margarine and refrigerator were brand names, although they never have been anything other than generics. Market research specialists know that there is always a "noise level" in a study of this kind produced by respondents who are either inattentive, antagonistic, or just plain stupid.

Name	Brand	Common	Don't Know
STP	90%	5%	5%
Thermos	51	46	3
Margarine	9	91	1
Teflon	68	31	2
Jell-O	75	25	1
Refrigerator	6	94	—
Aspirin	13	86	—
Coke	76	24	—

At any rate, this survey helped persuade the judge that Teflon had not become generic. As he said in his opinion, "The responses of the survey reveal that the public is quite good at sorting out brand names from common names." He was satisfied that the critical question—the principal significance of the term Teflon to the public—was answered satisfactorily by this survey and not by any of the other three surveys introduced as evidence in the case.

The final conclusion the judge reached was that Teflon continued to be a valid trademark and that Eflon was an infringement of Du Pont's rights.

Dictaphone

One of the hazards faced by the owner of a well-known trademark is that a lawsuit against an infringer may run into a counterattack claiming that the trademark is no longer valid because it has become a generic term. One familiar brand name that has gone through this experience is Dictaphone.

The history of Dictaphone began in 1907, when it was the winning entry in a contest among the employees of what was then called the Columbia Graphophone Company to find a name for its business phonograph products. In 1923 a newly organized company called Dictaphone Corporation bought the dictating machine division of Columbia.

Dictaphone has been a registered trademark in the United States since 1908, and it also has been registered in many foreign countries. Total sales of Dictaphone products exceed $1 billion; over $500,000,000 of these sales were made in the ten years from 1968 to 1978. Advertising expenditures during a sample ten-year period, 1964–74, were over $10,000,000. Dictaphone has consistently made over 1,000,000 direct mailings of sales literature to prospective customers per year.

In addition to appearing on dictating machines and supplies, Dictaphone has been used as a trademark for such other products as telephone answering equipment, multichannel recorders, calculators, facsimile transmission machines, and teaching machines. Dictaphone Corporation also has adopted a number of secondary marks with the prefixes Dicta- or Dict-, including Dictabelt, Dictet, Dictamate, and Dictamite.

Dictaphone has been careful about protecting its legal rights. Print advertisements typically carry a legend such as "Dictaphone and Dictabelt are registered trademarks of Dictaphone Corp." It has sued infringers, and it has opposed the registration of similar trademarks in the U.S. and elsewhere. Its own advertising carefully uses the expression "dictating machine" as the generic term for the major Dictaphone product, and this has educated both the consumer market and the industry. In addition, special advertising pointing out that Dictaphone is a trademark has been published. Dictaphone can be found in several dictionaries, which has been the kiss of death for some former trademarks, but Dictaphone, unlike those others, appeared in the dictionary with an initial cap and was identified as a trademark.

Against this background, Dictamatic came into the picture in 1972. The Portland, Oregon, distributor for Nyematic dictation equipment manufactured by Nye Products Company of Seattle, Washington, became the Portland representative for Lanier Business Systems in 1970 when Lanier acquired Nye Products. The distributor incorporated its business under the name of Dictamatic Corporation and began to use that name in 1972 when, for example, it appeared in the Yellow Pages for Portland, Tacoma, and Spokane.

The name Dictamatic was used by the Portland distributor's sales personnel in "cold calling," which is a major source of sales, in answering telephone inquiries, and in various other ways. It explained that it did this to identify itself as a dictating machine company because it believed Lanier was not widely recognized as a name in that industry.

Dictaphone Corporation filed a lawsuit for trademark infringement in the U.S. district court in Portland. As already indicated, Dictamatic countered with a claim that Dictaphone had become the generic term for dictation equipment in general. Dictamatic wanted not only to be free of any infringement claims against itself, but also to have all trademark registrations of Dictaphone canceled so that the term would lose its upper-case initial and become a word that anyone could use as a synonym for dictating equipment.

U.S. district Judge Skopil took a careful look at the evidence Dictamatic offered to support its counterclaim. One type of evidence was the testimony of over 30 individuals who said that, in their opinion, Dictaphone had become a widely used term to describe all kinds of dictation equipment and therefore was generic. But cross-examination by Dictaphone's attorney brought out the fact that the witnesses knew Dictaphone was a trademark and that they knew and used terminology like "dictating machine" or "dictation equipment" to describe the products on which the trademark Dictaphone is used. Also, most of the misuses of Dictaphone in a generic sense that these witnesses had heard were in casual conversations, calls for repairs, and other nonbuying situations.

Judge Skopil ruled that the only truly relevant evidence was the use of Dictaphone by persons seeking to buy dictation equipment. Personnel from competing companies testified that no more than 5 percent to 10 percent of prospective purchasers misused Dictaphone as a generic name for dictating machines. And even when they did misuse it, further inquiry developed that the customers usually realized their error.

Another type of evidence introduced by Dictamatic was a collection of newspaper "Help Wanted" advertisements, many of which used expressions like "Dictaphone operator" or "dictaphone secretary." Witnesses from several employment agencies testified about placing the ads. Once again, cross-examination established that each witness knew Dictaphone was a trademark.

Judge Skopil ruled that these employment ads were not competent to prove Dictamatic's point because they were not placed by or directed to buyers or sellers of dictation equipment. Dictaphone also answered this evidence by submitting its own collection of ads, from the identical newspapers, offering dictation equipment (mostly second-hand) for sale. Only 3 percent of these ads contained generic uses of Dictaphone, which the judge considered an insignificant figure. To him this group of ads, backed up by testimony from newspaper classified advertising managers, was good evidence that Dictaphone was known and used as a trademark by buyers and sellers of dictation equipment.

There was other evidence by which Dictamatic attempted to persuade Judge Skopil that Dictaphone had become a generic term, but he ruled against the counterclaim. The judge stated in his published opinion that "although its fame and familiarity have led to some misuse of 'Dictaphone' by the general public, the descriptive terms 'dictating machine,' 'dictating equipment,' and the like are well known and used by both Dictaphone's competitors and by the buyers of dictation equipment." He continued, "It is not necessary for others to use 'Dictaphone' to make the buyers understand what is being sold. Therefore, 'Dictaphone' is not generic."

On the question of infringement, Judge Skopil had very little difficulty in finding that there was a strong likelihood of confusion between Dictamatic and Dictaphone. They have the same number of letters and the same distinctive prefix. The suffix -matic is very common and nondistinctive. Prospective purchasers easily could believe that Dictamatic Corporation was associated with Dictaphone Corporation, particularly because the names were located so close to one another in the telephone book. In addition to that, there was evidence of misdirected mail, telephone calls, invoices, and checks.

The outcome was Judge Skopil's order prohibiting Dictamatic Corporation from any further use of Dictamatic or any other name with the prefix Dicta- or Dict- in the dictation equipment business.

Lights

Although it clearly was the first company to use Lights as a designation for cigarettes, Philip Morris was unsuccessful in an attempt to stop R. J. Reynolds from using Lights on Winston cigarettes.

Philip Morris added Lights several years ago to its established Marlboro line, which already included Marlboro 100s and Marlboro Menthols. When R. J. Reynolds came out with Winston Lights, Philip Morris responded with a lawsuit, alleging trademark infringement and unfair competition.

The basic question in the case was whether the word *Lights* is just a descriptive term that all companies in the cigarette industry are free to use, like "100s" or "Menthols," or whether it identified the Philip Morris product, in much the same way that Marlboro itself acted as an identifier of a particular brand.

It often happens in lawsuits of this type that the complaining party's own advertising and publicity come back to haunt it. The Lights case was no exception. The opinion quotes Philip Morris' promotional material, stating that "Marlboro Lights are for the smoker who enjoys the lighter taste of a low-tar and nictotine cigarette." Reynolds also produced a large quantity of evidence showing that the word *light* and its derivatives were widely used in a descriptive manner in the cigarette industry.

In addition, the judge ruled that Philip Morris really was not using Lights as a trademark. As he analyzed it, Morris used Marlboro as the trademark and Lights as a descriptive term to differentiate the low-tar, low-nicotine product from the other items in the Marlboro line, such as "Menthols" and "100s."

Philip Morris still had a string of other arguments, including the charge that Reynolds deliberately intended to create consumer confusion when it used Lights on its low-tar, low-nicotine version of Winston cigarettes. In reply, Reynolds pointed out that it certainly did not want any confusion between its light Winston cigarettes and Morris' light Marlboro cigarettes because 60 percent of its customers switched from regular Winstons to Winston Lights, and, if there had been confusion, some of them might have shifted to Marlboro Lights instead.

A final point raised by Morris in its effort to tag Reynolds with unfair competition was the claim that Reynolds intended to capitalize on the advertising investment in Marlboro cigarettes. Judge Stewart, who decided the case in the federal district court in New York City, explained the legal situation in these words:

> It is permissible in the American competitive economy for the second comer to endeavor to capture as much of the first comer's market as he can. The only limitation upon this activity in this context is that it must not be accomplished by confusing the public into mistakenly purchasing the product thinking it to be that of the competitor. While Reynolds did intend to compete in the market for lowered tar and nicotine cigarettes and to capitalize upon plaintiff's [Morris'] establishment of such a market, we find that it did not attempt to do so by consumer confusion.

An additional point in the case was the status of a registration of Light (not Lights) owned by Philip Morris. What had happened was that Morris ran a routine trademark search when it was planning to introduce Marlboro Lights. The search turned up an existing registration of Light for cigarettes, in the name of New Directions Film Company, a producer of TV commercials.

This presented an obvious conflict that had to be resolved in some way, or Philip Morris could have faced a lawsuit claiming that it was infringing on the registered trademark Light. Morris evidently conducted an investigation into the circumstances of the registration of Light by New Directions and turned up some evidence to the effect that it was based upon untrue statements about sales of the product in interstate commerce, a violation of the requirements for a federal trademark registration.

Morris instituted proceedings to have the registration of Light canceled on the ground that it had been "improperly and unlawfully" obtained. Those proceedings never were concluded. Instead, New Directions assigned its registration to Philip Morris, which became the new owner.

Judge Stewart found that he agreed with Philip Morris' original position about the invalidity of the Light registration obtained by New Directions. It followed that the assignment also was invalid, so that Morris got no benefit from it.

Philip Morris had attempted to cure the defects in the Light registration by making some sales of cigarettes under that trademark. Although it would not have made any difference in the final outcome of the case against Reynolds, Judge Stewart ruled that Morris' sales of Light cigarettes "have been insufficient to constitute the required good faith commercial use necessary to maintain the mark." As a result, the judge ordered the registration of Light canceled.

Lite

Miller Brewing Company, the fourth largest brewer in the country, won the first round in the series of lawsuits it brought to protect the brand name Lite. A federal district judge in western Wisconsin ordered G. Heileman Brewing Company to discontinue its Light label.

Lite reduced-calorie beer was introduced by Meister Brau in 1967. Faced with bankruptcy in 1972, Meister Brau sold several recipes and brands to Miller, including Lite, which by that time had been registered as a trademark in the U.S. Patent and Trademark Office.

Miller improved the taste of Lite beer, modified its label design, and adopted a new advertising approach. The revitalized Lite product sold approximately 50,000 barrels in the second half of 1973 and 400,000 barrels in 1974. In 1975 the brand went national, with sales exceeding the 2,500,000-barrel level, and estimated sales for 1976 were over 4,000,000 barrels. Meanwhile, advertising expense rose from $500,000 in 1973 to an estimated $12,000,000-plus in 1976.

Competitors naturally started to market reduced-calorie beers. Several of these used the word *light* on their labels. Miller reacted by going to court whenever it felt that "light" was emphasized to the point that it became the competitor's brand name.

Peter Hand Brewing Company, a small Chicago brewer, was the first. On the label for its "Peter Hand Special Pilsner Extra Light Beer," the word *Light* was the most prominent term, much more conspicuous than the name "Peter Hand." Miller sued Peter Hand for trademark infringement in federal court in Chicago.

Next came Joseph Schlitz Brewing Company, the nation's second largest, with a beer whose label displayed the word *Light* much more prominently than *Schlitz, Beer,* or *Special Lager.* Miller's lawsuit against Schlitz was filed in federal court in Milwaukee.

Next was Heileman, a regional brewer, but ranked seventh in the country. Although its label carried the name "Heileman" several times and also had the "House of Heileman" seal, the word *Light,* in the words of federal district Judge James E. Doyle, "was by far the most prominent and eye-catching word on the label."

As it turned out, the first decision was in the Heileman case.

Judge Doyle issued a preliminary injunction, which means that a full trial had not been held, but that the judge felt Miller's chances for ultimate success were sufficient to justify a temporary order halting the use of Light as a brand name.

Judge Doyle had to deal with several legal arguments. Heileman claimed that the Lite trademark was not valid because it is simply a descriptive term that any brewer is entitled to use. The judge noted that Miller was not using Lite with reference to the color of the product or its weight but rather to indicate that the beer was low in calories and less filling.

The legal problem is to draw the line between a descriptive term and a suggestive one. If the word used as a trademark gives some direct information about the product, it is descriptive. But if the word stands for an idea which requires an operation of the imagination to connect it with the product, it is suggestive.

Judge Doyle concluded that it would require some imagination to connect Lite with a beer that would cause its consumers to weigh less than those who drank regular beer. That put the word in the suggestive class, which made it a valid trademark.

As a good judge should, Judge Doyle then assumed, for the purposes of the argument, that Lite was descriptive after all. Descriptive terms can become valid trademarks if they are used and promoted so that the consumers recognize them as identifying the product of a particular manufacturer. To meet this requirement, Miller introduced a survey showing that a substantial proportion of beer drinkers (43 percent) considered Lite a particular brand of low-calorie or less-filling beer. (An additional 11 percent recognized "Miller Lite" and another 1 percent "Lite by Miller" as distinctive.)

Adding to the survey results the statistics about Miller's sales and advertising, Judge Doyle was satisfied that Lite—even if considered originally descriptive—had acquired distinctiveness as a trademark.

The final legal question was the basic issue of trademark infringement. In factual terms, were consumers likely to be confused?

The first point to notice was that Lite and Light are identical in sound. Therefore, as Judge Doyle said, "they cannot be distinguished in conversation among members of the public, in radio advertising, or in oral communications between customers and waiters or bartenders."

Lite and Light obviously have the same meaning. In addition, they are visually similar.

Judge Doyle explained that, although a person can tell the difference between the Miller product and the Heileman product when the bottles are placed next to one another, a side-by-side comparison is not the proper test for the likelihood of confusion. He pointed out that "Consumers are likely to rely on vague impressions and recollections when choosing a product, especially when the product is relatively low-priced." The correct test is "whether consumers with a rather indefinite recollection of the marks would be able to discriminate between the labels of the competing products or would tend to choose one product thinking it is the other, *when only one brand is in sight*" [emphasis added].

Applying this reasoning, Judge Doyle concluded that Miller was likely to prevail on the claim that Light, as used by Heileman, infringed on Miller's legal rights in its trademark.

Later in the year a federal Court of Appeals reversed Judge Doyle's ruling, stating in no uncertain terms: " 'Light' is a generic or common descriptive word when applied to beer," and "neither that word nor its phonetic equivalent [Lite] may be appropriated as a trademark for beer." In January 1978 the U.S. Supreme Court declined to review that decision.

The Heileman case, as noted, involved only a preliminary injunction. After the Supreme Court refused to grant a hearing, Miller announced its intention to pursue that litigation, along with the nine other pending cases in which Miller claimed infringement. But in April of 1978 a decision was issued in Miller's suit against Schlitz, and U.S. District Judge Gordon in that case ruled against Miller all the way.

The decision in the Schlitz case relied heavily on the Court of Appeals ruling in the Heileman case. Judge Gordon declared that, because the issues in both lawsuits were so similar, Miller did not even have the right to relitigate the validity of

Lite as a trademark for beer. He was aware, of course, that the Heileman decision dealt only with a preliminary injunction. Nevertheless, his analysis of the opinion led him to conclude that the Court of Appeals had given consideration to the merits of the entire case and found that Miller's claims to trademark rights in Lite were "fatally flawed."

Schlitz also formally requested Judge Gordon to direct the Commissioner of Patents and Trademarks to cancel Miller's federal registration of Lite as a trademark. Based on the "unambiguous holding" of the Court of Appeals in the Heileman case that Lite is a generic term for beer, the cancellation order was issued.

Next came the decision in a new case by Miller against Carling O'Keefe Breweries of Canada, which introduced Highlite low-calorie beer in February of 1978.

Although the Highlite product had not been sold in the United States, TV commercials advertising it were carried on U.S. stations located in Buffalo, New York. Federal District Judge Elfvin ruled that these broadcasts, even without U.S. sales of the product, were enough to infringe on Miller's trademark rights—if any.

Miller's objections to Highlite because of its similarity to Lite were rejected by Judge Elfvin on the basis of Miller's track record with Lite to date. He referred specifically to the cancellation order in the Schlitz case as undermining Miller's claimed trademark rights in Lite. But Miller also owned the long-established trademark High Life for beer, and evidently Carling did not challenge the validity of that mark. Judge Elfvin decided that Highlite was so close to High Life that consumers might be confused between them. He therefore issued a preliminary injunction against Carling, ordering the discontinuance of any use or advertising of Highlite in the U.S.

Meanwhile, Miller had appealed Judge Gordon's decision in the Schlitz case. The same Court of Appeals that had ruled against Miller in the Heileman case also ruled against Miller in the Schlitz case. Miller asked the Supreme Court to review both the Heileman and the Schlitz decisions, but its requests were turned down (most recently in 1980).

Some observers wonder why Miller took the trouble to launch the fight in the first place. Miller is owned by Philip Morris, which lost a similar battle when it claimed exclusive rights in Lights as a trademark for cigarettes. That was the case in which Philip Morris, maker of Marlboro Lights, tried unsuccessfully to stop R. J. Reynolds from marketing Winston Lights.

It is important to understand that nothing in any of the unfavorable decisions about the validity of Lite as a trademark would prevent Miller from using the word Lite on its labels and in its advertising as much as it wishes. The point of these decisions is that Miller cannot prevent other brewers from using light, or the phonetic spelling *lite,* for their own beers.

The Uncola

An unusual kind of dispute between major advertisers over trade symbols is the legal proceeding in which Coca-Cola tried to prevent the registration of The Uncola as a Seven-Up Company trademark. What was a competitor doing in a case like this anyway? Coca-Cola claimed basically that *uncola* was the equivalent of *noncola* and thus was a common generic term that no soft drink company should be permitted to monopolize. In situations of this kind, the Patent and Trademark Office examiner sometimes will throw out the application on his own, but there are occasions when it takes a competitor to bring the full story to the Patent and Trademark Office's attention.

It has been well established that a competitor has the legal right to raise this kind of question. Coca-Cola might not have had sufficient standing to object to The Uncola if it made only cola drinks, but Coca-Cola also manufactures such noncola beverages as Fanta, Fresca, and Sprite.

The 7Up product, of course, has been around for a long time. Promoting it as The Uncola got under way nationwide in early 1968, and advertising expenditures for the period 1968 through 1970 (the most recent year covered in the record of the legal proceeding) exceeded $45,000,000. Evidence in the case showed a dramatic increase in 7Up sales, which was attributed directly to the promotional campaign featuring the product as The Uncola.

Seven-Up starting imprinting The Uncola on cans of 7Up in March 1968 and on bottle caps in March 1969. (There is an indication of limited use of the term on cartons as early as December 1967.) The trademark application was predicated upon these uses of The Uncola on containers, since use in advertising does not qualify a term for trademark registration.

Seven-Up's consumer awareness studies showed that 70 percent to 75 percent of those interviewed associated The Uncola with 7Up. Coca-Cola attempted to counter this by a survey of its own taken of attendants in 413 places serving soft drinks; 383 of those interviewed reported that they had never received an order for "uncola."

The Patent and Trademark Office Trial and Appeal Board was impressed by the fact that the industry seems to use the term *noncola* rather than *uncola* as the common descriptive name for this broad class of soft drinks. It recognized that The Uncola does have a descriptive connotation but pointed out that Seven-Up is the only company that has used it to denote a noncola beverage. The Board, therefore, put it in the category of those terms that may start out as descriptive but acquire distinctiveness as the symbol of one particular manufacturer through widespread, exclusive sales and advertising. As such, the Board was satisfied that The Uncola met the standards for registrability and dismissed Coca-Cola's complaint.

Coca-Cola then filed a petition for reconsideration. Its fundamental argument continued to be that *uncola* is just a word that means the same thing as *noncola* and that a type of product can have more than merely one generic designation. For example, in the beverage industry itself, soft drink, soda water, soda pop, and pop are all used synonymously and are all generic designations that clearly could not be registered as any single company's trademark.

In Coca-Cola's view, adding the word *the* to *uncola* does nothing to increase the distinctiveness of the expression. On this point, Coca-Cola cited as legal precedent the refusal of the Patent and Trademark Office to allow G. D. Searle to register

The Pill for its oral contraceptive—a decision that was affirmed after Searle appealed.

The petition for reconsideration was denied, and Coca-Cola took an appeal to the United States Court of Customs and Patent Appeals, which handles trademark cases on appeal from the Patent and Trademark Office. In a unanimous opinion by the chief judge, the appellate court affirmed the ruling of the Patent and Trademark Office Board. Indeed, the court was even more impressed than the Board with the strength of Seven-Up's position.

The chief judge's opinion bears down hard on the point that The Uncola is not a generic term. The evidence satisfied the court that *noncola* was the only generic name for a soft drink not containing cola.

Going further, the court ruled that The Uncola never had been merely a descriptive term. Therefore, it was unnecessary to pursue the question of whether it had overcome an original deficiency and acquired distinctiveness as the result of Seven-Up's successful sales and promotional efforts.

It is clear from the appellate court's opinion that the testimony of Seven-Up's expert witness on word derivation was impressive. He testified that the term *uncola* was created in a manner contrary to normal English word construction. The combination of *un* with a noun, such as *book, desk,* or *cola,* would violate an English-speaking person's sense of idiom, according to the expert.

What all this boiled down to was the feeling that a member of the public would consider The Uncola a distinctive term— neither the generic name of, nor merely descriptive of, the product. As such, it was registrable by Seven-Up as that company's exclusive trademark.

Eveready

When a federal district judge decided in February 1975 that the well-known Eveready trademark was unenforceable against infringers because it simply described a characteristic of the product, the shock was felt not only by Union Carbide, but also by trademark owners and trademark lawyers throughout the country. To the great relief of almost everyone, that decision was reversed by the United States Court of Appeals in Chicago.

The history of the Eveready trademark goes back to 1898, when the American Electrical Novelty and Manufacturing Company started using the term Ever Ready as its trademark for various electrical products. In July 1901 the two words were combined, and the brand name Eveready appeared on electric batteries for the first time.

National Carbon Company took over the entire business of American Electrical Novelty and Manufacturing Company in 1914. Subsequently, National Carbon was succeeded by Union Carbide Corporation.

Eveready has been registered as a trademark for many years. Since 1966, Eveready flashlights, batteries, miniature bulbs, and similar products have been selling at the rate of over $100,000,000 per year. The statistics also showed that advertising and promotion expenses for Eveready products for the period 1943 to 1974 were more than $50,000,000.

The 1975 decision came in a trademark infringement lawsuit by Union Carbide against Ever-Ready, Inc. That company started in 1946 as an importer and distributor of electrical supplies and various gift items, including light bulbs and flashlights, sold under the Ever-Ready brand name. Carbide claimed that the use of the almost identical term would be likely to cause customer confusion, even though the product lines of the two companies were not identical.

The federal judge began his discussion of the legal issues by considering whether or not Eveready was a valid trademark. He relied largely on the definitions in the American Heritage Dictionary and decided that the combination of the words *Ever* and *Ready* means that the product is "constantly prepared or available for service." Applying this to Carbide's batteries and the other electrical products, the judge reached the "inescapable" conclusion that it means they are dependable and durable. Accordingly, he ruled that Eveready was descriptive, which means that the word did not qualify for trademark protection under federal law.

The next step in the analysis was to decide if Eveready, even though originally a descriptive term, had become so distinctive of Carbide's products through extensive use and advertising that it had turned into a good trademark despite its original deficiencies. This is what is known as acquiring a "secondary meaning."

The judge noted that the relevant evidence on this question included the amount and manner of use, direct consumer testimony, and consumer surveys. But, said the judge, length of use and volume of sales alone are not sufficient. Moreover, he went on, "The cost of advertising does not establish the success of it, but merely the effort to establish secondary meaning."

This judge looked primarily to survey evidence as a method of proving secondary meaning. He mentioned the two surveys Carbide had introduced on the likelihood of confusion between the trademarks but said that these surveys gave him no help on the secondary meaning issue.

That left Eveready as a descriptive term without secondary meaning and, therefore, not entitled to trademark protection. The judge, nevertheless, followed the logical progression by assuming, for the purposes of discussion, that Eveready was a good trademark and then considering whether or not it had been infringed by Ever-Ready.

The judge reviewed the facts and ruled that none of the products were directly competitive. He analyzed the evidence of actual confusion but dismissed it as the kind of "casual confusion by careless and inattentive people," which is insufficient to sustain a trademark infringement claim. He wrote disparagingly about the survey evidence that had been introduced on the confusion issue and concluded that it was entitled to very little weight.

The district judge, therefore, dismissed Carbide's suit, and Carbide appealed. The three-judge appellate court disagreed with the trial judge in almost every particular.

Perhaps the most important point in the decision of the Court of Appeals was a technical one with enormous practical significance. When the federal trademark law received its most recent overhaul in 1946, Congress included a provision that was intended to induce trademark owners to register their marks in the U.S. Patent and Trademark Office by making the rights of registered trademark owners more secure. If a registered trademark has been used continuously for more than five years, the owner may file an affidavit to that effect and the registration thereupon becomes what the statute calls "incontestable." There are exceptions to incontestability, but one of the benefits on which the trademark owner is supposed to be able to rely is that nobody can defend an infringement action against an incontestable trademark on the ground that it is a descriptive term. That issue, if there ever was any, cannot be reopened.

Surprisingly few cases have dealt with the meaning of this incontestability provision. The appellate court in the Eveready case gave it full effect. The statute says that the certificate of registration of an incontestable trademark is "conclusive" evidence of the owner's exclusive right to use it for the products or services listed in the certificate. Specifically, this means that an alleged infringer "faced with an incontestable registered mark cannot defend by claiming that the mark is invalid because it is descriptive."

The district judge had not even considered Carbide's claim of incontestability, and the Court of Appeals could have reversed on this point alone. However, tracking the district judge's analysis of the legal situation, the Court of Appeals went on to consider the other arguments in the case.

The Court of Appeals discussed the differences between descriptive and suggestive marks. It is only a descriptive term that fails to qualify for trademark protection; suggestive terms are valid trademarks.

The guiding principle is: "Generally speaking, if the mark imparts information directly, it is descriptive. If it stands for an idea which requires some operation of the imagination to connect it with the goods, it is suggestive."

According to the Court of Appeals, the trademark Eveready

"suggests the quality of long life, but no one in our society would be deceived into thinking that this type of battery would never wear out." Thus, it is not descriptive, but suggestive.

Following the same logical analysis, the Court of Appeals then went on to consider whether, if Eveready really was descriptive originally, it had acquired distinctiveness through use, i.e., secondary meaning. Contrary, again, to the district judge, the Court of Appeals felt that there was overwhelming evidence of secondary meaning. With specific reference to the surveys, the Court of Appeals was perfectly willing to use confusion surveys for whatever they showed on the question of secondary meaning and drew from them the conclusion that an extremely significant percentage of the people associated Eveready products with a single source.

Taking the final step, the Court of Appeals then went into the question of the likelihood of confusion. The opinion notes that, "Consumers often do not retain a clear impression of the precise form in which a mark appears. This is not due to carelessness, but rather is due to fallibility of the human memory."

On this analysis, the resemblances between Eveready and Ever-Ready far outweigh the differences. Moreover, the products of the two parties are sufficiently related to raise a strong likelihood of customer confusion.

The Court of Appeals was also impressed with the survey evidence. Two separate studies showed the percentage of the public who associated the defendant's Ever-Ready lamps and bulbs with Union Carbide, whether specifically or by identifying it as the same company that makes Eveready batteries. The lamp survey came in with 55.2 percent and the bulb survey with 60.6 percent. As the Court of Appeals noted, these percentages were substantially higher than those considered sufficient in other cases. Specifically, the opinion referred to cases where the survey results showed confusion percentages of 11.5, 25, 18, and 24.

It therefore was concluded that Eveready is a valid trademark that has become incontestable and that the use of Ever-Ready on lamps, bulbs, and similar electrical products is an infringement.

CHAPTER 12 Advertising Can Preserve Trademark Rights

Almost everyone engaged in advertising and marketing knows that some terms that are now accepted as the common names for products and are available for generic use by any manufacturer, originated as trademarks, which could legally be used only by a single company. Familiar examples are aspirin, cellophane, escalator, milk of magnesia, and shredded wheat. The most recent major judicial decision in this field added thermos to the list.

Exclusive trademark rights in these terms were lost because of a change of association in the consumer's mind. Instead of identifying a particular manufacturing source for a product (Chesterfield brand of cigarettes, Buick brand of automobiles), they came to signify the product itself, which might come from a number of competitive sources (Bayer brand of aspirin, Squibb brand of aspirin).

Essentially, it is advertising that creates the meaning for a trademark in the first place, and advertising may change that meaning into a generic term or preserve the validity of the trademark, depending on how it is used. *Time* magazine, in one of its own direct mail pieces, made the point indirectly:

> If you were not already familiar with these names, you might think that . . .
> *Eartha Kitt* is a soil testing outfit.
> *Cole Porter* is a chilly ale.

Duke Ellington won the Battle of Waterloo.
Van Gogh is a traffic sign for moving trucks.
Chester Bowles is a cabinet of salad ware.
Pearl Buck is a bejewelled dollar.

Similarly, establishing the meaning of any new trademark requires a process of consumer education, and this is primarily an advertising function. Sometimes the lesson is learned too well; the brand becomes so firmly established that the public starts to misuse the trademark as if it were a generic term for the product itself. Judge Learned Hand warned of the peril in a famous trademark opinion: "Its very success may prove its failure." If caught in time, this trend can be averted, and even reversed, by advertising directed to the specific objective of teaching proper trademark use.

To take a specific example: When American Cyanamid acquired Formica Corporation in 1956, it inherited a problem that tends to affect products in dominant market positions. Formica was so well known that many consumers were unaware of any other name for laminated plastic. This led to unnoticed substitutions at the retail level and a drop in market share. Cyanamid instituted a corrective program, which included a series of educational advertisements designed to strengthen Formica as a trademark. One of these showed a salesman, his face decorated with lipstick from the kisses of his happy customer, explaining to another salesman: "All I said was 'Certainly it's Formica,' and showed her the label."

Another pictured a salesman with a black eye, saying to his colleague, as the irate customer stalks out the door: "*You* tell the next one it's just as good as Formica."

Educational advertising may be addressed to the individual consumer, to the affected industry, or to publishers and writers who might otherwise tend to spread the misuse. It can be serious, lighthearted, or downright humorous.

The obvious similarities between a brand name and a personal name have set the theme for many trademark use advertisements, with frequent quotations from both Shakespeare and Gertrude Stein on the subject of roses. Less hackneyed approaches are also available.

Caterpillar Tractor Company, in a series of cartoons, pictured a poor fellow who keeps insisting his correct name is Mark Wayne, although he is introduced first as Mark Twain, then as Mark Layne, and finally is greeted as Mr. Cain. The copy reads:

> It's frustrating when someone misuses your name or confuses you with somebody else.
>
> We, too, feel badly when our name is misused—in connection with equipment we don't build.
>
> For instance, people sometimes call all track-type vehicles by the names Caterpillar and Cat.
>
> Which presents a problem. You see, Caterpillar and Cat are not common nouns. And they do not describe a type of locomotion.
>
> They are names denoting the manufacturer of a product—registered trademarks of Caterpillar Tractor Co. They should be used to identify *only* products we make.
>
> If your name has ever been misused . . . we think you'll understand our situation. Your help in correctly using our trademarks to refer only to our products will be appreciated.

Another use for the name theme is to explain that a manufacturer's trademark applies to a family of products, not merely a single item. An individual product name, therefore, must accompany the trademark for complete identification, and the resulting combination of generic term with trademark is just about the best possible way of preserving the manufacturer's legal rights.

Johnson & Johnson taught this important lesson with an advertisement showing an illustration of the familiar "While You Were Out" telephone message form tucked into the corner of an office desk blotter. The message is "Urgent—please call!" but it comes from "Miss Smith" with no further information. Under the headline "Which Miss Smith?" the ad reads:

> Full names are important, with products as well as people. Johnson & Johnson makes a whole family of products under the Band-Aid brand, from Band-Aid brand adhesive bandages to Band-Aid brand air-vent adhesive tape to Band-Aid spray antiseptic. We like to be talked about, but just as there's more than one woman named Smith, there's more than one product with the Band-Aid brand. A whole family of products carry the Band-Aid brand to indicate "made by Johnson & Johnson." So, always follow the "Band-Aid" brand with the product name.

The predecessor company of Chesebrough-Pond's once used a similar approach in an advertisement headed "What's Their *Whole* Name?" which showed photographs of famous persons with their first names followed by blank spaces for middle and last names. The body copy read:

> Vaseline, the registered trademark owned by the Chesebrough Mfg. Co., is not a complete name for any one product, but the brand word for the whole family of products made by that company.
> It should never be used alone, but always with the name of the product it designates, viz.: "Vaseline" petroleum jelly, "Vaseline" hair tonic, "Vaseline" lip ice pomade, etc. We'd appreciate it if you'd keep this in mind. Many thanks!

A number of years ago, Ethyl Corporation ran an extensive series devoted to the meanings of various names. With cartoon illustrations, the advertisements stated, for example, that Emily means "a nurse," Bertha means "bright, famous," Andrew means "manly, brave," and Philip means "lover of horses." The last panel in each ad explained that Ethyl is "a *trademark* name" and concluded:

It stands for antiknock fluid made only by the Ethyl Corp. Oil companies put Ethyl fluid into gasoline to prevent knocking.

The Ethyl trademark emblem on a gasoline pump means that Ethyl fluid has been put into high quality gasoline and the gasoline sold from that pump can be called "Ethyl."

A name, of course, is only one type of symbol. Du Pont has used the symbol theme effectively. In one of its educational advertisements, the illustration shows a glass slipper presented on a cushion. The headline reads, "Orlon and Dacron are trademarks, too"; and the body copy starts this way:

As the glass slipper distinguishes Cinderella, our trademarks distinguish the unique qualities and characteristics of our two modern-living fibers. "Orlon" distinguishes our acrylic fiber; "Dacron," our polyester fiber.

As we use and protect these trademarks, they become more meaningful and valuable to both consumers and to the trade.

Grammatically, a trademark is not a proper noun but a proper adjective (like the "French" in French dressing). One of the characteristics of any term in this category is the initial capital letter, and consistent use of that form helps greatly in maintaining the legal validity of the trademark.

Western Electric has used this principle as the theme of a series of advertisements for its Teletype Corporation subsidiary. Each advertisement started with the Teletype trademark in a different type face, and the name of the font served as the basis for the illustration and body copy. For example, one read:

This is 36 pt. Baskerville . . .
And, as Holmes would have said, "Elementary, my dear Watson"—Teletype, like all trademarks, needs an initial cap.

Another in the same series:

> This is 36 pt. Cloister Black . . .
> And even in this time-honored type face, registered
> trademarks like Teletype need an initial cap.

Dow Chemical Company teaches the same lesson in a different manner. One of its advertisements reads:

> Styrofoam® earns its letter. That *capital* "S." Styrofoam
> is a registered trademark for the specific brand of poly-
> styrene expanded plastic foam made by the Dow Chemi-
> cal Co. *Only* Dow makes Styrofoam brand insulation and
> buoyancy billets! So it always deserves the initial cap.
> All the other rules for proper trademark usage also
> apply to Styrofoam. Like other good trademarks, Styro-
> foam should be guarded by correct indentification. This
> avoids confusing people about the true source of a
> product.
> Please, hit that capital S when typing Styrofoam or
> mark it UC on proofs. We'll appreciate it. So will the
> trade. Thank you.

Almost identical copy serves the same purpose for another Dow trademark. This advertisement starts with:

> Polyfilm® needs a *capital* "P." It's a registered trademark
> for the specific brand of polyethylene film made by the
> Dow Chemical Co.

And the balance of the text, with obvious substitutions, is substantially the same as the Styrofoam ad.

The power of the initial capital letter to distinguish a trademark from an ordinary word in the language has been a recurring theme in Coca-Cola Company advertising. Back in 1950 a proper use series directed at publishers and editors used headlines like these, with appropriate illustrations:

coke in a shovel is a chore
but . . . *Coke* in the hand is a pleasure.

Another example:

coke burns
but *Coke* refreshes.

Coca-Cola also used variations of this type:

globe is a world map
but *Globe* is a newspaper.

Later versions also kept the product out of the headlines:

Life is a sentence . . .
but *Life* is a magazine.

The punning style of the Coca-Cola advertisements turned up with an entirely different twist in a Johnson & Johnson series that also used illustrations in pairs. One of these advertisements showed a printer examining some material that had just come off the press, and a cook at work on board ship. The accompanying headlines:

All galleys are not proofs!
All adhesive bandages are not Band-Aid adhesive bandages.

Another example displayed a man shoveling snow, paired with a newspaper photographer catching a woman standing over a corpse with a smoking pistol in her hand. The headlines in this advertisement read:

All scoops are not shovels!
All adhesive bandages are not Band-Aid adhesive bandages.

In a different series, Johnson & Johnson focused even more specifically on education for proper trademark use. The line "All adhesive bandages are not Band-Aid adhesive bandages" is retained in the body copy, but the illustrations show unusual uses of the product and the headline says:

> There may be many ways to use adhesive bandages . . . but there's only one way to use the Band-Aid trademark correctly . . . please say: "Band-Aid adhesive bandages."

A number of the advertisements described above use cartoon-type illustrations. An additional variation is to employ cartoon characters as the spokesmen for the advertising message. Kimberly-Clark Corporation put Little Lulu to work in this way, in addition to her other promotional functions for Kleenex products. For instance, under the headline "How is *your* trademark grammar?", Little Lulu appeared in the role of a schoolteacher. With the help of a conventional balloon around the words, it appears that she is saying, "The correct way is . . . ," while she points to a blackboard on which is chalked "Kleenex tissues." Beneath the illustration, the ad explains:

> The grammar book says: Trademarks are adjuncts— they must have a subject to qualify to be used correctly.
> Little Lulu says: To be grammatically correct, always say and write "Kleenex tissues" or "Kleenex towels" or "Kleenex table napkins."

Made to order for cartoon figures of children is the Crayola product of Binney & Smith. Daring to demonstrate an example of improper usage in print, one advertisement shows a little boy demanding of his older sister, "Gimme my crayolas!" She holds the box of crayons away from him as she answers, haughtily, "Not until you ask for them properly*" and the asterisk leads us to the body copy, brief and to the point:

Crayola® is a registered trademark or brand name of
Binney & Smith Inc. Say "Crayola crayons," please.

While many of the advertisements already described have a
light touch, some manufacturers prefer to approach the problem of proper trademark even more humorously. In 1957
Textured Yarn Company ran a trade paper ad that started like
this:

They Laughed When We Said We'd Sue (little did they
suspect we'd do anything to protect Tycora®).
Tycora is not a grand old name for everyone to use. *It's
a brand name* and relatively new.

Humble Oil had one with a big photographic illustration of a
suspicious-looking character clutching a chemical flask. The
headline was "What makes this man steal Varsol®?" It turned
out from the body copy that he was stealing the *name* Varsol by
using it in a generic sense for competing products manufactured by others. The advertisement continued:

That could take away our legal right to a brand name
that we've built into the standard of low odor and high
purity.
It gives our lawyers such a headache they have to take
aspirin. Then, when they remember what happened to
the "Aspirin" brand, they feel even worse.

Willys Motors has used a dowager character, complete with
lorgnette, to sugarcoat a whole list of rules for proper use of
the Jeep trademark. In one advertisement she is saying:

It just isn't cricket, my deah, to refer to "Jeep" vehicles
as "jeep-like," "jeepy," "jeep-type," etc. In our set, you
know, one *never* "jeeps around" or "goes jeeping." The
word "Jeep" should never stand alone as a verb or noun.
And the plural is never "Jeeps" but instead " 'Jeep'

vehicles." Properly speaking, chaps, one *should* link "Jeep" with the model name to designate a specific vehicle as in "Jeep" Universal. The word "Jeep" should *always* be capitalized—because "Jeep" is a registered trademark for vehicles made *only* by Willys Motors!

Equally justifiable, but perhaps more at home in industrial periodicals, is the serious advertisement that delivers its message straightforwardly and without frills. Magnaflux Corporation, for example, stated:

> Most people are proud of their names and what those names stand for in the community. We among them! "Magnaflux" is a trademark.

The body of the advertisement dealt in detail with the quality of the company, its products, and the service given to its customers.

Timken once built an advertisement around the phrase "Trademark Reg. U.S. Pat. Off." Under the heading "Little words that mean a lot" the copy explained:

> There's no room for compromise, doubt or question in those brief words above. They mean: "Timken" is the registered trademark of the Timken Roller Bearing Co. And that meaning is mighty important to you.
>
> The trademark "Timken" assures you of getting the highest quality tapered roller bearings, fine alloy steel bars, steel tubing or rock bits—all products of the Timken Roller Bearing Co.
>
> That's why it pays to remember that "Timken" *is* a trademark, not a type of product. That it isn't really a product of the Timken Co. unless it's backed up with this trademark.

Another example of the serious approach comes from Libbey-Owens-Ford which, after listing six facts about its registered trademark Thermopane, goes on to say:

We make these statements because the function of a trademark is to identify unequivocally the manufacturer of a product . . . and to eliminate the possiblity of confusion in the mind of the public concerning the producer of a specified product . . . and to assure that the customer gets what he orders.

We are sure that architects, contractors and others who are familiar with the superiority and advantages of *Thermopane* will welcome these statements [and] . . . will refrain from using our trademark in referring to any product not made by Libbey-Owens-Ford.

When Shakespeare wrote, "What's in a name? That which we call a rose by any other name would smell as sweet," he wasn't running down the value of a word, but merely pointing out the symbolic nature of the name applied to any object. Remember, the same Shakespeare also wrote, "Who steals my purse steals trash; . . . But he that filches from me my good name robs me of that which not enriches him, and makes me poor indeed."

The loss of exclusive legal rights in a name because it has turned from a trademark into a generic word can be a heavy financial blow to a manufacturer, as serious as the moral blow suffered by the man Shakespeare's character was talking about. As shown by the examples cited, advertising can play a powerful role in maintaining the status of a trademark and preventing its loss.

CHAPTER 13 Reference to Another's Trademark: Comparative Advertising

Chanel No. 5

The use in advertising of a comparative reference to a competitor's brand name raises questions ranging all the way from lack of good taste to legal liability for trademark infringement. In one unusual situation, Chanel, Inc., brought suit in federal court in California to stop a local perfume distributing company from advertising its product by comparing it with the famous Chanel No. 5.

The competitor in the Chanel case was a small company named Ta'Ron, run by a single individual. It promoted a line of perfume, cologne, and hair spray under the brand name Second Chance by advertising in *Specialty Salesman* magazine that its products "duplicate 100% perfect the exact scent" of Chanel No. 5. The ad also stated that "Ta'Ron's scientists have performed a masterful breakdown," and, "It has taken years to find the secret of positive duplication." The advertisement suggested making a comparison by means of a blindfold test. It also contained an order blank and a schedule of discount rates.

The federal judge summed up the overall effect of the advertisement by saying that it might "lead a resonable consumer or dealer to believe that 'Second chance' possesses all the distinctive qualities and properties of 'Chanel No. 5'." He pointed out that the invitation to make a comparison is really fictitious because the advertiser solicits mail orders and the dealer therefore could not have the opportunity of giving himself or his customers a blindfold test in advance. The judge also noted that this whole method of exploitation puts into the hands of unscrupulous retailers a method of passing off Second Chance as the equivalent of Chanel No. 5 or perhaps even claiming that it is the same product under a different label.

The court therefore issued a preliminary injunction stopping the use of the Chanel No. 5 brand name on the basis that the local distributor was unfairly taking a free ride on the good will of Chanel's registered trademark. In other words, it was prohibited from making any reference to the trademark Chanel No. 5 even on the assumption that the Second Chance product actually did duplicate the exact scent of Chanel No. 5. Subsequently, however, the United States Court of Appeals reversed that decision and ruled that the California distributor had full legal right to use the registered trademark Chanel No. 5 in describing its own product.

The Court of Appeals stated that, in the absence of misrepresentation or confusion of source or sponsorship, a seller in promoting his own goods may use a competitor's trademark for purposes of identification. The court took note of two major arguments against this viewpoint.

First, the establishment of commercial values in a trademark requires great effort, skill, and expense, so a competitor should not be permitted to take a free ride on the trademark proprietor's widespread good will and reputation. The second argument is that the use of someone else's trademark creates a serious threat to its distinctive quality and, if continued, might ruin the trademark by making it into a generic or descriptive term.

In analyzing these conflicting points of view, the Court of Appeals announced as a basic proposition that the only legally relevant function of a trademark is to provide information about the source or sponsorship of the product. In addition, the trademark protects its proprietor from diversion of sales through the use of the same or a confusingly similar trademark by a competitor, and the trademark owner's reputation also is protected from the injury that might occur if it were used by a competitor on inferior products. These, however, are purely private purposes, according to the court, although there is an important public purpose in the preservation of trademark rights as a means of identifying the product of the trademark proprietor.

Judge Browning, writing for a unanimous three-judge court, noted that a trademark makes effective competition possible in a complex, impersonal marketplace by providing a means through which the consumer can identify products that please him and reward the manufacturer by continuing to buy them. Without some such method of identification, informed consumer choice, and hence meaningful competition in quality, could not exist.

Judge Browning recognized the argument that protection of trademark values other than simple source identification would create serious anticompetitive consequences with little compensating public benefit. He cited some economists as authority for the proposition that advertising endows the trademark with sales appeal independent of the quality or price of the product to which it is attached. Thus, economically irrational elements are introduced into consumer choices, insulating the trademark owner from the normal pressures of price and quality competition. The opinion also noted that the economically irrelevant appeal of highly publicized trademarks might constitute a barrier to the entry of new competition into the market.

Going more deeply into the facts of the case, Judge Browning stated that "imitation is the life blood of competition." The opinion, quoting from an earlier decision, goes on to say: "It is the unimpeded availability of substantially equivalent units that permits the normal operation of supply and demand to yield the fair price society must pay for a given commodity." Judge Browning added that this public benefit might be lost if

the California perfume distributor could not tell potential purchasers that its product was the equivalent of the Chanel
product.

Putting it another way, Judge Browning wrote: "To prohibit
use of a competitor's trademark for the sole purpose of identifying the competitor's product would bar effective communication of claims of equivalence." If this were permitted to
happen, said Judge Browning, "the practical effect of such a
rule would be to extend the monopoly of the trademark to a
monopoly of the product."

In its broadest general terms, the opinion of the court means
that one who has copied a product sold under a trademark
may use that trademark in his advertising to identify the product he has copied, so long as the advertising material does not
contain any misrepresentations or create a reasonable likelihood that purchasers will be confused about the true source or
sponsorship of the products. Of course, this applies only when
the product is unpatented or otherwise is available for copying
without violating some other legal right.

In order to test the legal principle, Chanel assumed for the
purposes of this preliminary proceeding that the representation about exact duplication of the scent of Chanel No. 5 was
correct, and the opinion dealt with the facts on that assumption. In other words, the advertiser is permitted to tell the
truth and to use the Chanel trademark in doing so, but he may
not misrepresent.

The case was then sent back to the district court for trial.
The legal principle remains the same. A trial judge is bound by
the ruling of the Court of Appeals in the very same case. However, the decision after the trial demonstrates the practical
effect of how the comparative advertising rule works on specific advertising claims.

After reviewing the evidence, the trial judge concluded that
all of Ta'Ron's representations were untrue. The results of gas
chromatograph tests proved that the chemical composition of
Second Chance was not identical to Chanel No. 5, and the
scientific testimony established that it therefore could not

smell precisely the same. The claim that Second Chance duplicated the exact scent of Chanel No. 5 thus was a false representation.

The opinion does not make it clear whether Ta'Ron had any
scientists at all, or how many years of work had gone into the
effort, but there was no "masterful breakdown," since the
"secret of positive duplication" obviously had not been discovered. Ta'Ron had not succeeded in matching the scent of
Chanel No. 5. Those representations, therefore, also were
untrue.

Judge Harris, before whom the case was tried, made several
interesting observations about the marketing of perfume and
the effect of Ta'Ron's advertising on the Chanel trademark,
but the basic rule still stands that Ta'Ron can refer to Chanel
No. 5 in its advertising as long as it does not either misrepresent the facts or confuse the public into thinking that Second
Chance is manufactured or sponsored by Chanel.

One fact that was proved to the satisfaction of Judge Harris
was that the scent of Chanel No. 5 is a relatively unimportant
attribute of the product. The majority of the purchasing public, he found, did not buy Chanel No. 5 because of its scent.
Nevertheless, he also found that Ta'Ron's ad damaged Chanel
by destroying public confidence in its products, particularly
Chanel No. 5.

Further, Judge Harris noted that Ta'Ron had appropriated
and diverted business from Chanel without effort on its own
part. But, he ruled, this does not constitute unfair competition, because Chanel's large expenditures of money to develop
a market did not, by themselves, create legally protectable
rights. Judge Harris also concluded that the Ta'Ron product,
since it was packaged differently from Chanel No. 5, was not
likely to be confused by the consuming public with a product
made or approved by Chanel.

So Chanel was left with a partial victory. It established that
the three principal claims in Ta'Ron's ad were untrue, and this
was a violation of the federal law against false descriptions or
representations of a product.

But, as already explained, that did not prevent Ta'Ron from making a truthful reference to Chanel No. 5 in its Second Chance advertising. Since the Chanel product was unpatented, Ta'Ron was free to copy it as closely as it could, and the ruling of the Court of Appeals permitted it to state the facts in its comparative advertising, so long as it did so accurately.

Tylenol

Brand X is now just a historical curiosity. During the past several years comparative advertising that identifies the competitive product by its trademark has become an accepted practice. We have learned that, as a basic proposition, there is nothing illegal about using a competitor's brand name in advertising—but there are limits.

A recent example of court-imposed guidelines comes from the litigation concerning a pair of print and TV ads with such claims as: "Anacin can reduce inflammation that comes with most pain. Tylenol cannot." The analgesic ingredient in Anacin is aspirin, and this advertising campaign was part of the war going on between aspirin and the aspirin-containing products on one side and the newer nonaspirin pain relievers like Tylenol, which contain acetaminophen, on the other.

The two-sentence quote above comes from the print advertisement. The script for the TV commercial reads (in part):

> Your body knows the difference between these pain relievers [showing Tylenol and other pain products] and Adult Strength Anacin. For pain other than headache Anacin reduces the inflammation that often comes with pain. These do not. . . . Anacin reduces that inflammation as Anacin relieves pain fast. These do not.

The print ad was similar in content, except that it was directed specifically against Tylenol.

McNeil Laboratories, the Johnson & Johnson subsidiary that

makes Tylenol, protested to the networks, the print media, and the National Advertising Division of the Better Business Bureau, complaining about American Home Products Corporation, the maker of Anacin. Aside from a minor change required by ABC in the TV commercial, these protests were unsuccessful.

American Home, although the apparent winner of the dispute at this point, filed a lawsuit against McNeil for a court order to stop any interference with its advertising, claiming that the ads were truthful and proper. McNeil responded with a countersuit, alleging that a number of the statements in the Anacin ads were false and asking the court to order them discontinued.

Judge Stewart of the United States district court in New York City found the scientific evidence inconclusive on the effectiveness of aspirin in reducing inflammation, especially in normal dosages, and therefore did not rule on the superior benefit claims in that category. But the scientific evidence did establish that acetaminophen is just as effective as aspirin in reducing pain. Judge Stewart relied heavily on consumer reaction surveys to determine the meaning of the Anacin advertisements and concluded that Anacin falsely claimed itself to be a superior analgesic to Tylenol, specifically for conditions of inflammation.

Judge Stewart therefore ordered AHP to stop any advertising that represented Anacin as providing superior analgesia to Tylenol either generally, or for conditions associated with inflammation, or because Anacin reduces inflammation. AHP appealed unsuccessfully to the three-judge Court of Appeals, and it is the opinion of that court, written by Judge Oakes, that is discussed here.

The basic question is whether the challenged advertisements created a false impression. As Judge Oakes stressed, the law goes beyond condemning literal falsehoods. Otherwise, the opinion states, "clever use of innuendo, indirect intimations, and ambiguous suggestions could shield the advertisement from scrutiny precisely when protection against such sophisticated deception is most needed." Even an advertisement that is grammatically correct and literally true may have a tendency to mislead, confuse, or deceive the consuming public.

If factual evidence shows the advertising is literally false, the judge can make up his own mind. But an ambiguous claim is another matter, and the judges agreed that there was "deliberate ambiguity" in the Anacin ads. The issue then is what impression was created, not on the judge, but on the person to whom the advertisement was directed. Under these circumstances, consumer research is a proper kind of evidence to use, and Judge Stewart's reliance on it was approved by the Court of Appeals.

Two tests of the Anacin TV commercial were conducted. One, by Gallup & Robinson, was run approximately 24 hours after the broadcast of the commercial. Telephone interviewers talked with persons who said they had watched the accompanying program. The other, by ASI Market Research, was performed at special screenings, with the viewers questioned both during and one hour after the screening. The comments of the Court of Appeals are illuminating:

> Some of the people tested by both surveys either had bad memories or paid little attention to the television commercial, resulting in inaccurate descriptions, not only of the claims made but even of the products discussed. But such inaccuracies, we suppose, are to be expected in advertising research.

The ASI study was made for AHP, not McNeil, and therefore had extra impact in the lawsuit. This study was given substantial weight by Judge Stewart, and the Court of Appeals agreed that he had handled it properly.

In summary, the ASI test produced the recall that Anacin is a superior pain reliever generally, even though the advertisement was phrased in terms of comparing inflammation relief. An internal AHP memorandum deduced from the ASI report that "inflammation is a word that triggers pain association."

Since pain association is what both of the questionable advertisements were all about, the misleading comparative claim for Anacin over Tylenol became apparent. By claiming greater effectiveness against inflammation, which may or may not have been true, the ads created the impression that Anacin was more effective against pain, which was not true.

As a general principle, there is no legal objection to naming a competitive product in advertising. But if the comparative product claims are either just plain false or create a misleading impression, the makes of the competitive product has a legal claim that can be enforced by a court order.

CHAPTER 14 Updating Trademark Designs

Harper & Row

The process of modernizing corporate and brand identification logos keeps both marketing management and industrial designers busy. In 1969 Harper & Row, the well-known book publishing company, won a trademark dispute that demonstrates the value of preserving the essence of the old symbol even though it may be redesigned to appeal to contemporary tastes in graphics.

Harper's colophon has featured a torch ever since 1847 (when the company already was 30 years old). The original design showed one hand passing a torch to another hand, along with a motto in Greek from Plato's *Republic*. The design has been changed at least 20 times over the years, but a torch always was included. Even though other colophons were introduced from time to time, the torch design never was completely dropped. More recently, a modern, stylized torch has replaced the rather old-fashioned look of earlier versions.

The statistics on purchaser impact are rather impressive. Harper has published over 20,000 different works in all fields except legal books. During the last five years preceding the dispute, it sold over 60,000,000 books. During the period from 1957 to 1967, advertising and promotion expenditures totaled approximately $26,000,000. Well over 90 percent of all Harper books bear some version of the torch colophon. The colophon also appears in periodical advertising, in catalogs, and on retail displays.

In addition to publishing books, Harper & Row sponsors seminars, provides speakers for meetings, circulates films for school children, and provides other educational services. *Harper's,* a magazine now published by an independent company, is licensed by Harper & Row to use the Harper name and the torch emblem.

The conflict arose when an application was filed in the United States Patent and Trademark Office to register a design of a hand holding a torch as a trademark for educational services. Trademark rights were claimed by an organization called Young Americans for Freedom, Inc., which introduced its torch emblem in 1961. It particularizes its services as furthering the influence of conservative philosophy and policies by aiding the organization of politically conservative groups; organizing and sponsoring rallies, seminars, debates, and conventions; and providing materials and services to member groups, including films, speakers, study programs, and reports.

Young Americans for Freedom is a nonprofit membership corporation with some 500 affiliated chapters. It used the torch emblem on newsletters and other literature, manuals, letterheads, programs, application forms, and membership cards. It published a magazine called *The New Guard,* through which the organization provided a book-ordering service for selected titles (one of which was a paperback version of a book originally published by Harper & Row).

The legal issue was whether Harper could prevent the registration of Young Americans for Freedom's torch emblem on the theory that it resembled Harper's logo to such an extent that the public might think there is a connection between the two. Young Americans for Freedom argued strenuously that Harper had failed to show continuous use of any particular torch trademark and that Harper was entitled only to protection against a substantial duplication of its trademark on competing goods or services. The three-member Trademark Trial and Appeal Board in the Patent and Trademark Office disagreed; the Board ruled that, although Harper had indeed used a number of variations on the torch design, "it is quite apparent that a representation of a torch is the characterizing feature of its colophon."

Significantly, the Board responded to the argument that Harper's torch emblem is inherently a weak trademark because a purchaser buys a book by either title or author and would not ask, for example, for the book with the torch on it. The Board pointed out that this is inconsistent with the basic idea of a trademark. A trademark need not be used to buy goods; it can constitute a symbolic means of recognition of the source of the goods. The fact that a colophon may not be the immediate means for the purchase of books, therefore, does not make it inherently weak as a trademark. And the Board concluded with the comment that this argument also might be incorrect as a matter of marketing fact, because at least some members of the purchasing public would recognize the Harper colophon as a reflection of the publisher's concern for high standards of writing, integrity, competency, and other desirable attributes making up the Harper image, thus leading them to choose books bearing the familiar torch emblem.

The attempt of Young Americans for Freedom to draw distinctions between its activities and those of Harper & Row also failed to carry conviction with the Board. Although Harper is primarily a publisher and Young Americans for Freedom is an organization devoted to the propagation of a specific political philosophy, the Board pointed out that there is substantial similarity between their functions. Harper's does not promote any particular political philosophy, but its activities naturally publicize areas of political conflict and set forth various philosophical and political ideas. The books and other materials published by Harper's can reach the same audience that is appealed to by Young Americans for Freedom. What is more, the methods used by Young Americans for Freedom to disseminate its concepts include newsletters and other forms of literature, so that, in effect, it also is a publisher.

The Board therefore sustained Harper's objections to the registration of a torch emblem by Young Americans for Freedom. As already indicated, the conclusion was that persons familiar with Harper's torch colophon, on seeing literature bearing the torch emblem of Young Americans for Freedom, might well assume that Harper is sponsoring the organization's activities or that there is some other connection between them. The Board ruled that this would be detrimental and damaging to Harper in its relationship to the reading public and also with present and potential authors.

Maintaining the basic concept of the torch symbol through twenty-odd variations over a period of more than a century thus proved its worth in preventing the registration as a trademark of a specifically different representation of a torch used for somewhat different activities. The value in holding on to the fundamental symbol while modernizing the design should be apparent.

CHAPTER 15 Trademark Licensing

Introduction to the Subject

For some time, one of the growing branches of the complex marketing field has been the exploitation of trademarks or brand names by means of license agreements. Trademark licensing is legally permissible, but there are certain technical requirements that must be watched carefully. If the license agreement fails to comply with these legal technicalities, the owner of the trademark will be unable to protect it against infringements. In other words, the trademark proprietor no longer will have the exclusive right to use it, which, for practical purposes, means that the value of the mark has been destroyed.

The reason for this strict legal approach is that the trademark law is designed to protect the consumer as well as the trademark owner. The public has an interest in the way a trademark is used because one of the functions of a trademark is to assure the purchaser that he will get the same product time after time when he buys the same brand. If the trademark proprietor permits indiscriminate use of his identifying symbol, it might be applied to inferior merchandise and the public then would be deceived.

Only *controlled* trademark licensing is valid under the law. The owner of the trademark must specify the products on which the licensee is permitted to use the trademark, and he must supervise and control the quality of those products. So far as the public is concerned, the trademark will continue to identify its owner as the ultimate source of responsibility for the goods, and the trademark owner must assume the burdens of that responsibility or risk the loss of his rights.

It is worth noting that no such legal technicalities are required in connection with the licensing of copyrights or patents. This is another instance of the distinctions between trademarks on the one hand and copyrights and patents on the other.

Trademark rights are created by actual use that builds up recognition value for the brand name, and the law properly is concerned with the interests of the consuming public when questions of protecting and enforcing those rights arise. Copyrights and patents, by contrast, are absolute monopolies granted to authors and inventors under a special clause of the Constitution, and this kind of right can be licensed or not as the owner sees fit. One of the qualifications on patents and copyrights, however, is a time limit; once it expires, a patent or copyright falls into the public domain and everyone is free to make use of it without charge. But a trademark can be maintained in full force and effect indefinitely, provided it is not abandoned, and this perpetual right is an added reason why the law insists that a trademark be used properly.

The soft drink manufacturers pioneered trademark licensing. It was the economics of the industry that brought this about. Producers of the concentrated syrup found it impractical to service large areas from a limited number of plants, and they established a system of franchising local bottlers. Even with national advertising comparatively in its infancy, it was essential to make certain that the product of each bottler, sold under the same trademark, was identical. Basic uniformity came from the fact that the local bottlers all used the same syrup, procured from the company owning the trademark. In addition, franchise agreements in this industry traditionally impose elaborate quality controls on the licensees, who are required not only to use the proper formula in mixing the product, but also to maintain high standards of sanitation.

Other industries lending themselves to local investment and

coverage of relatively limited areas are particularly suitable for franchise systems. Frequently, services are involved, rather than goods, and service marks may be licensed under the same quality control standards that apply to trademarks. In addition to various kinds of fast food operations, familiar examples are dance studios and health clubs. The public interest in assuring that the same name identifies the same system of instruction or treatment is obvious in these fields. The license agreement must provide for rigid supervision and control in order to make certain that the consumer is not misled. The penalty for omitting to provide for uniformity of product or service, it must be remembered, is that the trademark proprietor will be unable to stop others from using his mark—even if the infringer is a former licensee who refuses to continue to pay royalties!

The examples given thus far relate primarily to the extension of an established brand name into new territories. Trademark licensing also may be used as a marketing technique in other ways. Instead of diversifying directly into a new product line, a trademark proprietor may license an existing producer in another industry to manufacture a line of goods under the licensor's trademark. This can happen, for instance, between perfume companies and apparel manufacturers—and vice versa. Many other products and services are readily adaptable to trademark licensing.

Controlled licensing also is—or at least should be—at the heart of merchandising programs for cartoon characters, television personalities, and similar properties. This happens to be a somewhat controversial area in which there is a contrary view that copyright protection, which does not require quality control, is a sufficient basis for licensing. The courts have not given a definite answer on this point yet, but the consequences of guessing wrong are so drastic that the risk hardly seems worth taking. Conservative practice requires the licensor of any property of this type to insist on quality control in order to protect his basic rights. Since the character or name functions as a merchandising symbol when applied to goods, it seems to have the qualities traditionally associated with trademarks, and this analysis supports the view that only controlled licensing would be proper.

Another controversial area in this highly technical field has been whether it is sufficient to reserve the right of control in the license agreement or whether actual control by the licensor is required. Here, court decisions have made it clear that the trademark owner must take the time and trouble actually to police the manufacturing operations of his licensee; otherwise the license will be declared invalid and the trademark will be unenforceable. This grows logically out of the idea that the proprietor of the trademark is responsible for whatever bears his brand name.

Despite the pitfalls and the uncertainties, trademark licensing continues to extend over larger and larger segments of the economy. There seem to be many enterprises that prefer a limited return in the form of a trademark royalty, as compared with the risks entailed in making capital investments for territorial or product expansion.

All-Weather Crete

The decision of a Connecticut judge in a comparatively unimportant suit for damages resulting from a leaking roof on a school in Hartford may have an enormous impact on the entire field of franchising. Whether it is a fast-food restaurant, a motel, a soft-drink bottling business, or some other enterprise, the typical franchise operation depends heavily on the consumer appeal of the franchisor's trademark.

A standard element in almost every franchise agreement is a license to use the franchisor's trademark. The problem in the Connecticut case grew out of the legal requirement that a trademark owner who permits a licensee to use his trademark must maintain control over "the nature and quality of the goods or services in connection with which the mark is used." Failure to exercise supervision over the licensee can lead to the loss of all rights in the trademark, so this requirement must be taken seriously. It is the basic reason for the detailed operating manuals and inspection procedures that form part of the usual franchise operation.

The leaking roof in Connecticut had been installed on a school building by Skyway All-Weather Crete Company. Skyway was the local licensee of Silbrico Corporation, owner of the registered trademark All-Weather Crete. The city of Hartford sued the general contractor who constructed the school and, in the same lawsuit, claimed damages against both Skyway and Silbrico.

According to the city's allegations, Silbrico has licensees for All-Weather Crete throughout the United States and Canada; it exercises control over the quality of the product as well as the methods for its application; Skyway followed Silbrico's specifications, but the All-Weather Crete product applied to the school roof was unsafe and defective and the leaks resulted from the defective design, formulation, and specifications of the product. The city of Hartford took the position that the franchisor, by exercising the quality control required by trademark law, became liable for defects in the product supplied by the licensee.

Discussions about the role of trademarks in marketing frequently mention that the trademark owner stands behind his product, that a trademark guarantees the quality of the product, and so forth. Extending this to a franchise situation, it could be said that the trademark owner, in a sense, takes the responsibility for the licensee's product, which he must do because of the quality control requirements of the trademark law.

Aside from a few suggestions in legal periodical articles, however, this kind of statement has not been taken literally as a warranty, which would create liability for damages. Trademark experts generally agree that Congress never meant to impose that kind of financial risk on a licensor when it wrote the quality control provisions into the 1946 trademark law.

The Connecticut judge acknowledged that the city of Hartford's claim was unique. He also recognized its great potential importance "in the light of the contemporary popularity of franchise agreements for the manufacture and sale by licensees of trademarked products."

As the published opinion points out, a trademark owner may extend the marketing area in which he exercises his rights either by expanding his own operations or by introducing his trademark into new territories through licensees. When the owner chooses the license route, he has a duty to exercise control over his licensees. Licensing without supervision by the licensor is the legal equivalent of abandoning the trademark, which means that the owner can no longer enforce his rights in it against anyone whether it is used with or without permission. The public is involved in this because the appearance of the licensor's trademark on uncontrolled products is considered to be deceptive to the consumer.

The judge then went into the product liability aspect of the claim. According to his analysis, the license agreement between Silbrico and Skyway guaranteed to the public that the roofing product sold under the All-Weather Crete trademark by Skyway was of the same nature and quality as Silbrico's product. The situation thus met the legal test for "strict product liability."

Silbrico tried to get the case against it dismissed by arguing that the city of Hartford was proceeding on an erroneous legal theory. As we have just seen, that argument failed to convince the judge.

The case was still at an early stage when this book went to press, but if there is a decision against Silbrico after trial, the legal responsibility of a trademark licensor for defective products sold by his licensee surely will be contested again on appeal. Meanwhile, the published opinion on this preliminary decision may stimulate other attempts to collect damages from licensors for acts committed by their licensees. At the very least, it is likely to lead to an increase in product liability insurance premiums for franchisors and, as a result, indirectly raise the prices of all franchised goods and services.

CHAPTER 16 Market Research as Legal Evidence in Trademark Cases

Excedrin; Bufferin

How far can a competitor safely go in simulating a brand name, a slogan, or the distinctive features of a package or label design? If the resemblance is sufficiently close so that the consuming public is likely to believe that the imitation is a product of the original manufacturer, then the competition is unfair and it can be stopped by court order.

But how does the judge know what is in the typical consumer's mind? This sounds like the kind of problem that ought to be solved by marketing research techniques, but comparatively little use has been made of these methods in litigation. The main reason for this appears to be the natural reluctance of courts to accept changes in traditional techniques of proving facts through a series of individual witnesses. However, there are some lawsuits in which opinion studies have been introduced as evidence, with the proper scientific backup to satisfy the judge of their reliability in such respects as questionnaire design, sampling methods, and overall freedom from bias; and this way of proving the likelihood of confusion has been receiving increased attention.

Bristol-Myers Company successfully used market studies in

obtaining a temporary injunction in 1966. Although this was a preliminary proceeding rather than a full trial, the ready acceptance by the judge of some simple, but effective, consumer tests has precedental value in future cases that raise similar issues of marketing psychology.

The Bristol-Myers litigation involved two of its well-known analgesic products, Excedrin and Bufferin. The suit was brought against Approved Pharmaceutical Corporation, which is a repackager of bulk drugs purchased from various suppliers.

The Excedrin package displays the brand name in red against a white background across the top half, with the slogan "Extra Strength Pain Reliever" and a list of symptom indications printed in white against a green background on the lower half. The label on the competing product was marked "Approved" at the very top, followed by the words *Extra Strength Pain Reliever* in red against a white background. The lower part of the label carried a list of symptoms nearly identical in arrangement to the one on the Excedrin package, also printed in white against a green background.

The Bufferin package is predominantly blue, with the brand name showing up strongly in white. Approved Pharmaceutical Corporation put out a similar product bearing a blue label with the words *Improved Buffered Aspirin* prominently displayed in white. One version of this label had *Buffered* appearing three times the size of the words *Improved* and *Aspirin*. After the lawsuit was started, this label was changed to make "Buffered" and "Aspirin" the same size.

Approved Pharmaceutical Corporation also had an analgesic product that it called Buffacin. The first four letters of this term were printed in white on blue, which is the color scheme of the Bufferin label, and the last four letters were printed in yellow on green, corresponding to the color scheme of the Anacin label. Although the manufacturer of Anacin analgesics was not a party to the suit, Bristol-Myers complained that the public would be misled into thinking that this product was an authorized combination of Bufferin and Anacin in a single tablet, or else that the brand name Buffacin simply would be confused with Bufferin itself (note that only two letters are different).

Two types of market studies were carried out for Bristol-Myers. The basis for one series was to determine whether or not a significant number of purchasers, under conditions of actual display and sale in a retail store, and unaware that they were participating in a survey, would be confused by the Approved Pharmaceutical label designs. Arrangements were made to set up a display of Bristol-Myers' Excedrin and also a display of Approved Pharmaceutical's competing product in a busy retail drug store. Every person entering the store during the survey period was handed a coupon offering a special low price on Excedrin.

A total of 277 persons attempted to redeem the Excedrin coupons. Of these, 39 customers, or 14.1 percent, chose the Approved Pharmaceutical imitation instead of the original.

The same technique was used to test the two different versions of the "Improved Buffered Aspirin" product against Bufferin. When the label with the outsized word *Buffered* was displayed, 24 out of 124 persons (19 percent) attempted to purchase the imitation in exchange for the Bufferin coupon. When the revised label was substituted, although the word "Buffered" no longer was emphasized, 43 persons out of a total of 161 (26.6 percent) selected the imitation product.

A totally different study was commissioned to measure the degree to which the public associated the slogan "Extra Strength Pain Reliever" with the product Excedrin. A nationwide sample of 1,567 respondents, selected on a statistical basis which the judge's opinion does not explain in detail but which he accepted as reliable, was interviewed. The respondents were asked, "What, if anything, do you associate with this phrase?" in connection with a list of well-known slogans of various manufacturers, including, of course, "Extra Strength Pain Reliever."

The results showed a substantial association ratio between the Bristol-Myers slogan and its product Excedrin. The published opinion does not include the statistical data, but it does report that the degree of identification was approximately the same as that achieved at the time by "The Champagne of Bottled Beer" with Miller High Life, "Progress Is Our Most Important Product" with General Electric, and "Put a Tiger in Your Tank" with Esso.

So far as Buffacin was concerned, no market research was undertaken, and the judge agreed none was necessary. Referring to this combination label, the judge said, "Its unfairness is evident from visual examination alone."

It is apparent from the opinion that the judge was influenced by the combination of similarities, and he might not have been so firm in his condemnation of the defendant's activities if only one product had been involved. The opinion speaks of the "purposeful design," "the imitative pattern," and the "intent to present their products to the public in a guise which would confuse ordinary purchasers." Nevertheless, the judge specifically ruled that the results of the market studies submitted by Bristol-Myers were sufficient by themselves to justify the issuance of the temporary injunction. Speaking of this evidence, the judge stated, "Independent of the inferences drawn from the proven pattern of imitation, and more than sufficient on its own footing on this motion, is the evidence before the court which clearly establishes that defendants' imitative labelling practices will produce substantial confusion."

This opinion can be read as an invitation to increase the use of marketing studies as legal evidence, especially in cases of trademark infringement and similar types of unfair competition, where the consuming public's state of mind is the basic legal issue to be decided.

7Up

A federal judge in Chicago ruled that Fizz Up infringes the trademark 7Up in a case whose most noteworthy feature was the use of marketing research techniques to produce evidence of consumer confusion.

The defending party at one time had used 1-Up as a trademark for a lemon-lime carbonated beverage. In 1958 it bought the rights to the trademark Fizz Up along with an inventory of bottles, labels, cartons, cases, crowns, and display materials from another bottler in Chicago. The latter had been warned by the Seven-Up Company, but there was no evidence that the purchaser had any knowledge of that incident.

At any rate, 7Up had been on the market since 1928, and nobody doubted its wide public acceptance, helped along by advertising expenditures in excess of $50,000,000. The judge decided that Fizz Up was so much like 7Up that confusion and mistake among purchasers was likely. He also found that Fizz Up was displayed in a manner that closely resembled the overall appearance of the 7Up labels, cartons, bottles, crowns, and cases. These conclusions by themselves would have been ample basis for a decision that Fizz Up was an infringing trademark, but the judge obviously was impressed greatly by the additional evidence of actual confusion presented by the Seven-Up Company in the form of two different consumer research projects.

The first of these was a survey conducted under the direction of Professor Steuart Henderson Britt of Northwestern University. This was a consumer reaction test consisting of a series of sidewalk interviews at nine different locations in Chicago. The judge's opinion states that the sample was "stratified and randomized." The city was divided into areas on the basis of existing statistical information concerning socioeconomic levels; the number of persons interviewed in each area was determined in proportion to population concentration; and the proper proportion in relation to population figures was allocated between the sexes and to various age groups. Finally, every third passer-by was interviewed until the prescribed number at each location had been reached.

The total number of respondents interviewed in this test was 999. The breakdown shows 48.0 percent males, 51.2 percent females, and 0.8 percent not recorded.

The questionnaire was simple in design. Each respondent was asked, "Do you ever buy soft drinks for yourself or your family?" He then was handed a bottle of Fizz Up and asked, "Have you ever bought this brand?" (If he failed to take the bottle, the interviewer held it up in front of him.) The next question was, "What soft drink company do you believe puts it out?" and the interviewer was instructed to record the answer verbatim. The only other question was a request for the respondent's name and address.

Of the 999 respondents, 250 (or 25.0 percent) answered "Seven-Up" or "I believe Seven-Up" to the second question. An additional 8.1 percent of respondents indicated some degree of indefinite connection with the Seven-Up Company, answering along the lines of "Is it Seven-Up?" or "I would guess Seven-Up."

As might be anticipated, the largest group didn't know who put out Fizz Up. This classification accounted for 51.3 percent of the repondents. Practically all the remaining persons interviewed gave specific answers, some of which probably were rather surprising to the parties involved. For example, no less than 65 individuals out of this group of 148 answered either Coca-Cola or Pepsi-Cola. The next most popular candidate was Canada Dry. A considerable number of companies received one vote each, including Dr. Pepper, Hires, and A&P.

Professor Britt's testimony explaining the consumer reaction test runs to several hundred pages in the typewritten trial transcript. In addition, both a supervisor and an interviewer testifed about the way in which the test had been conducted, and all the interviews were put into evidence as exhibits along with a tabulation of the results.

Evidence of this general type has been used in trademark infringement cases before. The presentation of the second consumer research project, however, is believed to be unique. This evidence was secured by one of Seven-Up's lawyers by interviewing shoppers in a supermarket. The unusual feature is that the interviews were recorded by a concealed sound motion picture camera and later projected in court.

These interviews were conducted in the immediate vicinity of a Fizz Up display in the supermarket. Each person who passed the place where the lawyer had stationed himself was handed a bottle of Fizz Up and asked, "What soft drink company do you believe puts out this drink, 'Fizz Up'?" Out of a total of 232 interviews, 86 respondents answered "Seven-Up."

The individual who operated the camera took the witness stand to explain the technical details of the equipment and the manner in which it was concealed. He verified the fact that the inverviews were recorded accurately, but also explained the technical difficulties he had experienced, which resulted in the partial or total loss of a number of interviews that actually had been conducted. These problems with the equipment ranged from running out of film at inconvenient times to inexplicable loss or garbling of the sound. In addition, the camera jammed on several occasions and it was necessary to call in representatives of the manufacturer. Only the recognizable interviews shown in the courtroom were included in the tabulated results, which indicated that 37.0 percent of the respondents believed Fizz Up was a product of the Seven-Up Company.

The judge summed up the evidence as follows:

> Both the reaction tests and the movie interviews produced credible evidence of confusion on the part of a substantial percentage of the approximately 1,000 persons interviewed in the reaction tests and of the large number of those interviewed in the supermarket in the Homewood area as reflected by the movie and that such interviews were truly reported in plaintiff's evidence; from all of plaintiff's evidence aforesaid the court finds that the use by the defendants of the accused trademark in marketing their product has caused, and is likely to cause, confusion or mistake and to deceive purchasers as to the source of defendants' goods and to cause a substantial percentage of purchasers to believe that defendants' product was actually produced by the plaintiff.

Some readers may be curious about how the motion pictures got into evidence. The defendants objected on the ground that the filmed interviews were hearsay and that they would be deprived of the opportunity of cross-examining the persons appearing on the screen. Counsel for Seven-Up responded with the statement that they were not trying to prove the truth of what the respondents stated; their claim was not that Fizz Up actually was put out by the Seven-Up Company. The purpose of the motion pictures, they argued, was simply to demonstrate the reaction of the persons interviewed in the grocery store itself when presented with the allegedly infringing product. With that explanation, the judge overruled the objection and accepted the evidence.

CHAPTER 17 Imitation of Packaging and Design Features

Mycostatin

E. R. Squibb & Sons makes, among about 1,200 other prescription products, a tablet under the trademark Mycostatin for the treatment of a vaginal fungus infection. The chemical or generic name of the drug is nystatin.

Premo Pharmaceutical Labs, Inc., is a generic drug manufacturer. It began to produce a nystatin tablet in 1976, long after Squibb had established itself as the market leader with its Mycostatin brand.

In 1969 Squibb introduced a unified graphic design for all its prescription product packages to establish visual identification for both health professionals and consumers. The principal feature of this graphic display is two thin dark brown parallel stripes, at different distances from the ends of the package, on a buff-colored background. Distinctive packaging is about the only way a consumer can relate a prescription drug to a particular manufacturing source because the manufacturer's name ordinarily is removed by the pharmacist before the package reaches the customer.

The Mycostatin product is packaged in a carton with the typical Squibb brown-and-buff graphics. The carton also has a tear-away gatefold panel, intended for removal by the pharmacist. This panel shows the Squibb trademark, but its principal purpose is to provide detailed technical information that normally is seen only by the physician and pharmacist.

The Mycostatin tablet itself has a beveled edge and is wrapped in gold foil. Neither one of these features has any necessary connection with the product; the tablet could be blister-packed, for example, and a competing brand of nystatin tablet actually has a nonbeveled edge.

To complete the description, a package insert accompanies each carton of Mycostatin tablets. Competitive brands of nystatin also include package inserts to instruct the user.

The Premo product was unbranded and sold simply under the generic name nystatin. Premo's carton copied the Squibb color scheme and design. It included a gatefold designed to be removed by the pharmacist. The tablets themselves had a beveled edge and were wrapped in gold foil. The package insert duplicated Squibb's, including the Spanish version on the reverse side.

United States District Judge Constance Baker Motley, who was in charge of the case, said that "with the gatefold removed, the two products are virtually indistinguishable." Squibb's director of advertising testifed that even he could not tell the difference between a box of Mycostatin tablets and a box of Premo's generic tablets without the gatefolds, unless he compared the type faces used for the rubber-stamped control number and expiration date.

Statistics showed that approximately two-thirds of the patients who receive a prescription for nystatin are repeat users. Premo's president said that his company was particularly interested in cultivating this repeat market. He testified that he wanted the customer to be satisfied she was receiving the right product. If the patient has been used to Mycostatin tablets and then received Premo's nystatin tablets, she would have no concern. There wouldn't be anything to question because the package looked the same. An unfamiliar package might raise questions, he explained.

Judge Motley had a different way of looking at it. She ruled that Premo intentionally copied the Mycostatin "trade dress" and therefore had committed unfair competition against Squibb.

Premo was ordered to stop imitating Squibb's packaging and also to pay over to Squibb all the profits it made on nystatin tablets in the copied trade dress. Judge Motley also included a somewhat unusual provision that ordered Premo to recall from the trade all unsold quantities of its nystatin tablets in the infringing packages and deliver them to Squibb, along with its inventories of the deceptive packaging items and the printing plates for producing them, so that Squibb could destroy all infringing material.

It should be noted that Premo was not stopped from making and selling nystatin tablets. It remained free to do so provided that it did not imitate Squibb's graphics or other distinctive packaging features.

The Mycostatin lawsuit was very much like a typical trademark infringement case—except that Premo didn't even use a brand name. The combination of elements in Squibb's graphic display and packaging functioned as a symbol to identify its products and therefore was the equivalent of a conventional trademark for marketing purposes. Situations like this are reminiscent of earlier days when many customers were illiterate and relied on the shape and color of a tag or label to identify a brand of goods they wanted to buy. Most customers for prescription drugs today might as well be illiterate because they frequently are not even aware of either the brand name or the chemical name of the product, which often is too complicated to remember anyway, so they also rely on shapes, colors, and other design features.

Clairol

A former regional sales manager for Clairol started his own cosmetics business under the name of Andrea Dumon, Inc., and decided that one of its products should be a cream hydrogen peroxide modeled after what Clairol calls "Pure White Creme Developer." The product itself was not patented, and there was no question about the right of a competitor to imitate it. The basis of Clairol's complaint was that Andrea Dumon selected an almost identical bottle and used very similar graphics.

The Clairol product had been something of a marketing breakthrough beginning with its introduction to the beauty salon trade in 1958 and the retail market in 1960. When Andrea Dumon came on the scene several years later, Clairol's "Pure White Creme Developer" was the leading product in its field.

The face of the Clairol bottle used a distinctive color scheme of alternating mustard-gold and black elements. A crown design appeared at the top in gold. Then came the trademark Clairol in black. Below that was a horizontal bar in gold, extending about 50 percent of the distance around the bottle. Next was the name of the product, with the words *Pure White* and *Developer* in black and the word *Creme* in gold. The background was the product itself, which is a white cream.

The Clairol container was a stock bottle that probably meant very little by itself. But Andrea Dumon chose a substantially identical stock bottle for its product.

The Dumon bottle also used alternating mustard-gold and black. At the top of the face there appeared a design in gold which, although not a crown, occupied approximately the same amount of space as the Clairol crown design. Below the design came the Andrea Dumon name in black. Next was a horizontal gold bar that extended almost the same distance as Clairol's gold bar, although Dumon's bar was plainer in design. Then came the name of the product, with the words *White* and *Developer* in black and "Creamed Peroxide" in gold. And the white cream color of the product provided the background.

At the trial one of the principal pieces of evidence was a rough sketch drawn by Dumon's sales manager for use by the artist who prepared the final art work for the container. A visual comparison demonstrated that the sketch had been copied directly from Clairol's bottle. And there were handwritten instructions on the sketch, which resulted in spacing the various graphic elements in such a way that they corresponded to the main features of the Clairol bottle design.

The trial judge concluded that the appearance of Clairol's container was sufficiently distinctive to serve as an identifying symbol to the purchasing public and that the Andrea Dumon package was a deliberate imitation intended to divert trade from Clairol by making the same overall visual impression on the consumer. Andrea Dumon then took the case to the Illinois appellate court, asserting two main points in support of its appeal.

The first Dumon argument was based on the policy of federal law encouraging imitation as a spur to free competitive enterprise. The theory is that competitors should be allowed to copy anything not protected by a patent or a copyright because this is good for the competitive system under which our economy operates.

The trial judge had gone into that question, and he ruled that the leading Supreme Court precedents on the subject dealt only with the copying of *products*, not their trademarks or their packaging; if the container design is sufficiently distinctive so that copying it would tend to confuse the purchasing public, another company that does copy it has committed a type of unfair competition.

The Illinois appellate court agreed that the Supreme Court precedents were limited, as the trial judge had ruled, and, of course, Clairol had made no claim that copying the cream peroxide product was illegal.

Therefore, the trial judge's order requiring Andrea Dumon to discontinue all use of the confusingly similar design was sustained on appeal.

The second point of the Andrea Dumon appeal was that the trial judge had improperly applied the Illinois Deceptive Practices Act to the case. This state law basically is a recodification of general principles of unfair competition (otherwise known as deceptive trade practices) developed through court decisions over the years. The appellate court agreed with the trial judge on this argument also, stating that the Illinois Deceptive Practices Act clearly was intended to provide a remedy for precisely the type of situation that was created by the activities of Andrea Dumon.

The Illinois state law provided the basis for a substantial award of money to Clairol. The statute contains a provision to the effect that costs or attorneys' fees, or both, may be assessed against a defendant only if the court finds that he has wilfully, i.e., deliberately, engaged in a deceptive trade practice. The trial judge did find a wilful violation on the part of Andrea Dumon and accordingly entered judgment in favor of Clairol for $20,616 in attorneys' fees and costs, in addition to an injunction prohibiting Dumon from any further use of the imitative container design.

This monetary award is unusual in such a case, and it suggests that the Illinois Deceptive Practices Act really may have put teeth into enforcement against so-called "knock-off artists," who otherwise might get away with only a court order to cease and desist. The appellate court also agreed that this award of money was proper under the circumstances and affirmed the judgment of the trial judge in all respects.

Rolls-Royce

A Florida-based company named Custom Cloud Motors, Inc., marketed a kit designed to convert a Chevrolet Monte Carlo into what they suggested be called a Custom Cloud, but which looked very much like a Rolls-Royce. The kit sold for approximately $3,000 and included a considerable amount of material, such as fenders, to be attached to the Monte Carlo; but its most noticeable features were a radiator grill very much like the Rolls-Royce grill, a hood ornament closely resembling the Rolls-Royce "flying lady," and a rectangular emblem which, instead of the name Rolls-Royce separated by an RR monogram, contained the words *Custom Cloud* separated by a CC monogram.

Predictably, the Rolls-Royce organization took a dim view of this. Both Rolls-Royce Motors Ltd., the British manufacturer, and Rolls-Royce Motors, Inc., its exclusive U.S. distributor, brought suit against Custom Cloud Motors. They also included its advertising agency and a Chevrolet dealer who had been installing the kits. The court action was based primarily on trademark infringement. The Rolls—RR—Royce insignia is a registered trademark in the U.S., and so is the "flying lady" ornament and also the model name Silver Cloud.

The kit manufacturer argued that there was no infringement because there was no competition between what it was doing and the sale of Rolls-Royce automobiles, so that nobody could be confused. It also claimed the legal right to copy the Rolls-Royce designs because they were neither patented nor copyrighted. In addition, it pointed to differences in detail between each of the challenged elements of the kit and the Rolls-Royce design, including differences in the name and the insignia.

The case came up in the U.S. district court in New York, where the judge decided to concentrate on a section in the federal trademark law that prohibits the use of a "false designation of origin." The judge wrote in his opinion that he found "without hesitation that the design of the Custom Cloud grill, including the statuette and the insignia, is such as to falsely represent that its origin is Rolls-Royce."

Rolls-Royce conducted a "mini-survey" of 100 persons who were stopped at random in midtown New York. They were shown the cover of the March 1976 issue of *Car & Driver* magazine, with the lettering hidden. The cover photograph was a Chevrolet Monte Carlo automobile converted by means of the Custom Cloud kit. Sixty-five out of the 100 respondents identified the car in the picture as a Rolls-Royce. Four individuals said that it was an imitation Rolls-Royce. Only 23 out of the 100 identified the car as something other than a Rolls-Royce.

As the court's opinion points out, although there have been various changes in body designs from time to time, Rolls-Royce has used the same distinctive grill for many years. As a result, "It has become a universally recognized symbol of the quality of the Rolls-Royce automobiles."

The ornament on top of the Custom Cloud grill, said the judge, was almost identical to the Rolls-Royce "flying lady."

And the insignia, although it had different wording, was in the "same shape and styling" as the Rolls-Royce insignia.

The judge also was impressed with the connection between the name Custom Cloud and the familiar Rolls-Royce model Silver Cloud. There was evidence to the effect that persons familiar with Rolls-Royce and other expensive automobiles often refer to the Silver Cloud simply as "the Cloud."

In concluding his opinion, the judge wrote: "This is an obvious case where the promoters of a new product are attempting to capitalize deceptively upon the well established reputation of another party, built up over long years of dealings with the public, and based upon a large expenditure of money and effort both in the production of the product and in advertising." He therefore ordered an injunction, pending trial, to stop all further distribution or promotion of the Custom Cloud kit.

After reviewing their position in light of the judge's ruling, the defending parties decided to capitulate. They agreed to have a permanent injunction issued against them, and Custom Cloud Motors has gone out of business.

Tenuate

So-called generic drug manufacturers produce the chemical equivalents of brand name products for sale under their generic names. So long as there is no patent covering the original product, this kind of manufacturing is legal. But the laws governing unfair competition set some limits on what the generic drug manufacturer can do.

Merrell-National Laboratories, a subsidiary of Richardson-Merrell, makes appetite suppressant tablets under the registered trademarks Tenuate and Tenuate Dospan. These are known as DEP products from their chemical name—a typical jawbreaker, diethylpropion hydrochloride.

DEP tablets are available only on a doctor's prescription. They are used in cases of obesity when accompanied by such other disorders as hypertension, cardiovascular disease and diabetes, or in pregnancy.

The Tenuate tablet is circular, about ⅜ of an inch in diameter and ⅛ of an inch deep, with beveled edges, and is colored aqua. The Tenuate Dospan tablet is long and narrow, capsule-shaped, about ¾ of an inch in length and ⅛ of an inch thick, with beveled edges, and is colored white.

A generic drug manufacturer named Zenith Laboratories also makes DEP tablets. Although other DEP manufacturers use different sizes, shapes, and colors, Zenith produces two versions that are almost identical in size, shape, and color to the Tenuate and Tenuate Dospan tablets of Merrell-National Laboratories. In addition, Zenith's promotional literature describes its DEP products as "similar to" and "comparable to" Tenuate and Tenuate Dospan.

Merrell-National was able to document several instances where two drug stores in New Jersey filled prescriptions calling for its DEP brand name tablets with DEP products made by Zenith. It also uncovered an incident in which Zenith's wholesale distributor shipped Zenith's DEP tablets to a druggist who had ordered Merrell-National's DEP tablets. A lawsuit was filed against Zenith, its distributor, and the two drug stores that had filled Tenuate prescriptions with the Zenith product. Chief Judge Lawrence A. Whipple of the federal district court in New Jersey issued an order stopping any further substitution of the Zenith product for the Merrell-National product and prohibiting the advertising of Zenith's product as anything other than a generic diethylpropion hydrochloride. Zenith also was ordered to discontinue making DEP products in shapes and colors similar to those used by Merrell-National.

The actual substitution of one company's product for a similar one made by another company is a classic type of unfair business practice that has been considered illegal for centuries. Passing off a cheaper product for a more expensive one of similar appearance was a common form of unfair competition in much earlier days, when many customers could be fooled easily because they were illiterate.

Judge Whipple, therefore, did not have a very difficult decision to make in ruling against the retail drug stores. The legal status of the generic drug manufacturer was not quite so clear, and this also was true of the wholesale distributor, except for the incident where it substituted the Zenith product when a druggist ordered Tenuate tablets.

Is it unfair to copy the color and shape of a product when there is no patent protection on the chemical substance itself? After all, Zenith and its distributor did not label their DEP tablets with Merrell-National's registered trademarks, Tenuate and Tenuate Dospan.

Looking back into the legal precedents, Judge Whipple found nothing in New Jersey law that was directly in point. However, similar questions had come up in other courts in the country. The basic rule was stated this way in a 1976 federal Court of Appeals case: "It is unfair competition for a person to put a product into a dealer's hands which a producer can reasonably anticipate may be easily passed off as the goods of another."

Applying this principle to the imitation of the color and shape of Merrell-National's DEP tablets, Judge Whipple concluded that Zenith and its distributor were acting illegally because they sold an "instrumentality of trade" that could be passed off as the Merrell-National product.

CHAPTER **18**

International Problems

The Trademark Registration Treaty

At a diplomatic conference in Vienna in June 1973, some 50 countries adopted the text of an international trademark registration treaty that is intended to simplify procedures for obtaining legal protection for trademarks around the world.

The United States was a strong supporter of the new treaty through its drafting stages and was an active participant in the Vienna conference. The treaty provided that it could not go into effect until it had been ratified by at least five countries, and that did not happen until 1980, when the Soviet Union joined four small African nations that had ratified it earlier. The treaty has no effect on any nonmember country, and the United States has not yet ratified it.

Aside from the treaty members in their relations with one another, a company that wishes international protection for its trademarks must file a separate application in each foreign country. This requires a local attorney or agent, the preparation of legal documents that fit the particular country's requirements and language, and, naturally, the payment of a government filing fee.

There are approximately 200 countries that are prepared to receive such an application and to issue a trademark registration certificate if everything is in order.

Major U.S. companies seeking protection for their brands in foreign markets frequently file in 50 to 100 countries, and sometimes more.

The new Trademark Registration Treaty (known as TRT) will reduce the paperwork and make the entire procedure easier. Just one application will have to be filed in a central office in Geneva called the International Bureau. It will be on a simple form, in the applicant's choice of English or French. Printed forms will be supplied free of charge.

The application will list the classifications of goods or services for which the trademark is to be registered (an international classification system already in existence will be used for this purpose) and the countries where protection is desired. The applicant's own country may be one of those listed. The International Bureau then will issue a registration certificate and notify the appropriate government department in each of those countries. However, this is only the beginning.

Trademark registration procedures and requirements vary greatly throughout the world. For the most part, TRT does not attempt to unify these by requiring changes in local practice. Each government will treat the international registration as the equivalent of a local application. If approved, the international registration will be given the same effect as a local registration.

In many countries registration of a trademark is virtually automatic, and that will continue under TRT. The government departments in those countries will issue registrations in response to TRT applications just as they do in response to local applications. If there should be a conflict with someone else's trademark, it is up to the company claiming the conflict exists to commence legal proceedings. Unless that happens, the trademark owner operating under TRT will have no need for any direct dealings with that country nor any need to engage a local attorney or agent.

In other countries the procedure involves an official check for trademark conflicts and sometimes different kinds of legal obstacles as well. These countries (the United States is one of them) also will continue to follow their regular procedures with TRT applications.

One significant difference required by TRT is that if any

obstacle does turn up, a final decision will have to be reached within 15 months, or else the government department, before the expiration of 15 months, must notify the International Bureau of a possible refusal, stating the legal grounds on which the objection is based.

Within a reasonably short time, therefore, the TRT applicant either will have a trademark registration effective in all the countries on his list, or at least will know what specific difficulties remain to be ironed out (if they can be) in those countries where some legal obstacle has arisen. The registration will be effective for ten years. If the trademark owner wishes to add more countries, he can do so by filing another simple form with the International Bureau. He also can delete classes of goods or services if he wishes to limit the extent of his protection (perhaps in order to avoid conflict with a third party in a field that is commercially unimportant to the owner).

One of the great features of TRT is the simplicity with which renewals and changes of ownership can be accomplished. A single renewal application filed with the International Bureau every ten years will keep the trademark in force in all the designated countries. At the time of renewal, the trademark owner can exclude specific countries if he wishes, or he can exclude specific classes of goods or services from the coverage of his trademark registration.

If a trademark changes hands, which happens frequently in corporate acquisitions or mergers, one simple form filed with the International Bureau will be sufficient. Similarly, if the trademark owner changes its corporate name, a single document sent to the International Bureau will substitute the new name in the official records of all countries involved.

Naturally, fees will have to be paid under TRT. It is not anticipated that there will be substantial cost savings, if any, as compared to the multiple government fees now required, although there should be significant economies in the reduction of paperwork. Also, local representatives will no longer be needed, except where trouble develops.

Even the system of fee payments will be simplified, however, because a single payment in Swiss francs to the International Bureau will cover everything. This payment will vary depending on the countries listed and the number of classes of goods or services for which protection is requested. The International Bureau will distribute most of what it collects to the individual countries, to help them defray the costs of the services their own government departments will continue to perform.

The success of TRT as something useful for the business community obviously will depend on how many countries ratify it. If the membership of TRT remains at only five countries after several more years have gone by, it probably will have to be considered a failure.

But why shouldn't every country rush to join TRT, since it seems to offer so many advantages over the present system? There are two principal reasons.

In the first place, there is another international trademark registration arrangement in effect, and a number of European countries belong to it. The United States, England, and many other countries, big and small, have resisted joining that other arrangement because of one complexity. It requires that a trademark applicant first have a registration in his home country, and the international registration automatically loses its effect if the home registration is not renewed or is canceled.

Although the membership of this arrangement is not very large, the countries making use of it have expressed satisfaction, and they may not be willing to join TRT in addition. At least they are not likely to join early, although they may come along later if experience demonstrates that TRT is achieving widespread acceptance in other parts of the world.

The second reason is that some of TRT's minimum requirements will make it necessary for certain countries to change their domestic trademark laws. The United States is the country that would need the greatest change. U.S. law requires that a trademark be in actual use in interstate or foreign commerce before an application to register it can even be filed. The minimum standard under TRT is quite different; no country can cancel a trademark on the ground of nonuse for at least three years after its registration. Therefore, the United States would have to change its system and provide for the registration of unused trademarks before we could ratify TRT.

As a kind of counterbalance for this, TRT would permit us to provide that no action for infringement could be brought on the basis of an unused trademark.

Despite the official support for TRT from the U.S. government, there are many people in this country who believe our present system of requiring use of a trademark before registration should not be changed. On the other hand, we are practically alone in this regard. Almost every other country allows registration of a trademark without use, although the registration in many countries is subject to cancellation if the trademark has not been put into use within a specified period of years.

Most of the rest of the world finds us out of step; they don't understand why we insist on having the mark put into use and then subjecting the owner to the hazards of a possible rejection of his trademark application.

Indeed, it is an open secret that many U.S. companies get around this requirement by making minimal use of a trademark, perhaps one small shipment with a simple black-and-white label on the product, to support the filing of an application. They then wait to see if they can get a registration before starting commercial use.

In an era when increased international cooperation clearly is the trend, it would seem desirable for the United States to change its trademark system and get in step with the rest of the world. But Congress is going to have to be convinced of this, on practical as well as ideological grounds, before the United States can even qualify to become a member country of the Trademark Registration Treaty.

Wells Fargo

The opinion of a United States District Judge in Nevada in a case concerning the famous Wells Fargo trademark illustrates the difficulties American companies face in protecting their trademarks against unauthorized use in foreign countries.

The present Wells Fargo & Co. is a California-based corporation that traces its history back to 1852, when a predecessor started the express and stagecoach services that played such a well known part in the development of the West. Wells Fargo & Co. now is engaged primarily in banking, although it also is involved in restaurant services, the travel agency business, and toy manufacturing.

One of the sidelights that emerged from the lawsuit is the fact that the Wells Fargo armored car business belongs to an unrelated company, a Delaware corporation named Baker Industries, Inc. In an effort to avoid confusion, let us follow the same procedure that the judge used in his opinion and call Wells Fargo & Co. "the Bank" and the armored car company "Baker."

In the summer of 1970 Baker and the Bank discovered that there was a corporation in Nevada named Wells Fargo Express Company (which we had better call "the Nevada corporation"). A threatening letter complaining about the unauthorized use of the Wells Fargo name brought no response, so Baker and the Bank filed suit against the Nevada corporation in September of that year.

Investigation revealed that the Nevada corporation was owned by still another company using the Wells Fargo name. This was Wells Fargo Express Company, A.G., organized under the laws of Liechtenstein, a tiny European country that was known mostly to stamp collectors until comparatively recent times when financiers discovered its highly desirable tax and corporate laws.

In a further effort to keep the cast of characters straight, this fourth company will be known here as "the Liechtenstein corporation." The Bank and Baker subsequently added the Liechtenstein corporation to the lawsuit, charging it with having registered Wells Fargo as its trademark in various foreign countries.

The Nevada corporation had been organized in 1961, but it was completely dormant until late in 1968. Then it opened an office in Las Vegas and later hired an inventor to work on various new product possibilities, including a coin-handling device that would reject slugs and counterfeits. It was listed under the heading "Research and Development" in the Las Vegas Yellow Pages.

Three weeks after the lawsuit was filed, the Nevada corporation changed its name to Modern Research, Inc. Less than one month later, the stock of the corporation was purchased by the New York lawyer who represented it in this case.

Because it never had much activity and because its corporate name no longer contained the expression Wells Fargo, the Nevada corporation asked the court to dismiss the case against it. At the same time, the Liechtenstein corporation also sought dismissal, on a variety of grounds. The opinion, which runs an unusual thirty printed pages, deals only with these preliminary phases of the lawsuit.

So far as the Nevada corporation was concerned, the judge ruled that it had to stand trial on the question of whether the Bank and Baker suffered any pecuniary damage from its operations, minor though they were, and on whether a court order might be appropriate to compel it to give up all use of the name Wells Fargo.

As the judge pointed out, the Nevada corporation insisted that it had the right to use the corporate name Wells Fargo Express Company. This is a legal issue that remained to be litigated in spite of the voluntary name change to Modern Research because the corporation might have changed its name back again if the issue were left undetermined in the lawsuit.

The more interesting part of the decision, in light of the preceding section about the Trademark Registration Treaty, deals with the Liechtenstein corporation and the foreign trademark registrations of Wells Fargo. We can leave aside the technicalities of whether the Nevada corporation could be made reponsible for the acts of its parent company in foreign countries and whether the Liechtenstein corporation was properly brought before the court in Nevada.

Fundamentally, the Bank and Baker argued that the use and

registration of the name Wells Fargo by the Liechtenstein corporation was causing grave injury to their worldwide good will
and would prevent them from expanding into international
markets. But the judge pointed out that registration of a trademark in the United States is not international in scope; it gives
protection only in this country. If the Bank and Baker wanted
international protection for their trademark, they should have
taken appropriate steps to register it in the foreign countries
of their choice.

Moreover, the acts of the Liechtenstein corporation might
very well have been lawful in the countries where it operates.
As noted in the discussion of TRT, there are numerous countries where a trademark can be registered by merely filing an
application, without any requirement that it be used. And in
such countries the registration may be legal regardless of the
fact that the trademark in question happens to be well known
in the United States.

At any rate, the Bank and Baker had not succeeded in bringing forth evidence to convince the federal judge in Nevada
that the foreign registrations of Wells Fargo were in any way
defective in the particular countries that had issued them to
the Liechtenstein corporation.

For this and other reasons, the judge dismissed the case so
far as the Liechtenstein corporation was concerned. That decision, however, was reversed by the Court of Appeals, which
ruled the judge had not applied the proper legal standards to
the question of whether or not the Liechtenstein corporation
was subject to suit in a United States federal court in Nevada,
and sent the case back for reconsideration. The law books
show no developments since that reversal in 1977. Conceiv-
ably, the Bank and Baker, should they wish to continue the
fight, will have to proceed in foreign countries, where they
may or may not be successful. It is possible that a foreign court
will agree that the name Wells Fargo has such a worldwide
reputation that it is unfair for an unrelated company to use it
without authorization, but that is not a foregone conclusion.

Many companies have found themselves in the position

where they had to buy "their" trademarks from foreign nationals who took advantage of the opportunity to get registrations in their own names, perhaps just for the purpose of a little commercial blackmail.

Would the situation in the Wells Fargo case have been any different if the Trademark Registration Treaty were in effect? Not necessarily. But if the new treaty had gone into operation before the Liechtenstein corporation started collecting foreign registrations, the chances are that either the Bank or Baker, or both of them, would have filed under the treaty for foreign protection of the Wells Fargo trademark. And that would have blocked the Liechtenstein corporation, which would not have been able to obtain conflicting registrations of the identical trademark.

As matters now stand, the Wells Fargo decision demonstrates the need for companies with international interests to secure protection for their trademarks on a country-by-country basis wherever they feel that their business, present or prospective, justifies the expense.

CHAPTER 19 Trademarks and the Public Interest

All of us are consumers, and—whether we are conscious of it or not—we all live by trademarks. The alarm clock that wakes you up; the toothpaste, toothbrush, and soap you use in the bathroom; the plumbing; the towels—all of these products have trademarks. And, while you are getting dressed (in various pieces of trademarked clothing), perhaps you turn on your RCA, Zenith, or Sony television set. If you tune in the "Today" program, you may see the NBC peacock—a registered service mark. "Today" and "NBC" are service marks too; so are "CBS," the CBS "eye" design, "ABC," and the titles of their shows. The name of your morning newspaper is its trademark, and almost every advertisement in the newspaper features at least one trade or service mark. So it goes from morning till night. The Patent and Trademark Office has estimated that the average American is exposed to approximately 1,500 different marks every day.

In accordance with its legal definition, a trademark distinguishes goods supplied by a particular manufacturer or merchant from similar goods manufactured or sold by others. The trademark is the means through which a consumer can choose among competing products. It is a symbol that lets a purchaser identify goods that have been satisfactory in the past and reject those that have failed to provide satisfaction. The same applies to marks used for services.

The impact of trademark law on the consumer sometimes is overlooked. The entire law of trademarks, however, depends upon consumer psychology. Questions of both registrability and infringement of trademarks are decided on the basis of what is believed to be going on in the mind of the consumer.

Consumer satisfaction sometimes is simply a matter of whim or style or taste. But the trademark always is the identifying symbol that enables the consumer to make the choice. If you happen not to like the flavor of a particular brand of toothpaste or mouthwash, the trademark is the symbol that tells you not to buy it again. On the other hand, if you find a brand of toothpaste or mouthwash whose taste you do like, the trademark on the container leads you back to a repeat purchase of a satisfactory item. The same system lets the consumer select the quality as well as the kind of product he or she wants to buy.

The consuming public is an unnamed third party in every trademark infringement case. When a trademark proprietor sues an infringer, he is doing at least two things. First, he is protecting his own pecuniary interests by suppressing a form of unfair competition. At the same time, he is also protecting the public from being deceived or misled.

The law defines the infringement of a trademark in terms of its impact on the public. Trademark infringement is illegal because it interferes with the marketing process in which the consumer chooses goods by their trademarks. An infringing mark is one whose use is likely to cause confusion or mistake, or to deceive.

It is well-established legal doctrine that the enforcement of private trademark rights is in the interest of the consumer. Back in 1882 the United States Supreme Court explained that a trademark proprietor is entitled to legal protection, "not only as a matter of justice to him, but to prevent imposition upon the public."

This theme has been reiterated consistently through the years. For example, the influential federal Court of Appeals in New York recently stated that the protection of the public is the fundamental consideration in the law of unfair competition.

Considering all this emphasis on the protection of the purchasing public through the medium of trademarks, it is rather surprising to find that consumer advocates are opposed to the trademark system. This negative attitude seems to be based on the same fundamental misunderstanding that also leads some consumer advocates to condemn trademarks as a form of monopoly.

Trademarks traditionally have been linked with patents and often with copyrights as well. Trademarks are registered by the same United States government office that issues patents. From a global viewpoint, the United Nations agency known as the World Intellectual Property Organization administers the international treaties dealing with patents, trademarks, and copyrights. In spite of these traditional links, the legal basis for a trademark is entirely different from the legal basis for a patent or a copyright.

Both patents and copyrights are exclusive rights granted by the federal government under the specific authority of the Constitution to protect "writings" and "discoveries." The Constitution requires that patents and copyrights be issued only for limited times. Because of the "limited times" restriction, the invention protected by a patent, and the literary, musical, or artistic work protected by a copyright, fall into the public domain when their terms expire. This means that they become available for free use by anyone who wishes when the expiration date arrives and forever afterward. Meanwhile, the economic protection provided by the patent and copyright has stimulated the inventor and author to disclose the results of their creative processes. The public gets the information contained in the patent as soon as it is issued, and the information contained in the copyrighted work as soon as it is published. If the inventor or author did not have legal protection against infringers, he would tend to keep his creations secret. By inducing disclosure to the public, the patent and copyright systems fulfill their Constitutional purpose "to promote the progress of science and the useful arts," by which the writers of the Constitution meant to include scholarship, literature, and invention.

By contrast, trademarks are simply marketing symbols.

They differentiate goods or services provided by one supplier from similar ones provided by another. A trademark is not a "writing" or a "discovery," as those terms are used in the Constitution.

Congress itself has been confused about the relationship between trademarks and patents or copyrights. The first trademark statute purportedly was based on the patent and copyright clause of the Constitution. The Supreme Court had to set Congress straight by declaring that statute unconstitutional.

Trademarks cannot be protected under the same legal theory as patents and copyrights. All federal trademark legislation after that first unconstitutional attempt by Congress has been based on the commerce clause of the Constitution. A trademark cannot be registered unless it is used in commerce that is subject to regulation by Congress, which ordinarily means use in interstate or foreign commerce.

The owner of a patent can exclude anyone else from making, using, or selling the patented invention. A copyright proprietor can prevent anyone else from copying his work, either directly or in the form of a translation or adaptation. A trademark owner, on the other hand, has only the limited right to stop the use of an identical or similar mark where confusion, mistake, or deception are likely to occur.

The word *monopoly* has a particularly unfavorable connotation in the American economy because our economic system is based on free enterprise. This is not the place to argue whether patents and copyrights are "good" or "bad" monopolies (although both history and economics support the statement that patents and copyrights are at least defensible exclusive grants), but, as a matter of terminology, patents and copyrights could be called monopolies of a sort. The point here is that trademarks are different; they do not deserve the epithet *monopoly* at all.

The basic confusion concerns the definition of the word *monopoly*. In strict economic terms, the ownership of real estate or tangible personal property could be classed as a monopoly.

These are obvious examples of exclusive legal rights that our society does not consider objectionable. Also, we have many monopolies that, if not completely "good," at least are acceptable compromises with reality. The most common examples are the regulated utility companies.

The evil connotation of the word *monopoly* originated centuries ago when sovereigns arbitrarily granted exclusive industrial rights to favored individuals. Currently the unfavorable implications of the word *monopoly* come from its antitrust context. However, the antitrust laws condemn only monopoly power that was acquired by exclusionary acts and that substantially controls a relevant competitive market.

It therefore is at least questionable whether the word *monopoly* can properly be applied to a trademark at all. The Supreme Court has said, "In truth, a trademark confers no monopoly whatever, in a proper sense. . . ." If a trademark is a monopoly at all, it is a monopoly only in the limited sense that the trademark proprietor can prevent the use of the same or a similar symbol under circumstances where confusion, mistake, or deception is likely to occur.

If the trademark is a word, the owner of the mark has not removed it from the English language. "Ivory" is a well-known trademark for soap products, but that does not monopolize it for all purposes. Anyone is free to use the word *ivory* to name the material in an elephant's tusk or to describe a color. "Ivory" can even be used as someone else's trademark if the goods or services for which it is used are not so closely related to soap products that a prospective purchaser would mistakenly assume a connection between their supplier and the owner of the trademark "Ivory" for soap. The same could be said for "Arrow" shirts or "Camel" cigarettes.

Critics of the trademark system sometimes suggest that competitors ought to be permitted to share in the good will of highly successful trademarks. But that is simply another way of saying that trademark infringement should be condoned under some circumstances. The competitive system does not demand such extreme steps. The idea that a branded product can be so successful that its trademark is a barrier to competitors wishing to enter the market is fallacious. The market is self-correcting. A successful product known by its trademark is an invitation to the industry to introduce competing products under their own trademarks.

The ultimate goal of a free market economy is success by fair means. It is not true that competition in any form is necessarily good. Only fair competition serves the basic purposes of our economy. Trademark infringement, under the guise of sharing in someone else's good will or otherwise, is a form of unfair competitions and, as an Illinois court opinion said, "Unfair competition is not competition at all in the truest sense of the word."

In the words of the U.S. Court of Appeals for the Fifth Circuit, "The essence of competition is the ability of competing products to obtain public recognition based on their own individual merit." Without trademarks the "public recognition" of "competing products" would not be possible. It is strange that trademarks should be attacked as anticompetitive when their basic purpose is to facilitate the operation of the competitive process.

The theoretical economic model of a free enterprise system in which interchangeable goods are offered for sale by an indefinite number of suppliers can function without any trademarks. The indiscriminate application of classical economic theory to a modern industrial system for which it is no longer entirely suitable may explain the hostile attitude of some consumer advocates toward trademarks.

One of the great changes the industrial revolution made was to separate the producer from the consumer. In recent history, increased industrialization has increased the spread. This is a far cry from earlier and simpler times when the consumer knew the artisan who made the article he bought, or the farmer who grew the food he brought home to be served at his table. Technological improvements result in larger and larger production units. Advances in transportation methods make it possible to deliver goods to what used to be considered impossibly remote markets. Self-service retailing takes the consumer even farther away from direct touch with the manufacturer.

Trademarks are the symbols that bridge the wide gap between the producer and the consumer. The trademark allows the consumer to identify the product with its manufacturer. In a figure of speech that has been traced back to H. G. Wells, the trademark lets the manufacturer "reach over the shoulder" of the retailer straight to the consumer.

The popularity of a successful trademark obviously can increase a manufacturer's market share. But that is what the competitive system is all about. Increased consumption requires larger production facilities. In the long run this leads to economies of scale and therefore lowers prices. In addition, it must be recognized that the freedom to introduce a new product carries with it the possibility of failure as well as success. The free private enterprise system that is so basic in our society does not protect particular competitive enterprises against loss. What the free enterprise system protects is the competitive economy as an institution.

A world without trademarks would be very hard to imagine. When everything comes in a plain brown wrapper, the incentive to try to make a better product is thrown into complete reverse. The incentive is to produce the lowest possible quality because the consumer will not be able to tell the difference and therefore will not be in a position to retaliate against any particular producer. Under those conditions, said Edward S. Rogers, acknowledged dean of the trademark bar, "There could be no pride of workmanship, no credit for good quality, no responsibility for bad." That could be the ultimate result if the opponents of the trademark system had their way.

Competition in modern society would be impossible unless the consumer had the means for distinguishing similar goods supplied by different producers. The most a successful trademark can do is persuade a consumer to try the product—once. A trademark alone does not have the monopoly power to force the public to buy something it does not want. Consumers use trademarks to identify products they would like to avoid as well as products they would like to purchase again.

In a comparative advertising case decided in 1968, the U.S. Court of Appeals in California said that trademarks, as a means of identifying the products of their owners, serve an important public purpose. The trademark makes effective competition possible in a complex, impersonal marketplace. It does this by providing the consumer a means of identifying products that please him and then rewarding the producer with continued patronage. Without this method of product identification, informed consumer choice could not exist.

In protecting the consumer and maintaining meaningful competition, the trademark system serves the public interest.

CHAPTER 20 How to Use a Trademark Properly

Trademarks must be handled with care because improper use literally can destroy them. Under federal law, rights in a registered trademark are forfeited "when any course of conduct of the registrant, including acts of omission or commission, causes the mark to lose its significance as an indication of origin"; and courts apply the same principle whether or not the mark has been registered.

The purpose and function of a manufacturer's trademark are, quoting the federal statute once again, "to identify his goods and distinguish them from those manufactured and sold by others." If a trademark is used properly, it will remain the exclusive property of its owner forever. But if the consuming public comes to treat a trademark as the name for a type of product, rather than a designation for one particular brand of the product, it will no longer "identify" and "distinguish" the goods of one manufacturer. The trademark then has become a generic term, and that means it is available for anyone to use.

History shows that the manufacturer's own advertising or labeling is frequently at fault when a trademark is lost by conversion into a generic term. This is essentially what went wrong with such well-known examples as aspirin, cellophane, celluloid, escalator, kerosene, lanolin, linoleum, milk of magnesia, shredded wheat, and thermos. The fact that these valuable assets could have been destroyed unintentionally is what makes it necessary to have some rules for the proper usage of trademarks.

What happened to those well-known former trademarks?

They started out with an arbitrary, trademark significance. But their meanings changed in the mind of the consumer, and they passed into the language as ordinary words because that is the way in which the general public came to understand and use them.

The former trademark "escalator" provides an example of how the manufacturer itself sometimes contributes to the change of meaning. It is possible to visualize an Escalator brand of moving staircase and also, perhaps, a Westinghouse brand of moving staircase, an Otis brand of moving staircase, and so forth. But when the Otis Elevator Company advertised in magazines like Architectural Forum, claiming "the utmost in safe, efficient, economical elevator and escalator operation," it was using the admittedly generic term *elevator* and the alleged trademark *escalator* in precisely the same fashion. By failing to distinguish between the trademark term for one product and the generic term for another, the manufacturer helped to prove that the term *escalator* had lost its significance as an indication of origin, and had become merely a synonym for the term moving staircase. The advertisement quoted in this paragraph was an exhibit in the proceeding in the United States Patent and Trademark Office that led to the cancellation of the Escalator trademark registration, which had been on the books for fifty years.

Unfortunate results like these can be prevented by proper advertising and labeling practices. Just as poorly constructed advertising helped to change escalator and the other terms listed above from trademarks into generic terms in the public mind, so proper use can maintain the significance of a trademark.

Proper trademark use would be almost automatic if we could train ourselves to remember that a trademark is classified grammatically as an adjective—actually a proper adjective (like the "Russian" in Russian dressing or the "Boston" in Boston baked beans, although those designate types rather than brands). A trademark identifies a particular brand of some product; it is not the name of the product itself and therefore is not a noun. It tells the consumer something about the product; it modifies the name of the product and thus is an adjective. Conversely, since a trademark is an adjective, there must be a noun for it to modify, and that noun, of course, is the generic name of the product. It is wise to remember, also, that a trademark is a *proper* adjective because a proper adjective, like a proper noun, is entitled grammatically to an initial capital letter.

The key principle in proper trademark usage is that a trademark always must be identified *as* a trademark. It has to be distinguished from the mere name of a product. The public must recognize the trademark, not as an identification of the product alone, but as the identification of some particular manufacturer's version of that product. This basic point can be made by observing the following rules.

1. The first and most important rule is to use the generic name of the product in association with the trademark. It would be bad taste in this discussion to refer to actual trademarks as examples, unless they have been the subject of legal rulings. In order to avoid stepping on anyone's toes, therefore, let us organize the hypothetical Empire Manufacturing Company, which produces, among other imaginary products, a washing machine under the trademark Gremlin. Applying the rule to this hypothetical product, the technique is a very simple one. In its advertising, the Empire Manufacturing Company should not refer simply to a Gremlin; it should advertise a Gremlin *washing machine* or a Gremlin *automatic washer*.

A simple test to apply to advertising copy is this: Would a complete thought be expressed if the trademark were omitted from the sentence? For example, in the sentence "Get Your Clothes Cleaner with a Gremlin Washing Machine," you can eliminate the trademark Gremlin, and the remainder will still read sensibly as an example of English grammar—although certainly not a very good piece of advertising copy: "Get Your Clothes Cleaner with a Washing Machine."

The version with which this must be compared is "Get Your

Clothes Cleaner with a Gremlin." That sentence will be destroyed grammatically if the trademark is eliminated; it then would read "Get Your Clothes Cleaner with a."

It must be born in mind that this is simply a test. If the advertising copy passes the test, the next step is to put the trademark back into the sentence.

If the advertisement only says "Get Your Clothes Cleaner with a Gremlin," there is no generic name used in association with the trademark, and the consuming public is likely to come to think of the term *Gremlin* as the name of a particular kind of washing machine. If this happens to be a new type of automatic washer, the danger is increased. And if, instead of an automatic washer, it is an entirely new product, the danger is very great indeed. The public is likely to attach the trademark to the new product unless the manufacturer gives the public a generic name to use for the product itself. For example, let Empire now invent an electrostatic dry cleaner that makes all of the dirt simply drop right out of your clothes. If Empire were to advertise "Dry Clean Your Clothes with a Gremlin," it would not be providing enough language for the consumer to distinguish between a product name and a trademark.

This is reminiscent of the Escalator moving staircase problem that was mentioned earlier. The same rule would require writing Gremlin washing machine or Gremlin automatic washer or Gremlin electrostatic cleaner in order to insure against the possibility that the public will treat the trademark Gremlin as a generic term rather than as a brand name.

2. The second rule for making sure that the consuming public recognizes a trademark *as* a trademark is to use a trademark notice in advertising and labeling. The federal statute provides three alternate versions that can be used for trademarks registered in the United States Patent and Trademark Office. You have the choice of "Registered in U.S. Patent and Trademark Office" or the abbreviated version "Reg. U.S. Pat. & Tm. Off." or simply the letter R enclosed within a circle, thus: ®. It is important to remember that these notices can be used only when the trademark already has been registered in

the United States Patent and Trademark Office. If you make deliberate use of a false registration notice and the Patent and Trademark Office finds out about it, they will refuse to register your trademark, and the mark also may be unenforceable in court against an infringer as a kind of penalty for using the false notice.

The simplest and least conspicuous version of the trademark notice, of course, is the letter R enclosed within a circle. It is not necessary to use these circle-R notices to such an extent that they become obtrusive. If a trademark registration notice appears with the first or the most prominent use of the trademark in an advertisement or on a label, it is not essential that the notice be repeated each time the trademark is used after that.

The circle-R notice need not spoil the aesthetic appearance of the advertisement. It can be quite small provided, of course, that it remains legible.

There is no prescribed style for the letter R in this form of notice, and there is no reason why it should not be set in a style of type that harmonizes with the rest of the printed matter. One of the country's largest advertising agencies produced a style sheet for its art directors some years ago, giving them circles of various sizes with capital Rs of various designs enclosed within them. To satisfy any art director who might want to select his own typeface for the letter R, the sheet even contained some blank circles as a sort of do-it-yourself kit.

The circle-R notice conventionally goes "on the shoulder" of the trademark; that is, it fits in the same relative position as a footnote reference would appear. However, even this is subject to variation because the statute does not prescribe any particular location; it simply requires that the notice appear "with the mark as used." Some companies integrate the circle-R within the logotype version of the trademark.

The longer forms of notice, "Registered U.S. Patent and Trademark Office" or "Reg. U.S. Pat. & Tm. Off.," rather obviously do not fit in body copy. The conventional way to use them is as footnotes.

The asterisk, or dagger, or whatever other form of footnote reference you prefer, should appear in the body copy or the headline against the first or most prominent appearance of the trademark, and the notice will run as a footnote at the bottom of the page. It can even appear at the top of the page or run vertically at the side if that seems preferable.

When a trademark has not yet been registered in the Patent and Trademark Office, you may use a footnote that says, for example, "Trademark of Empire Manufacturing Company" or simply "Trademark." It has become quite common to use the letters TM in small caps as a notice for an unregistered trademark. This TM notice conventionally runs in the same relative position as the circle-R notice, that is, generally on the shoulder of the trademark.

The filing of an application in the United States Patent and Trademark Office is not the same as getting a registration. It is improper to use one of the statutory forms of notice until after the certificate of registration actually has been issued. Some manufacturers like to use "TM pending" or words to that effect. The federal statute makes no provision for this, but there certainly is no objection to notifying the public that a trademark application is pending; such a notice, of course, helps in the essential task of identifying the trademark *as* a trademark.

Another variation is the trademark that is registered under a state law but not in the United States Patent and Trademark Office. The word "Registered" is correct under those circumstances or, if you prefer, "Trademark Registered" or "Registered Trademark."

Some manufacturers and advertising agencies think that a notice like "Reg. U.S. Pat. & Tm. Off." is a bit too austere, and they also may prefer to avoid the circle-R notice, which, to some art directors at least, appears to clutter up the advertisement. There is no reason why the required information cannot be sugar-coated in some fashion, such as by making it part of a slogan that runs at the bottom of the page. For a number of years, a boy's shirt manufacturing company used to run a line like this underneath the signature of every advertisement: "Donmoor is a trademark for knit shirts that make boys look and feel great." Clearly, this kind of treatment provides the required notice to the consumer that the brand name is being claimed as a trademark and is not the generic designation for a type of product. And, if the trademark has been registered in the United States Patent and Trademark Office, the circle-R notice can be used in association with the trademark in a legend of this type.

A declaratory statement, possibly in small type at the bottom of the page, is also useful in dealing with an advertisement that mentions several different trademarks. Instead of putting a circle-R notice or a footnote reference next to each trademark in the headline or body copy, a legend along the following lines can be used: "Gremlin, Widget, and Whatsis are trademarks of Empire Manufacturing Company. Reg. U.S. Pat. & Tm. Off."

One other method of clearly designating a trademark is to use the word "brand" after it. The appearance of the word brand between the trademark and the generic term makes it unmistakably clear that it is a trademark. Some well-known examples of marks treated in this way are Scotch brand tape and Pyrex brand glassware. This use of the word "brand" teaches the consumer unconsciously that Scotch is not a generic designation for a type of tape nor Pyrex a generic designation for a type of glassware; each term is a trademark.

3. Another technique to insure that a trademark will be recognizable as such is to display the mark with some form of special typographical treatment. At a bare minimum, the mark should be capitalized. (It is a proper adjective, remember.) Nothing contributes more strongly to the impression that a trademark is generic than its appearance in lower case letters.

There are many other forms of special typographical treatment that can be used to help make it clear that a trademark is not being used generically. For example, the trademark may appear in all caps, in quotation marks, in hand-lettered form, in a frame, in italics, in bold face, underscored, set larger than body copy, in a different type face, or in a different color from the balance of the text. One effective device is the use in body copy of a miniature version of the logotype form of the trademark, scaled to the type size selected for the rest of the copy.

There should be a special form for the trademark, and it is important to stick to it. Many companies issue style sheets and specifications, sometimes in the form of engineering drawings, giving the exact proportions of the letters and the proper relationships among all parts of the mark. To avoid blurring the image of the trademark in the consumer's mind, a standard form of trademark display should be established, and appropriate steps should be taken to see that this form is used without departure. This is not to say that a trademark cannot be modernized under appropriate circumstances. If such a program is adopted, however, the idea should be to pick one new form and stick to that.

4. The next rule for proper trademark use is to avoid having the trademark appear in an incorrect grammatical form. Do not use the trademark as a noun. Specifically, do not pluralize it, because that suggests it is a noun. For example, going back to our hypothetical line of Gremlin products, it would be wrong to refer to "a full line of Gremlins." If the trademark itself ends with the letter "s," do not create a false singular form by dropping the "s." Also, avoid using the trademark as a verb. Do not say "Gremlin your clothes."

Moreover, do not use a trademark in the possessive. It is erroneous to use such an expression as "The Gremlin's remarkable service record." The correct form would be to invert the order of the sentence and introduce the generic term, for example, "The remarkable service record of the Gremlin washing machine."

5. A final rule is not to vary the trademark by using it as the basis for other language forms, such as abbreviations or coined words. Don't change the spelling, insert or delete hyphens, make one word into two, or combine two words into one. Changes in the form of a trademark tend to detract from its status because they suggest to the consumer that it is just an-

other word that is subject to variation or grammatical manipulation.

Going back once again to our hypothetical clothes washer, an advertising campaign might be developed around the idea of "gremlination" as a new treatment for the housewife's wash. This would quickly break down the distinctiveness of the trademark and it is just the kind of thing that ought to be discouraged.

Moving beyond these five rules, it is possible to build an advertisement affirmatively around a trademark and thus forestall any possible loss of trademark significance. A good example is United Fruit Company's series for Chiquita brand bananas. One of these advertisements showed a partly-peeled banana with the Chiquita brand seal visible in a three-quarters view. It carried the headline: "Before you peeled this banana, what told you it would be this good?" And the answer, which appeared opposite the label that bears the trademark, read "This seal."

The body copy of the advertisement started this way: "That Chiquita Brand seal says a lot about a banana. It says that *this* banana has been as pampered and protected as a banana should be. All the way from the tree to your grocer's." After an explanation about the special packing arrangements used for Chiquita brand bananas, the advertisement continued: "So look for the seal on the peel. It's the one way to tell the best of the bananas from the rest of the bananas." This advertiser was teaching the public that the significance of its trademark, in the words of the federal trademark law, is "an indication of origin."

Another example of advertising directed specifically to a trademark is the "body tattoo" series by Fruit of the Loom, Inc. The trademark appears as a tattoo on some portion of the model's body, and the standard headline reads "My brand is Fruit of the Loom." The copy then lists a wide variety of products available under the Fruit of the Loom trademark.

Advertising also can be used in a positive educational campaign to insure against improper trademark use or consumer misunderstanding. Xerox Corporation adopted a humorous tone for its series of educational advertisements. One had a headline that takes up most of the page, reading "WE INTER-RUPT OUR ADVERTISING FOR A WORD FROM OUR LAWYERS." The body copy says:

> Xerox is a trade name and a registered trademark.
> As a trade name, it stands for Xerox Corporation. As a trademark, it identifies our products.
> And it shouldn't be used when referring to anybody else's copier, duplicator, paper or whatever. (Let them use their own name.) Lawyer or not, remember that. O.K.?
> We return you now to our regularly scheduled advertising.

It would be wrong to pretend that every single trademark needs the same degree of care. Provided you understand what you are doing, there are many situations in which the rules discussed above need not be followed to the letter.

For instance, a number of companies make it a practice to use a house mark and also individual product marks. The house mark Nabisco of National Biscuit Company (now Nabisco, Inc.) is a leading example. A trademark of this character obviously requires much less concern than a mark applicable to an individual product because the chances of the house mark becoming thought of as a generic term are quite remote.

There is one particular danger of using a house mark in association with a product mark that ought to be mentioned, however. If not carefully controlled, the house mark can cause trouble for the product mark. To go back to our hypothetical company and its washing machine, if the advertising should talk about Empire Gremlin, it might be taken to imply that Empire is one variety of Gremlin washing machine, which in turn creates the implication that other companies also make their own versions of Gremlin washing machines. You can see that this would put our famous trademark Gremlin in about the same category as Escalator or any of the other lost trademarks mentioned previously. At the very least, be sure to have a generic term when you use the house mark and the product mark in tandem; Empire Gremlin washing machine is not nearly so bad as the Empire Gremlin. But notice what Nabisco does; the house mark and the product mark are always separated. For example, you may see an advertisement for Ritz crackers by Nabisco, but not an advertisement for Nabisco Ritz crackers.

A trademark may be used for a whole line of products rather than just a single item. The product line mark provides another situation in which less care is necessary, because there is much less risk of the trademark becoming generic. Del Monte is an example of a famous trademark owned by a company that simply does not use product marks. As almost everybody knows, there are Del Monte peaches, Del Monte pears, and Del Monte fruits and vegetables of numerous varieties. The general counsel of Del Monte Corporation (then known as California Packing Corporation) once published an article in which he said, among other things, "Obviously, there is no danger of consumers going to the corner grocery seeking a can of peaches and asking for a can of del monte." The typical consumer is not even going to think of a trademark like Del Monte without having a mental image of it in initial caps. The status of this trademark is secure because it is not limited to a single product, and the public therefore cannot misunderstand its function and take it to be a product designation as distinguished from an indication of origin.

Another very important influence on the danger of losing trademark rights is the advertiser's share of the market. If a large number of competitive products are available, it is likely that the consuming public has been educated without realizing it into distinguishing among different versions of the same type of competing item. Accordingly, each trademark will serve the function of identifying origin even if the generic term is omitted, as it must be confessed it frequently is.

Let us think, for example, of the cigarette industry, where we have Camel, Chesterfield, Lucky Strike, Salem, Winston, etc. Similarly, the automobile industry has Buick, Cadillac, Chevrolet, Ford, Lincoln, Plymouth, and many more. Among household items, consider detergents—we can think quickly of Dash, Cheer, Bold, and others.

Why is it possible to talk about buying a Buick or smoking a Chesterfield or getting a box of Cheer without using the generic term for the product and yet not lose the trademark? The reason is that the consumer understands what product is being talked about or written about in the advertisement. It is as if the generic term were there in brackets. A memorable example that proves the point is the Volkswagen advertisement that has a headline reading: "Here's what to do to get your Volkswagen ready for winter:"—and the entire rest of the page is blank. This is a very clever idea, but it would be a complete waste of time and money unless all or substantially all of the consuming public knew that Volkswagen was a brand of automobile. And, of course, all or substantially all of the consuming public *does* know that Volkswagen is a trademark for a kind of automobile. The generic term is understood so clearly and completely that it need not appear in the advertisement.

The generic term can be omitted safely only when the context is so clear that no ambiguity is created. If we are talking about oceans, it will be enough to say "the Atlantic," and everyone will understand; the proper adjective Atlantic does not become a synonym for all oceans. Some trademarks achieve this status effortlessly; in other instances, habitual use without the generic name must be recognized as a danger signal that calls for corrective action. Trademark owners should be on the alert to make certain that their valuable property rights do not slip away because the terms that started life as proper adjectives are converted into common nouns in the minds of the consuming public. The worst possible situation is when the consumer starts asking his or her friends, "What brand of _____ do you use?"—and the blank space is filled, not with a generic product name, but with your trademark.

A final word should be said about internal communications. Bad trademark usage sometimes begins with the trademark proprietor itself, in careless speech, written memos, and correspondence. It then has a way of moving out to suppliers and customers. Poor advertising and labeling practices frequently follow. And that is the beginning of the end for the neglected trademark. The trademark owner should be sure that its own employees do not err. Leaflets or manuals explaining the principles of proper trademark use and why they are important to the financial well-being of the company frequently are published for this purpose. The same educational material can be distributed to suppliers and industrial customers so that they will learn to avoid misuse and the mark will continue to retain, in the statutory language, "its significance as an indication of origin." If so, it will never expire; the trademark can go on functioning forever as a proprietary symbol and a valuable marketing tool.

Index of Trademarks Mentioned

Entries in *italics* indicate detailed discussion in text.

Legal Reference Notes

Page(s)

34 Rolls-Royce: *Wall* v. *Rolls-Royce of America, Inc.*, 4 F.2d 333 (3d Cir. 1925).

34 Kodak: *Ex parte Galter,* 96 U.S.P.Q. 216 (P.O. Ex-in-Ch. 1953).

37–40 Ultra Brite and Ultra-Dent: *Colgate-Palmolive Co.* v. *Warner-Lambert Co.*, 184 U.S.P.Q. 380 (T.T.A.B. 1974).

41–43 Textron and Tectron: *Textron Inc.* v. *Thor Electronics Corp.*, 173 U.S.P.Q. 753 (T.T.A.B. 1972).

51–53 Mountain King and Alpine King: *Masterpiece of Pennsylvania, Inc.* v. *Consolidated Novelty Co.*, 368 F. Supp. 550 (S.D.N.Y. 1973).

53–56 Comsat and Comcet: *Communications Satellite Corp.* v. *Comcet, Inc.*, 429 F.2d 1245 (4th Cir. 1970), rev'g 300 F. Supp. 559 (D. Md. 1969), cert. denied, 400 U.S. 942 (1970).

56–59 Continental: *Continental Motors Corp.* v. *Continental Aviation Corp.*, 375 F.2d 857 (5th Cir. 1967).

59 Justice Frankfurter's quote: *Mishawaka Rubber & Woolen Mfg. Co.* v. *S. S. Kresge Co.*, 316 U.S. 203, 205 (1942).

59–61 Tornado and Vornado: *Vornado, Inc.* v. *Breuer Electric Mfg. Co.*, 390 F.2d 724 (C.C.P.A. 1968), aff'g 147 U.S.P.Q. 370 (T.T.A.B. 1965).

61–63 Tylenol and Extranol: *McNeil Laboratories, Inc.* v. *American Home Products Corp.*, 416 F. Supp. 804 (D.N.J. 1976).

62 Dramamine and Bonamine: *G. D. Searle & Co.* v. *Chas. Pfizer & Co., Inc.*, 265 F.2d 385 (7th Cir. 1959), rev'g 159 F. Supp. 878 (N.D. Ill. 1958), cert. denied, 361 U.S. 819 (1959).

62 Brylcream and Valcream: *Harold F. Ritchie, Inc.* v. *Chesebrough-Pond's, Inc.*, 281 F.2d 755 (2d Cir. 1960), rev'g 176 F. Supp. 429 (S.D.N.Y. 1959).

62 Cheracol and Syrocol: *Upjohn Co.* v. *Schwartz,* 246 F.2d 254 (2d Cir. 1957), modifying 131 F. Supp. 649 (S.D.N.Y. 1954).

63–68 Spray 'N Vac and Spray & Vacuum: *Glamorene Products Corp.* v. *Boyle-Midway, Inc.*, 188 U.S.P.Q. 145 (S.D.N.Y. 1975).

68 The Uncola: *Coca-Cola Co.* v. *Seven-Up Co.*, 497 F.2d 1351 (C.C.P.A. 1974), aff'g 178 U.S.P.Q. 309 (T.T.A.B. 1973).

Page(s)
101 Paulsen for President: *Paulsen* v. *Personality Posters, Inc.*, 59 Misc. 2d 444, 299 N.Y.S. 2d 501 (S. Ct. 1968).

102–105 The Greatest Show On Earth: *Ringling Bros.-Barnum & Bailey Combined Shows, Inc.*, v. *Chandris America Lines, Inc.*, 321 F. Supp. 707 (S.D.N.Y. 1971).

109 Broken Doll: *International Film Service Co.* v. *Associated Producers, Inc.*, 273 Fed. 585 (S.D.N.Y. 1921).

109 That's Right, You're Wrong: *Ott* v. *Keith Massachusetts Corp.*, 309 Mass. 185, 34 N.E. 2d 683 (1941).

109 Slightly Scandalous: *Jackson* v. *Universal International Pictures, Inc.*, 36 Cal. 2d 116, 222 P. 2d 433 (1950).

109 Yukon Jake: *Paramore* v. *Mack Sennett, Inc.*, 9 F.2d 66 (S.D. Cal. 1925).

109 Nick Carter: *Atlas Mfg. Co.* v. *Street & Smith*, 204 Fed. 398 (8th Cir.), cert. denied, 231 U.S. 755 (1913), 232 U.S. 724 (1914).

110 Frank Merriwell: *Patten* v. *Superior Talking Pictures, Inc.*, 8 F. Supp. 196 (S.D.N.Y. 1934).

110 Alice in Wonderland: *Walt Disney Productions, Inc.* v. *Souvaine Selective Pictures, Inc.*, 98 F. Supp. 774 (S.D. N.Y.), aff'd, 192 F.2d 856 (2d Cir. 1951).

110–113 Playboy: *HMH Publishing Co., Inc.* v. *Brincat*, 504 F.2d 713 (9th Cir. 1974), modifying 342 F. Supp. 1275 (N.D. Cal. 1972).

111–112 Esquire (slippers): *Esquire, Inc.* v. *Esquire Slipper Manufacturing Co., Inc.*, 243 F.2d 540 (1st Cir. 1957), vacating 139 F. Supp. 228 (D. Mass. 1956).

113–116 Penthouse: *Penthouse International, Ltd.* v. *Dyn Electronics, Inc.*, 196 U.S.P.Q. 251 (T.T.A.B. 1977).

116 Ebony: *Johnson Publishing Co., Inc.* v. *McLendon*, 133 U.S.P.Q. (T.T.A.B. 1962).

116 Esquire (restaurant): *Esquire, Inc.* v. *Esquire Bar*, 37 F. Supp. 875 (S.D. Fla. 1941).

116 Life: *Time, Inc.* v. *Life Television Corp.*, 123 F. Supp. 470 (D. Minn. 1954).

116 Look: *Cowles Magazines, Inc.* v. *Andrew Jergens Co.*, 115 U.S.P.Q. 92 (Comm'r 1957).

116 Playboy: *HMH Publishing Co., Inc.* v. *Brincat*, 342 F. Supp. 1275 (N.D. Cal. 1972) mod., 504 F.2d 713 (9th Cir. 1974).

Page(s)

116   Seventeen (dresses): *Hanson v. Triangle Publications, Inc.,* 163 F.2d 74 (8th Cir. 1947), aff'g 65 F. Supp. 952 (E.D. Mo. 1946), cert. denied, 332 U.S. 855 (1948).

116   Seventeen (girdles): *Triangle Publications, Inc. v. Rohrlich,* 167 F.2d 969 (2d Cir. 1948), modifying 73 F. Supp. 74 (S.D.N.Y. 1947).

116   Seventeen (luggage): *Triangle Publications, Inc. v. Standard Plastic Products, Inc.,* 241 F. Supp. 613 (E.D. Pa. 1965).

116   Vogue (ladies' hats): *Vogue Co. v. Thompson-Hudson Co.,* 300 Fed. 509 (6th Cir. 1924), cert. denied, 273 U.S. 706 (1926).

116   Vogue (modeling school): *Conde Nast Publications, Inc. v. Vogue School of Fashion Modelling, Inc.,* 105 F. Supp. 325 (S.D.N.Y. 1952).

117–121   Dracula: *Lugosi v. Universal Pictures,* 172 U.S.P.Q. 541 (Cal. Super. Ct. 1972), rev'd, 70 Cal. App. 3d 552, 139 Cal. Rptr. 35 (1977), aff'd, 25 Cal. 3d 813, 160 Cal. Rptr. 323, 603 P. 2d 425 (1979).

118   Gene Autry: *Autry v. Republic Productions, Inc.,* 213 F.2d 667 (9th Cir. 1954), modifying 104 F. Supp. 918 (S.D. Cal. 1952), cert. denied, 348 U.S.858 (1954).

119   Al Capone: *Maritote v. Desilu Productions, Inc.,* 345 F.2d 418 (7th Cir. 1965), aff'g 230 F. Supp. 721 (N.D. Ill. 1964), cert. denied, 382 U.S. 883 (1965).

119   That Was The Week That Was: *Young v. That Was The Week That Was,* 312 F. Supp. 1337 (N.D. Ohio 1969), aff'd per curiam, 423 F.2d 265 (6th Cir. 1970).

120   Baseball card case: *Haelan Laboratories, Inc. v. Topps Chewing Gum, Inc.,* 202 F.2d 866 (2d Cir.), cert. denied, 346 U.S. 816 (1953).

121–124   Laurel and Hardy: *Price v. Hal Roach Studios, Inc.,* 400 F. Supp. 836 (S.D.N.Y. 1975).

124–127   Joe Namath: *Namath v. Sports Illustrated,* 80 Misc. 2d 531, 363 N.Y.S. 2d 276 (S. Ct.), aff'd, 48 A.D. 2d 487, 371 N.Y.S. 2d 10 (1st Dept. 1975), aff'd mem., 39 N.Y. 2d 897, 386 N.Y.S. 2d 397, 352 N.E. 2d 584 (1976).

126   Shirley Booth: *Booth v. Curtis Publishing Co.,* 15 A.D. 2d 343, 223 N.Y.S. 2d 737 (1st Dept.), aff'd mem., 11 N.Y. 2d 907, 228 N.Y.S. 2d 468, 182 N.E. 2d 812 (1962).

Page(s)

126 Flores: *Flores* v. *Mosler Safe Co.*, 7 N.Y. 2d 276, 196 N.Y.S. 2d 975, 164 N.E. 2d 853 (1959), aff'g 7 A.D. 2d 226, 182 N.Y.S. 2d 126 (3d Dept. 1959).

127 Howard Hughes (biography): *Rosemont Enterprises, Inc.* v. *Random House, Inc.*, 366 F.2d 303 (2d Cir. 1966), rev'g 256 F. Supp. 55 (S.D.N.Y. 1966), cert. denied, 385 U.S. 1009 (1967).

127–129 Howard Hughes (game): *Rosemont Enterprises, Inc.* v. *Urban Systems, Inc.*, 72 Misc. 2d 788, 340 N.Y.S. 2d 144 (S. Ct.), modified, 42 A.D. 2d 544, 345 N.Y.S. 2d 17 (1st Dept. 1973).

129–132 Paladin: *Columbia Broadcasting System, Inc.* v. *DeCosta*, 377 F.2d 315 (1st Cir.), cert. denied, 389 U.S. 1007 (1967); on remand, 383 F. Supp. 326 (D.R.I. 1974), rev'd, 520 F.2d 499 (1st Cir. 1975), cert. denied, 423 U.S. 1073 (1976).

132–134 Hugo Zacchini: *Zacchini* v. *Scripps-Howard Broadcasting Co.*, 433 U.S. 562 (1977), rev'g 47 Ohio St. 2d 224, 351 N.E. 2d 454 (1976).

134–138 Hazel: *Booth* v. *Colgate-Palmolive Co.*, 362 F. Supp. 343 (S.D.N.Y. 1973).

136–138 These Boots Are Made For Walkin': *Sinatra* v. *Goodyear Tire and Rubber Co.*, 435 F.2d 711 (9th Cir. 1970), cert. denied, 402 U.S. 906 (1971).

136–137 Up, Up and Away: *Davis* v. *Trans World Airlines*, 297 F. Supp. 1145 (C.D. Cal. 1969).

136–137 Bert Lahr: *Lahr* v. *Adell Chemical Co.*, 300 F.2d 256 (1st Cir. 1962), rev'g 195 F. Supp. 702 (D. Mass. 1961).

139–142 Bug: *Volkswagenwerk Aktiengesellschaft* v. *Rickard*, 175 U.S.P.Q. 563 (N.D. Tex. 1972), modified, 492 F.2d 474 (5th Cir. 1974).

142 Coke: *Coca-Cola Co.* v. *Busch*, 44 F. Supp. 405 (E.D. Pa. 1942).

142 Bud: *Anheuser-Busch, Inc.* v. *Du Bois Brewing Co.*, 73 F. Supp. 338 (W.D. Pa. 1947), rev'd on other grounds, 175 F.2d 370 (3d Cir. 1949), cert. denied, 339 U.S. 934 (1950).

144 Kelly Spinner: *Foster Cathead Co.* v. *International Tool Co.*, 149 U.S.P.Q. 859 (T.T.A.B. 1966).

144 Nuclide: *In re Nuclide Corp.*, 149 U.S.P.Q. 853 (T.T.A.B. 1966).

Page(s)

144 Sudsy: *Roselux Chemical Co.* v. *Parsons Ammonia Co.*, 299 F.2d. 855 (C.C.P.A. 1962), rev'g 124 U.S.P.Q. 524 (T.T. A.B. 1960).

144–145 Pasteurized: *Helena Rubinstein, Inc.* v. *Ladd*, 219 F. Supp. 259 (D.D.C. 1963), aff'g 131 U.S.P.Q. 152 (T.T.A.B. 1961), aff'd, 141 U.S.P.Q. 623 (D.C. Cir. 1964); see also *Application of Helena Rubinstein, Inc.*, 410 F.2d 438 (C.C. P.A. 1969).

145 Shampoo Plus Egg: *In re Helene Curtis Industries, Inc.*, 125 U.S.P.Q. 352 (T.T.A.B. 1960).

145 Aspirin, Cellophane, Linoleum, Milk of Magnesia, Shredded Wheat: See notes to p. 247 for these and other similar lost trademarks.

146–147 Q-Tips: *Q-Tips, Inc.* v. *Johnson & Johnson*, 108 F. Supp. 845 (D.N.J. 1952), aff'd, 206 F.2d 144 (3d Cir.), cert. denied, 346 U.S. 867 (1953).

148–152 Thermos: *American Thermos Products Co.* v. *Aladdin Industries, Inc.*, 207 F. Supp. 9 (D. Conn. 1962), aff'd *King-Seeley Thermos Co.* v. *Aladdin Industries, Inc.*, 321 F.2d 577 (2d Cir. 1963), mod. denied, 289 F. Supp. 155 (D. Conn. 1968); remanded, 418 F.2d 31 (2d Cir. 1969); modified, 320 F. Supp. 1156 (D. Conn. 1970); policing order, 320 F. Supp. 1156 (D. Conn. 1970).

152–156 Yo-Yo: *Donald F. Duncan* v. *Royal Tops Mfg. Co.*, 343 F.2d 655 (7th Cir. 1965), rev'g 141 U.S.P.Q. 567 (N.D. Ill. 1964).

156–160 Teflon and Eflon: *E. I. DuPont de Nemours and Co.* v. *Yoshida International, Inc.*, 393 F. Supp. 502 (E.D.N.Y. 1975).

156 Cellophane: *DuPont Cellophane Co.* v. *Waxed Products Co.*, 85 F.2d 75 (2d Cir. 1936), modifying 6 F. Supp. 859 (E.D.N.Y. 1934), cert. denied, 299 U.S. 601 (1936).

156 Thermos: See note to pp. 148–152.

159 Aspirin: *Bayer Co.* v. *United Drug Co.*, 272 Fed. 505 (S.D. N.Y. 1921).

160–164 Dictaphone and Dictamatic: *Dictaphone Corp.* v. *Dictamatic Corp.*, 199 U.S.P.Q. 437 (D. Ore. 1978).

166–171 Lite and Light: *Miller Brewing Co.* v. *G. Heileman Brewing Co.*, 427 F. Supp. 1192 (W.D. Wisc.), rev'd, 561 F.2d 75 (7th Cir. 1977), cert. denied, 434 U.S. 1025 (1978); *Miller Brewing Co.* v. *Jos. Schlitz Brewing Co.*, 605 F.2d 990 (7th

Page(s)

Ill. App. 3d 641, 303 N.E. 2d 177 (1973), cert. denied, 419 U.S. 873 (1974).

224–226 Rolls-Royce: *Rolls-Royce Motors Ltd.* v. *Custom Cloud Motors, Inc.*, 190 U.S.P.Q. 157 (D.N.J. 1977).

226–228 Tenuate: *Merrell-National Laboratories, Inc.* v. *Zenith Laboratories, Inc.*, 194 U.S.P.Q. 157 (D.N.J. 1977).

228 Federal Court of Appeals quote: *Union Carbide Corp.* v. *Ever-Ready, Inc.*, 531 F.2d 366, 384 (7th Cir.), cert. denied, 429 U.S. 830 (1976).

233–237 Wells Fargo: *Wells Fargo & Co.* v. *Wells Fargo Express Co.*, 358 F. Supp. 1065 (D. Nev. 1973), rev'd, 556 F.2d 406 (9th Cir. 1977).

240 U.S. Supreme Court quote: *Manhattan Medicine Co.* v. *Wood*, 108 U.S. 218, 223 (1882).

240 Federal court of appeals statement: *Norwich Pharmacal Co.* v. *Sterling Drug, Inc.*, 271 F.2d 569 (2d Cir. 1959).

242 U.S. Supreme Court—Trademark statute unconstitutional: *Trade-Mark Cases*, 100 U.S. 82 (1879).

243 U.S. Supreme Court quote: *United Drug Co.* v. *Theodore Rectanus Co.*, 248 U.S. 90, 98 (1918).

244 "Unfair competition is not competition at all": *Schulenburg* v. *Signatrol, Inc.*, 33 Ill. 2d 379, 212 N.E. 2d 869 (1965), cert. denied, 383 U.S. 359 (1966).

244 "The essence of competition": *Standard Oil Co. (Kentucky)* v. *Humble Oil & Refining Co.*, 363 F.2d 945, 954 (5th Cir. 1966), cert. denied, 385 U.S. 1007 (1967).

245 "There could be no pride of workmanship": Rogers, The Lanham Act and the Social Function of Trade-Marks, 14 L. & Contemp. Prob. 173, 175 (1949), republished (excerpts), 62 Trademark Rep. 255, 257 (1972).

246 1968 comparative advertising case: *Smith* v. *Chanel, Inc.*, 402 F.2d 562, 566 (9th Cir. 1968).

247 Aspirin: *Bayer Co.* v. *United Drug Co.*, 272 Fed. 505 (S.D.N.Y. 1921).

247 Cellophane: *DuPont Cellophane Co.* v. *Waxed Products Co.*, 85 F.2d 75 (2d Cir. 1936), modifying 6 F. Supp. 859 (E.D.N.Y. 1934), cert. denied, 299 U.S. 601 (1936).

247 Celluloid: *Celluloid Mfg. Co.* v. *Cellonite Mfg. Co.*, 32 Fed. 94 (D.N.J. 1887).

Page(s)

247   Escalator: *Haughton Elevator Co.* v. *Seeberger*, 85 U.S.P.Q. 80 (Comm'r 1950).

247   Kerosene: *Bennett* v. *North British and Mercantile Ins. Co.*, 81 N.Y. 273 (1880); see *H. A. Metz Laboratories, Inc.*, v. *Blackman*, 153 Misc. 171, 177, 275 N.Y.S. 407, 414 (N.Y. Sup. Ct. 1934).

247   Lanolin: *Jaffe* v. *Evans & Sons, Ltd.*, 70 App. Div. 186, 75 N.Y.S. 257 (1st Dept. 1902).

247   Linoleum: *Linoleum Mfg. Co.* v. *Nairn*, L. R. 7 Ch. Div. 834 (1878); see *Centaur Co.* v. *Heinsfurter*, 84 Fed. 955, 958-9 (8th Cir. 1898).

247   Milk of Magnesia: *McKesson & Robbins, Inc.* v. *Charles H. Phillips Chemical Co.*, 53 F.2d 342 (2d Cir. 1931), modified on rehearing, 53 F.2d 1011 (2d Cir, 1931, cert. denied, 285 U.S. 552 (1932).

247   Shredded Wheat: *Kellogg Co.* v. *National Biscuit Co.*, 305 U.S. 111 (1938).

247   Thermos: *American Thermos Products Co.* v. *Aladdin Industries, Inc.*, 207 F. Supp. 9 (D. Conn. 1962), aff'd, *King-Seeley Thermos Co.* v. *Aladdin Industries, Inc.*, 321 F.2d 577 (2d Cir. 1963); mod. denied, 289 F. Supp. 155 (D. Conn. 1968); remanded, 418 F.2d 31 (2d Cir. 1969); modified, 320 F. Supp. 1156 (D. Conn. 1970); policing order, 320 F. Supp. 1156 (D. Conn. 1970).